The Real Church

CHURCH OF SWEDEN
Research Series

Göran Gunner, editor
Vulnerability, Churches, and HIV (2009)

Kajsa Ahlstrand and Göran Gunner, editors
Non-Muslims in Muslim Majority Societies (2009)

Jonas Ideström, editor
For the Sake of the World (2010)

Göran Gunner and Kjell-Åke Nordquist
An Unlikely Dilemma (2011)

Anne-Louise Eriksson, Göran Gunner,
and Niclas Blåder, editors
Exploring a Heritage (2012)

Kjell-Åke Nordquist, editor
Gods and Arms (2013)

Harald Hegstad
The Real Church (2013)

The Real Church
An Ecclesiology of the Visible

HARALD HEGSTAD

☙PICKWICK *Publications* · Eugene, Oregon

THE REAL CHURCH
An Ecclesiology of the Visible

Church of Sweden Research Series 7

Copyright © 2013 Trossamfundet Svenska kyrkan (Church of Sweden). All rights reserved. Except for brief quotations in critical publications or reviews, no part of this book may be reproduced in any manner without prior written permission from the publisher. Write: Permissions, Wipf and Stock, 199 W. 8th Ave., Suite 3, Eugene, OR 97401.

Translated from *Den virkelige kirke: Bidrag til ekklesiologien*, by Harald Hegstad (Trondheim, Norway: Tapir, 2009)

Scripture quotations are from the New Revised Standard Version Bible, copyright © 1989, Division of Christian Education of the National Council of the Churches of Christ in the United States of America. Used by permission. All rights reserved.

Pickwick Publications
An Imprint of Wipf and Stock Publishers
199 West 8th Avenue, Suite 3
Eugene, Oregon 97401
www.wipfandstock.com

ISBN 13: 978-1-62032-145-4

Cataloguing-in-Publication data:

Hegstad, Harald.

The real church : an ecclesiology of the visible / Harald Hegstad.

Church of Sweden Research Series 7

x + 248 pp. ; 23 cm. Includes bibliographical references and index.

ISBN 13: 978-1-62032-145-4

1. Church. I. Title. II. Series.

BV600.2 H45 2013

Manufactured in the U.S.A.

Contents

Preface / vii

1 Introduction / 1
   What Does It Mean to Believe in the Church?   1
   Between Systematic and Practical Ecclesiology   3
   Confessional Context and Biblical Basis   7
   Recent Developments in Ecclesiology   10

2 The Church: People Gathered in the Name of Jesus / 14
   The Starting Point: the Church is a Fellowship of People   14
   Matthew 18:20 as a Starting Point for Understanding the Church   17
   The Continuing Presence of Jesus by the Holy Spirit   20
   The Church as the Body of Christ   25
   Understanding the Church from an Eschatological Perspective   30
   The Holiness of the Church   34
   The Eschatological Reservation: "Not Everyone Who Says Lord, Lord . . ."   38
   A Heavenly Church?   44
   The Presence of Jesus in Word and Sacrament   49

3 Sociological and Theological Perspectives / 56
   The Nature of Social Reality   56
   Is the Church a Result of Human Work or the Work of God?   62

4 Sent Out into the World / 67
   Church and Creation   67
   Gustaf Wingren on Church and Creation   72
   Church and Culture   76
   The Church and the Mission of God   80

Contents

    The Church's Healing Ministry   86
    The Diakonia of the Church   89
    Diakonia and Politics   92
    The Church Catholic   95

5   Fellowship with One Another / 97
    The Church as Koinonia   97
    Visible and Tangible Fellowship   101
    The Church as Moral Community   106
    Folk Church as Christian Fellowship   109
    The Church as Public   116
    The Fellowship and the Individual   122

6   The Church as an Organization and Institution / 126
    The Church as an Organization from a Sociological Perspective   126
    The Church as an Institution   130
    Is the Institutionalization of the Church Theologically Untenable?   135
    Church as a Legally Ordered   138

7   A Fellowship of Ministries / 142
    A Traditional Distinction between Clergy and Lay   142
    A Diversity of Ministries   145
    The Lutheran Case: The One Ministry of the Church   149
    Unified Structure or Different Ministry Patterns   152
    Instituted by God?   155
    Pastoral Ministry   158
    Ordination to Ministry   161
    All Christians Have a Ministry   163
    The Leadership and Governance of the Church   166

8   Worship: As Gathered in the Name of Jesus / 171
    What Does It Mean to Be Gathered in the Name of Jesus?   171
    The Distinctiveness of Christian Worship   173
    Historical and Contemporary Sources   176
    Worship as Sign   179
    What Should and Should Not Be Included in the Worship Service   184
    Various Elements of the Worship Service   186

Contents

The Time, Place and Form of the Worship Service   194
The Worship Service as a Ritual   197
The Worship Service as a Place to Experience God   199
The Worship Service of the Real Church   200

9   **The Universal Church as the Fellowship of Local Churches / 203**

The Universal Church   203
Church Splits and Moves towards Unity   207
Unity between Local Churches   210
Types of Unity   212
Mutual Accountability   217
Church Organizations as Ministering on behalf of the Churches   220
Church and Small Groups   223

10   **Epilogue: Building Up the Real Church / 227**

Bibliography / 231

Index / 241

Preface

THIS BOOK IS A result of many years of work in the field of ecclesiological studies. I started my career as a rather traditional systematic theologian who was mainly concerned with analyzing the works of other theologians about the church and other matters. It was while being employed at the Center for Church Research (KIFO) in Oslo that I was introduced to empirical methodology and social scientific perspectives as a way to investigate the church. This experience gave me a desire to incorporate my original training as a systematic theologian with this methodological approach. I was left with a nagging question: what is the relationship between doctrinal and theological statements about the church and the empirical reality of the church? Often when the issue of the empirical church was discussed in certain circles among theologians and church officials, I experienced a resistance and even an immunization strategy. Whatever data researchers would provide regarding the situation of the church, this did not seem really to affect the theological appraisal. This sort of response was clearly rooted in the traditional division between the visible and the invisible church. The visible church was left to empiricists and the practitioners, while the invisible was the domain of theologians. On reflection, I found this way of thinking increasingly unsatisfactory. This book is an attempt to resolve this issue at the heart of where the idea of the invisible church arose, namely in the area of systematic theology. As I will show throughout this book, a sound theological interpretation of the church does not necessitate this division. In fact, there is a better alternative: It is the concrete, visible church that is the only real church. Ecclesiology should therefore be an ecclesiology of the visible church.

This book was first published in Norwegian by Tapir Academic Press (*Den virkelige kirke,* 2009). After its publication it received a lot of attention. The arguments raised in this book were not I realized, just limited to a Norwegian context, but were relevant to the ongoing international debate in ecclesiology. I therefore decided to make this book more avail-

Preface

able to a wider audience. I would like to thank the Research Council of Norway who made the translation of this book possible by a generous grant. I would also like to thank the Church of Sweden Research Unit for including this book as volume seven in *Church of Sweden Research Series*.

In an early stage of the process, John W. Kaufman, PhD, translated an excerpt of the two first chapters. The main body of translation work has been completed by Bradley Long, MPhil, who also revised John's first text in order to bring it in line with the style of the rest of the translation. The translation process has been a joint collaboration between the author and translator, with drafts and comments going back and forth. While I was understandably keen to see my views expressed as accurately as possible, Bradley accepted no compromise in making the text readable in English. I am thankful for this working relationship which has proved to be a rich experience. During this process we both learnt a lot about issues like, the interplay between translation and interpretation, and how different cultural and theological contextualizations (he an Englishman and an Anglican, I a Norwegian and a Lutheran) influences how things are written, as well as how they are read. For example, our discussions about capitalization would be worth a separate report!

During the translation process minor alterations, omissions and additions were made, which makes the present work an *English edition* of the work, rather than just simply a translation.

The writing of this book was for the most, a solitary enterprise. At the same time, I recognize that such a work is dependent upon, and is part of a wider scholarly community. I am therefore immensely indebted to the teachers, colleagues and students, both nationally and internationally, to whom I have had the privilege to be taught by, had fruitful discussions with, given critique, have worked with, and have become friends with. The names are clearly too many to be mentioned. I am also thankful to be part of the vibrant ecclesial community of the Church of Norway, both at a local and diocesan and national level. This has contributed in a special way to my interest and reason for writing this book.

I am especially thankful to the MF Norwegian School of Theology, which is a wonderful place to learn and to teach. What I particularly like about this institution is its uncompromising commitment both to serving the academy and the church. This dual commitment is one to which I adhere and continues to shape me as a theologian.

Oslo in Lenten 2012
Harald Hegstad

1

Introduction

WHAT DOES IT MEAN TO BELIEVE IN THE CHURCH?

FROM THE VERY BEGINNING, the Christian faith has been a fellowship phenomenon. Jesus himself gathered the first group of disciples, and after his death the Christians continued to meet in his name. Based upon faith in Jesus, Christian congregations, denominations and movements have grown and developed in various times and places. Viewed from the perspective of faith, this fellowship aspect of the Christian faith is not merely coincidental, but it is of major importance. This is witnessed in the historic Creeds and confessions of the church. Here the word *church* is used to indicate this fellowship dimension. In the Nicene Creed, for example, it states: "We believe in . . . one holy, catholic, and apostolic church," and in the Apostles' Creed, "I believe in . . . the holy catholic church, the communion of saints."[1]

So what does it mean to *believe in the church*? Normally, when we speak of believing in something, it is usually something we cannot experience directly. According to the Letter to the Hebrews, faith is "the assurance of things hoped for, the conviction of things not seen" (Heb 11:1). We say that we believe in God because God cannot be experienced in the same way as other things in the world. If we understand belief in the church as being similar, this means that the church we believe in cannot be experienced. With such a starting point, it is not surprising that many theologians have referred to an invisible or hidden church, beside or behind the empirical church. The concept of *church* has thus attained a sort of duality: on the one hand, we have the church we believe in but cannot experience, and on the other hand we have the church we experience.

---

1. Kolb and Wengert, *Book of Concord*, 22–23.

Furthermore, the obvious disjunction between what is said in the confessions of the church (for example, that the church is one and holy), and the church as we experience it (divided and most often characterized by anything but holiness) points in the same direction. Is it then the invisible church that is one and holy and not the visible one?

While such a model apparently solves certain issues, it also creates others. One issue is how we should actually conceive of such an invisible church and how it is related to the people who belong to the church. Another issue is if theological concerns are so focused upon the invisible church then less attention is paid concerning the visible church. In a way, the church in the here and now becomes something *unreal* in relation to theological ideas about the church. Finally, there is the fact that it is difficult to find support in the New Testament for the notion of an invisible church. In the New Testament the church is, first and foremost, understood as a real and visible fellowship of believers.

In this book I will argue that the question of what it means to believe in the church cannot be understood by introducing a distinction between the visible and the invisible church. My thesis is that there is only one church, namely the church as visible and one that can be experienced in the world. When we confess our faith in the church according to the historic creeds, this is the church we are referring to. This is the only church, the real church. This church is a fellowship of believers, gathered in the name of Jesus around the Word and the sacraments. This confession about the church can be understood as statement of faith because it expresses the belief that this fellowship has a special relationship with the triune God, through the presence of the resurrected Jesus, by the Spirit. Believing in the church means believing that Jesus is speaking truthfully when he promises that "where two or three are gathered in my name, I am there among them" (Matt 18:20).

Such an understanding of the church presupposes seeing the church from an *eschatological* perspective. From the perspective of faith, the church is understood in light of its future as a sign and an anticipation of that fellowship between God and humans which will be brought about by the forthcoming kingdom of God. Statements about the church as one and holy must not be understood as statements about an invisible church behind the visible, but about the church in light of its eschatological destiny.[2]

---

2. This will be discussed in more details in chapter 2.

Introduction

The fact that I believe this Christological and eschatological perspective is more apt key for ecclesiology than the traditional distinction between visible and invisible does not mean this distinction does not represent important theological concerns. Not least, it represents an important critical perspective *vis-à-vis* the actual church. As I will show, such concerns can be maintained within alternative theological framework.

BETWEEN SYSTEMATIC AND PRACTICAL ECCLESIOLOGY

If believing in the church implies that we can say something about the church we experience, this has consequences for theological statements about the church. The belief in the invisible church, has often led to an ecclesiology that primarily deals with theological *ideas* about the church, rather than the church as concrete reality. Such an ecclesiology finds its sources in the work of other theologians and in doctrinal documents from various ecclesial traditions. The extent to which there is an interest in the empirical reality of the church has largely been understood as applying a theological understanding of the church to the practical church life.

If ecclesiology is more concerned about the visible church, rather with the invisible, this will influence the way we do ecclesiology. First, this will result in a lessening of the gap between a theological understanding of the church and other academic disciplines. If theology deals with the visible church, the very same church may also be studied from the perspective of historical and social sciences. It is important to clarify how the theological understanding of the church is to be related to, and integrated with, perspectives and results from other disciplines.

Second, if the concrete and empirical church becomes the object of ecclesiology, this means that theology cannot simply see the church as a doctrinal topic. Theology must also take into account what the church actually is. Ecclesiology is not only about the church from a theoretical point of view, but a doctrine of the church as we experience it in reality.

An ecclesiology that sees the church from different angles has its proponents, as exemplified by Don S. Browning's practice-theory-practice-model from his book *A Fundamental Practical Theology*.[3] Understanding the theological project as essentially practical, he distinguishes between four movements in the theological enterprise: descriptive theology, historical theology, systematic theology, and strategic practical theology. The

---

3. Browning, *A Fundamental Practical Theology*.

merit of this model is twofold: it attempts to keep the different theological disciplines together within a comprehensive understanding of theology, and it proposes a way of relating practice and theory to each other. Theology is not understood as theory divorced from practice, but as reflection built upon practice, and related to practice. It starts from practice and returns to practice. It starts with the descriptive movement to outline and interpret empirical realities. This descriptive work raises theological questions that have to be worked through in the light of Christian history, tradition and doctrine. In historical theology questions from practice are related to central texts and events of the Christian faith, including the Bible. In systematic theology a critical and philosophical perspective is further added to the theological process by discussing normativity and the validity of truth claims.[4]

Building on the results of the three first phases, strategic practical theology "brings the general fruits of descriptive theology and practically oriented historical and systematic theology back into contact with the concrete situation of action."[5] It asks the question for means, strategies, and rhetoric that should be used in the concrete situation. Contrary to the traditional view, this phase of practical theology is not to be understood as an application to the practice of theology as a theoretical discipline, but rather as "the culmination of an inquiry that has been practical throughout."[6]

When applying this model to ecclesiology, we can see how the first phase entails the necessity of a descriptive ecclesiology which, in the best possible way, can try to understand the church in actual reality. Such a descriptive or empirical ecclesiology not only relates to other disciplines and their results (interdisciplinary), but also integrates within one's own academic work, concepts, methods, and perspectives from other disciplines (intradisciplinary). Not least, this requires the use of empirical methods and theoretical perspectives borrowed from the social sciences.[7] Historical ecclesiology examines the church throughout history and how the church has been interpreted theologically, starting from the New Testament up to the present day. The task of systematic ecclesiology is to

---

4. Ibid., 47–54.
5. Ibid., 55.
6. Ibid., 57.
7. Van der Ven, *Practical Theology*, 101–2.

Introduction

understand the church doctrinally and dogmatically. Systematic ecclesiology should also relate to the church as concrete existence. At the same time it should be general enough so as to include insights that are not restricted to the given context. Finally, a strategic practical ecclesiology should revise the fellowship and practice of the church according to what the church is called to be.

In recent years, this desire to work towards a theology that is more related to the concrete and empirical church has been endorsed by other theologians as well. For example, the issue of ecclesiological methodology have been raised by the Roman Catholic theologian Nicholas M. Healy.[8] Healy points out, that a basic weakness in contemporary ecclesiology has been the fact that it has primarily worked with abstract ecclesiological *models*, rather than being related to the empirical church.[9] A result of this way of thinking has led to an ecclesiology that has idealized the church, rather than dealt with the *sinfulness* of the church. Instead of using this model, Healy calls for a *practical-prophetic* ecclesiology that can help the church carry out its mission.

Healy underlines the limited value of ecclesiological models, and points to the fact that such models are in practice understood and applied in very different ways, depending upon the theological framework in which they are used and often includes a predisposed understanding of the church.[10] The aim of ecclesiology should be a reflection of the concrete identity, rather than the formulation of general statements concerning the *nature* of the church.[11]

---

8. Healy, *Church, World, and the Christian Life*. Another example of a similar line of thought is presented by the fellow Roman Catholic scholar Roger Haight in his three-volume work on ecclesiology: Haight, *Christian Community in History*. Haight describes his objective as: "The primary object of the study of ecclesiology is the empirical church. To phrase the same thing somewhat differently, the subject matter of ecclesiology is the concrete community that exists in history, although not without hope in its eschatological fulfillment" (ibid., vol. 3, p. 35). In comparison to Healy, Haight is more concerned with history. His presentation is, to a greater degree, a presentation of the history of *the understanding of the church*, rather than of the concrete church in history.

9. The idea of ecclesiological models to which Healy refers to has been developed, among others, by Avery Dulles in *Models of the Church*. Dulles' work can be described as comparative ecclesiology. Dulles attempts to understand the ecclesiology of various theologians as expressions of a limited number of *models* that interpret biblical conceptions of the church in relation to concrete situations.

10. Healy, "Some Observations on Ecclesiological Method," 54.

11. Ibid., 57–60; *Church, World, and the Christian Life*, 154–85.

I agree with Healy's concerns that ecclesiology should relate to the concrete church. However, I disagree with Healy that ecclesiology should never attempt to formulate general statements concerning the basic identity of the church. Of course, we can never arrive at a final formulation of the church's identity. Furthermore, both the Bible and Christian tradition are so rich and varied that *any* attempt at formulating what the church is, in more general terms, will clearly represent an incomplete and one-sided picture. However, this is not to undermine the necessity of such a project, but instead it is a continual reminder that all theological constructs are works in process and imperfect.

I believe we should distinguish between different stages of a theological and ecclesiological work. While a practical, descriptive ecclesiology is primarily an examination of the church at a given point in time and space, systematic, dogmatic ecclesiology is an attempt to formulate a valid understanding of the church that goes across time and space (without becoming decontextualized). An ecclesiology that *only* deals with the church in a specific context is problematic, especially when we consider the theological conviction that the church is the *same church* that exists in different places and at different times.

It is important that the stages of practical and systematic theological development are not removed from one another. In order to avoid this, theologians need to be able to communicate and work across the different stages. To do this, we need to see the object of study for both practical and systematic ecclesiologies in such a way they recognize that they are dealing with the *same* object. For dogmatic ecclesiology, this means that all work regarding ecclesiological *ideas* should be considered with an awareness of what these ideas refer to, namely the real, visible church.

Having acknowledged that there are different stages of theological and ecclesiological work, this present book will primarily come under the category of systematic ecclesiology. I will therefore, not investigate the concrete reality of the church and its historical and social preconditions.[12] Within the framework of systematic theology, I will examine the theological *understanding* of the church. However, in line with my understanding of the concrete and visible church as the real church, I will make reference to the *relationship* between the general doctrinal understanding

---

12. As such, this book is different from the example given by Johannes A. van der Ven in his book: *Ecclesiology in Context*, which takes as its starting point the conditions of the church in contemporary society.

Introduction

and the empirical reality of the church. In order to do this I will also make connections between the theological perspectives and perspectives from other academic disciplines, especially the social sciences.

CONFESSIONAL CONTEXT AND BIBLICAL BASIS

Even though systematic theology is practiced by individual theologians, it is not without a certain ecclesial context. As I understand it, systematic theology is on behalf of the church and for the benefit of the church. As Karl Barth states in his classical definition of dogmatics: "As a theological discipline dogmatics is the scientific self-examination of the Christian Church with respect to the content of its distinctive talk about God."[13] According to Barth, theology is exercised on behalf of the church and is the investigation of the content of the church's faith and doctrine. At the same time, as indicated by his use of the expression "scientific self-examination," Barth suggests a critical perspective. Theology is not simply a reproduction and apologetic of what the church thinks and does, it is also a critical enterprise. For Barth the criterion for such criticism is given in the *object* of theology, namely God and God's self-revelation as witnessed by the Bible.

The ecclesial context of systematic theology (including ecclesiology) can never be just about the church in general, because the church exists only in and through specific denominations and ecclesial traditions. Any account of ecclesiology has to be placed within a certain context and confessional tradition. As a Lutheran, I write from within the Lutheran tradition. My Lutheran background will therefore influence both the sources I use and my line of argument. Non-Lutheran readers will notice the references I make to the Lutheran confessional documents and in particular the Augsburg Confession. Within a Lutheran framework this is a normal part of doctrinal discourse. The confessional documents do not have the same authority as the Bible, but they are regarded as the primary, authoritative interpretation of the biblical gospel. These confessions, nevertheless, also serve as ecumenical documents in the sense that there is not much in them that is not also to be found within other confessional traditions. These have to be interpreted as documents as set within a certain historical context, and distinctions have to be made between their

---

13. Karl Barth, *Church Dogmatics*, vol. I/1, 3.

central doctrinal content and the conceptual and philosophical framing of this content.

Ecclesial affiliation is not only a general denominational or confessional affiliation, it is also an affiliation to a church as placed within a concrete, cultural and social setting. Even if the ecclesiology of this book is not limited to a single context, it will be evident to the reader that I am part of the Nordic "folk church" by the examples and references I make.

The fact that ecclesiology is exercised *within* a specific ecclesial context, is not to limit ecclesiology *by* this context. There are inherent ecclesiological reasons why this is so, due to the fact that there is only *one* catholic and apostolic church. Any account of ecclesiology cannot be limited therefore to only one section of the church. However, it still remains true that this one church only exists within and through concrete *churches*. In other words, ecclesiology always takes place in a specific setting. Even if the ecclesiology proposed in this book has its primary frame of reference within a certain context and tradition, it is not limited to just the Lutheran church, nor is it only written just for Lutherans. Its theme is the Christian church in general, and it is written for an ecumenical readership. With this in mind, I will refer to, and dialogue with, theologians from variety of denominational backgrounds.

When proposing a theological argument that is not only limited to a certain confessional framework, this raises the question of what precisely is the basis for a theological argument. What may be very convincing argument within a confessional setting does not necessarily mean it will have the same value within a wider ecumenical setting. For example, the sources and creedal documents of a particular tradition might contradict and even be in opposition to those of other churches. In the recent ecumenical discourse, there has been an increased awareness of the primary role of the Bible for ecumenical theology. Building upon this common authoritative source, ecumenical rapprochement has often been advanced by a collaborative and renewed reading of the Scriptures. An important aspect of this progress has been to incorporate the insights of modern historical exegesis. This has helped to provide common ground, one that goes beyond traditional confessional readings of the biblical texts.

Following this development, references to biblical exegesis (primarily New Testament) will play an important role in this book. This is not to say that I hold simplistic, Biblicist position, whereupon one imagines that all questions can be simply answered by referring to isolated texts or

Introduction

to interpreting the Bible without consideration of how it has been understood throughout history.

Using biblical texts as a basis for ecclesial unity has been questioned by, among others, Ernst Käsemann in a famous essay, "The Canon of the New Testament and the Unity of the Church." In his view, the New Testament does not contain one consistent doctrinal system, but rather it includes variety of contradicting doctrinal positions. This means the canon of the New Testament does not constitute the unity of the church; on the contrary it provides the basis for the multiplicity of the confessions.

Käsemann is obviously correct when he says that the New Testament cannot be used as a doctrinal handbook. There are not a seamless amount of proof texts that can support a clear cut theological system. Rather, the various books, and groups of books, all have their own specific theological profile and emphasis. This, of course, also applies to a New Testament understanding of the church, a fact that is demonstrated in an assortment of historical studies made of New Testament ecclesiology.[14] However, it is an oversimplification to draw the conclusion that there are *no* unifying New Testament elements in understanding the church. While exegetes may have historical interests as their primary focus and make deliberate choices in what differences and contradictions are to be highlighted, a theological exegesis in the service of the church will also look for unifying elements. These unifying elements are not to be found elsewhere other than in the central content of the New Testament gospel of Jesus Christ. Biblically based ecclesiology thus has to be theologically and Christologically founded.[15] The possibility of such an exegesis, in contrast to Käsemann's view, is historically valid as verified by the aforementioned role of biblical exegesis in ecumenical dialogue.

For the purposes of this book, this means that the biblical material will play a crucial role. When applying this material, I will distinguish between the use of concepts and the lines of thought presented by the different books and groups of books. At the same time, I will focus on recurring themes as a common basis for a New Testament understanding of the church. As with other questions, the core of the New Testament message is to be found in the gospel of Jesus Christ. For ecclesiology, the belief in Jesus as Son of God and savior of the world is basis for any theo-

14. See e.g., Roloff, *Die Kirche im Neuen Testament*, and Collins, *The Many Faces of the Church*, which include bibliographies of similar studies.

15. Cf. the reflections concerning this question in Küng, *Church*, 15–23.

logical interpretation of the church.¹⁶ Above all, this is reflected in the understanding of the church as a fellowship which gathers in the belief that Jesus is present among those who gather in his name.

Even if the New Testament is the primary and normative basis for all Christian theology (including ecclesiology), doctrinal theology cannot be confined to an account of New Testament theology. Systematic theology is distinguished from biblical theology by the use of concepts and philosophical ideas that are not necessarily identical to those of the New Testament. While the New Testament reflects the experiences of the first Christian generation, systematic theology has to take into account the experiences and reflections of latter generations, while also addressing the challenges and needs of the church of today. Systematic theological ecclesiology has to reflect upon the meaning of the continuous existence of a fellowship of believers who assemble in Jesus name.

RECENT DEVELOPMENTS IN ECCLESIOLOGY

In recent years there has been a greater emphasis placed upon the empirical church as the object for ecclesiology and for doing theological empirical research about the church. While this present work wants to contribute to this trend, there is good reason to make reference to other significant ecclesiological developments which have been of importance for the thesis presented in this book.

A very important contribution in the development of the ecclesiological debate has undoubtedly been the reorientation of Roman Catholic theology articulated by the Second Vatican Council (1962–1965), not least by the Dogmatic Constitution on the Church, *Lumen Gentium*.¹⁷ Since Vatican II we have seen the publication of important and innovative works made to ecclesiology, from Roman Catholic, Eastern Orthodox and Protestant theologians.¹⁸ Besides the contributions made by indi-

---

16. According to Roloff, *Die Kirche im Neuen Testament*, 11–12, the common Christological foundation is the main unifying element of New Testament ecclesiology.

17. Published in *Teachings of the Second Vatican Council*. Cf. also the Decree on Ecumenism (*Unitatis Redintegratio*).

18. Other theologians who have been important influence in my work on ecclesiology are notably: Hans Küng (e.g., *Church*), Jürgen Moltmann (e.g., *Church in the Power of the Spirit*), John Zizioulas (e.g., *Being as Communion*), Wolfhart Pannenberg (e.g., *Systematic Theology*) and Miroslav Volf (e.g., *After Our Likeness*). For a comprehensive overview of recent ecclesiology see Kärkkäinen, *Introduction to Ecclesiology*. From the Norwegian

Introduction

vidual theologians, ecclesiological questions have also played a key role in various ecumenical documents. Although these documents are far from uniform, it is still possible to identify some common trends. Some of these trends can be summarized as follows:

(a) The work of ecclesiology has much more ecumenical profile nowadays than it ever had before. Earlier, ecclesiology was formulated within different confessional traditions, and was often polemically orientated to distinguish it from other traditions. Ecclesiology was seen as a means to articulate a particular confessional character, and was often used to show the ecclesial superiority of one's own church compared to other churches. Ecumenical developments in contemporary theology are now moving ecclesiology in another direction: First, the question of church unity has become a central theme of ecclesiology. Confessional ecclesiology often makes reference to conversational partners from other denominations, be they bilateral or through ecumenical organizations.[19] Second, the discussion of ecclesiological issues not only takes place within the various denominations, or polemically between denominations, but crosses confessional lines of demarcation. This is especially true of ecclesiological research within academic theology, which generally moves across confessional affiliations. Roman Catholic and Protestant theologians refer to each other even if their respective confessional affiliations still are of importance for their particular viewpoints. We can see theological and practical ecclesial developments and movements across denominations, which in various ways, also contributes to ecclesiology.[20] Third, the *subject* of ecclesiology is increasingly not just about individual churches, but the Christian church in a more general sense. This has also become a distinguishing feature among many Roman Catholic ecclesiologists whose

---

context, I am indebted to the work of Ola Tjørhom (e.g., *Kirken—troens mor*).

19. An important document from a Norwegian point of view is the Porvoo Common Statement, which in 1992 established communion between Anglican churches in Britain and Ireland with Lutheran churches in the Nordic and Baltic regions. In order for this to happen, it was necessary to work on the differing views concerning ecclesiology before an agreement could be reached. See *Together in Mission and Ministry*, cf. Tjørhom, *Apostolicity and Unity*.

20. For example, Charismatic theology, feminist theology and liberation theology. We can see denominational borders also being crossed with shared concerns about evangelization, church planting, and church growth.

work has come to represent not only their own denomination, but that of the church as a whole.[21]

(b) There has been a growing tendency to stress the church's character as *fellowship* (Greek: *koinonia*; Latin: *communio*). This emphasis was a central theme in the Second Vatican Council' teachings on the church, and has ever since been an important motif in further ecclesiological presentations.[22] In the ecumenical movement *koinonia* ecclesiology, is a key when it comes to work towards greater fellowship between the churches.[23] To the extent that we view the church fellowship as something real (and not merely as something spiritual and mystical), this too is an important theme when it comes to relating theological and sociological perspectives about the church to one another. An important factor in this reorientation has undeniably been the major changes in the social formation of the major European churches over the last two centuries. From being the religious dimension of society as a whole, the churches have gradually lost much of their religious hegemony. In many European countries the church membership is a minority compared to the population as a whole. Even in countries where the church members are still the majority of society, the church as both institution and fellowship in relationship to society has a more independent identity. This has led to internal consolidation where churches and congregations are increasingly being seen as distinct fellowships. One outcome of this development has been an increased awareness of the *local congregation's* role. This can be seen in ecclesiological scholarly works and within the practical theological context. Not least, this is reflected in the material about church planting and church growth, which to a large extent, also focuses upon the

---

21. Both Johannes van der Ven and Nicholas M. Healy can be interpreted as *postecumenical* ecclesiologists. Simply stated, this assumes that ecclesiology is about the Christian church in the broadest sense. When van der Ven in his ecclesiology focuses on the Roman Catholic Church, this is for practical and not evaluative reasons (*Ecclesiology in Context*, xiii). Healy defines the object of his ecclesiology as reflecting all the Christian groups who accept the Nicene Creed (*Church, World, and the Christian Life*, 6).

22. Dulles, *Models of the Church*, 47-62.

23. For example, see the statements made by the Lutheran World Federation at Curitiba (Hjelm, *I Have Heard the Cry of My People*); the World Council of Churches at Canberra (Kinnamon, *Signs of the Spirit*); Faith and Order report at Santiagio de Compostela (Best and Gassmann, *On the Way to Fuller Koinonia*); and the report from the Ecumenical Research Institute at Strasbourg *Communio/Koinonia*. I will return to this point in more detail in chapter 5.

Introduction

local congregation. A result of seeing the church as a distinctive fellowship has put the issue of the correlation between ecclesiology and ethics on the agenda. As moral community the church upholds certain moral standards for its own fellowship and provides a challenge to the ethical and political matters of society.[24]

(c) A marked feature of the theology of the last few centuries has been a renewed awareness of the Christian *eschatology*. This is not only seen as one of many truths, but is understood as the key to understanding Christian faith and theology, and also the church. Accordingly, Christian existence in the here and now is understood in light of the end of history with the second coming of Jesus. With Jesus' life, death and resurrection, God's kingdom is made present in the world. The life of the church and of individual Christians is therefore, characterized by the tension between what is already given, and what is not yet realized. The rediscovery of the essential role of eschatology within theology has furthermore been an important influence in ecclesiology.[25]

(d) The awareness of a church as a pilgrim people moving towards the final consummation, while also acknowledging that the church has lost its majority position in society, has led to a new awareness of the church's *mission*. According to this interpretation, mission is not just a part of the church's history, but is its call that runs throughout all ages. Mission is not only one of many activities the church engages in, but is paramount to understanding the church in its fullness. The church should not just *do mission*, but is by nature a *missional church*.[26]

---

24. Jürgen Moltmann and Stanley Hauwerwas have, in their various ways, helped to shed light on these issues, see Rasmusson, *Church as Polis*.

25. Wolfhart Pannenberg and Jürgen Moltmann are theologians who have contributed to giving eschatology greater significance for theology in general, which in turn, has influenced ecclesiology. Cf. Pannenberg, *Systematic Theology*, vol. III; Moltmann, *Church in the Power of the Spirit*.

26. Van Gelder and Zscheile, *Missional Church in Perspective*.

2

The Church: People Gathered in the Name of Jesus

At the beginning of the previous chapter, I asked: what does it mean to believe in the church? In this question we are implicitly asking what the nature of church is, and how this relates to the church we experience. In this chapter I will suggest an answer to this question. In essence, the church is a visible and concrete fellowship between people as defined by its relationship with the triune God.[1] The church becomes the church when people gather in the name of Jesus and believe that Jesus himself, through the Spirit, is made present in their midst. As such, the church is both a sign and an anticipation of the fellowship between God and people with the forthcoming kingdom of God.

THE STARTING POINT: THE CHURCH IS A FELLOWSHIP OF PEOPLE

In the theological debate about how to understand of the church, I believe there is one particular aspect that is often neglected, either because it is so obvious or because its significance is overlooked, namely that the church (whatever we may think of the church) *consists of people*. In classical doctrinal formulations about the church, this is either clearly stated or implied. For example, in the Augsburg Confession article VII it states: "The church is the assembly of saints (*congregatio sanctorum*) in which

---

1. A terminological qualification: When talking about the church in this sense, I use concepts like "visible," "concrete," and "tangible" interchangeably, or I use the expression the church "as we experience it." I am also using the concept "empirical" in the same general way, except when referring more specifically to social scientific methodology.

the gospel is taught purely and the sacraments are administered rightly."[2] This statement raises numerous points that necessitate further discussion, for example, what requirements must be met to say when the gospel is rightly taught, or what does it mean when the members of the church are holy? In any case, this text makes it clear that *the church is a specific group of people.*

This understanding of the church's core identity is also outlined by Martin Luther in article XII of the Smalcald Articles: "God be praised, a seven-year-old child knows what the church is: holy believers and 'the little sheep who hear the voice of their shepherd' [John 10:3]."[3] The formulation in the Apostles' Creed of "the communion of saints" (*sanctorum communio*)[4] also presupposes that the church consists of people who are in a specific relationship with one another. In other words, they are a community or a fellowship.[5]

Rather surprisingly this very core aspect of the church has often been placed in the shadow of other aspects of the church's identity. This is largely due to the fact that the church as an institution often has been viewed, more or less, independently from the fellowship upon which it is based. This is not to say that there is anything necessarily wrong with such a (inevitable) process of institutionalization.[6] Such a practice becomes more of an issue when the primary identity of the church is displaced and obscured by secondary features. For example, this can occur when the church building, or say the organization and hierarchy of the church are associated as being the actual church separate from its core as a fellowship of people.

2. Kolb and Wengert, *Book of Concord*, 43. Please note that when the Lutheran confessions are cited in English, the text is taken from this edition. When the German or Latin text is referred to the source is *Die Bekenntnisschriften der evangelisch-lutherischen Kirche*.

3. Kolb and Wengert, *Book of Concord*, 324–25.

4. According to Werner Elert (*Abendmahl und Kirchengemeinschaft*, 5–16) "*sanctorum*" can also be interpreted as the plural of "*sancta*." If this is the case, then the statement could be translated as "communion with the holy things," i.e., the bread and wine of eucharist. This interpretation does not necessarily contradict the idea of the communion of saints: In both cases, we are speaking about a fellowship of people. Cf. the discussion at Skarsaune, *Troens ord*, 130–31, which concludes in support of a communion of persons.

5. I will consider in more depth the understanding of the church as fellowship in chapter 5.

6. I will consider in more detail the question of the church as an institution in chapter 6.

This core notion of the church can also be found in the New Testament. Here the church is not seen as an abstract or institutional entity, but as a fellowship of people who have faith in Jesus Christ. The word we usually translate as *church* comes from the Greek word *ekklesia*. In secular usage the Greek word simply means a political gathering of citizens. In the New Testament, however, *ekklesia* also alludes to the Hebrew word *kahal*, which is used in the Old Testament to refer to the people of Israel gathered in the presence of God (Deut 23:2–8; 1 Chr 28:8; Mic 2:5). The way the term is used in the New Testament can just as well be translated *congregation* as *church*. This is related to the fact that the term can refer to both the local congregation of believers (Acts 8:1; Gal 1:2) as well as to the fellowship of Christians all over the world (Gal 1:13), although the first meaning is more prevalent.[7]

Both the term itself, and its use in the New Testament presuppose not only a group of people, but a group of people that *gathers together*. For this reason the term *ekklesia* can also be translated as *assembly*. The assembly is the fellowship who gathers together for worship.[8] A similar understanding of a congregation as a group of people who gather together can be found in the use of the Latin terms *communio* and *congregatio* as found in the Creeds.

It is important that we do not set these two meanings off against each other, but allow them to be heard simultaneously. *Ekklesia* is both *the act of coming together* (to fellowship/to commune) and the *group that comes together* (the fellowship/the community). The church is not only present in the worship service, but continues to be the church beyond the formal gathering. The same God who calls people together, also sends people out, not only as individuals but as a fellowship (Matt 28:16–20).[9]

The gathering together of a group of people for specific activity is something that can be described empirically and sociologically. What distinguishes the theological perspective from a purely sociological one is the belief that this group has a particular relationship with God and is part of the work of God in the world. According to the theological perspective, in its most profound sense, what takes place is initiated by God: it is God

---

7. Küng, *Church*, 79–87.

8. For a more in-depth description of the concept of the worship service, see chapter 8.

9. Küng, *Church*, 104: "Ekklesia, like 'congregation,' means both the actual *process of congregating* and the *congregated community* itself." See chapter 5.

The Church: People Gathered in the Name of Jesus

who gathers his[10] church, and it is God who leads each individual into the fellowship of the church. Furthermore, when the congregation gathers, it is not only with the purpose of meeting each other, but is with the purpose of meeting God. The very reason for coming together in Christian worship is motivated by the belief that God makes himself present.

MATTHEW 18:20 AS A STARTING POINT FOR UNDERSTANDING THE CHURCH

In his ecclesiological work Miroslav Volf takes as his starting point, what he calls the "definition of the church" of Matthew 18:20: "For where two or three are gathered in my name, I am there among them." Volf points out that this verse in fact has been a key verse in ecclesiological thinking ever since the days of the early church, for example in the writings of Ignatius and Tertullian.[11] In agreement with Volf, I believe this verse is a suitable starting point when considering the nature of the church.[12] In some traditions this verse has been understood as a statement about the fellowship of believers within the church (*ecclesiola in ecclesia*), rather than being primarily about the church. However, this delimitation is not in keeping with the original meaning or supported by later significant readings of this passage.

When understood as a statement about the church, Matthew 18:20 becomes an interesting verse to start our inquiry, precisely because it combines the concrete and empirical ("For where two or three are gathered in my name") with a statement about the divine presence in the world ("I am there among them").

In many ways, Matthew 18:20 describes the church in its nucleus form, both chronologically and in content.[13] Chronologically, it was the small group of disciples gathered in the name of Jesus that preceded lat-

---

10. I here follow the Biblical practice of referring to God by the masculine form of the pronoun, even if God clearly is beyond human gender differences.

11. Volf, *After Our Likeness*, 135–37.

12. Ibid., 136: "I will join this long tradition by taking Matt. 18:20 as the foundation not only for determining what the church is, but also for how it manifests itself externally as a church. *Where two or three are gathered in Christ's name, not only is Christ present among them, but a Christian church is there as well,* perhaps a bad church, a church that may well transgress against love and truth, but a church nonetheless."

13. The widespread view of the day of Pentecost as the *birthday of the church* is questionable. We could see the birth of the church as being the time Jesus called his disciples.

ter developments of the church. At the same time, there is a priority in content: The only thing that can give an organization or institution the status of *church* is the presence of the resurrected Jesus Christ among the people gathered in his name. The church can lack everything else, but not this essential dimension.[14]

Based on Matthew 18:20, we see that the church is an encounter between the risen and glorified Jesus and his disciples. Although these words are spoken by the earthly Jesus, they are nevertheless spoken with the promise of Jesus' continued presence to be with them, even when he is no longer together with them in the same manner as during his earthly life. Jesus' presence is connected to a very specific situation: First, people must be gathered together. Jesus' presence is thus connected to fellowship and not to the individual. "Two or three" should be understood as a minimum, and not as the maximum. One person alone is not a fellowship, in the very least only two or three people are a fellowship. Second, people must come together *in the name of Jesus.* In New Testament terminology, an action that takes place in the name of Jesus is an action that takes place on behalf of Jesus and in the name of Jesus. This also applies to praying to God: "Very truly, I tell you, if you ask anything of the Father in my name, he will give it to you" (John 16:23). A similar promise is made in the verse prior to the promise of Jesus' presence when two or three are gathered in his name: "Again, truly I tell you, if two of you agree on earth about anything you ask, it will be done for you by my Father in heaven" (Matt 18:19). These examples shed light on the type of gathering Jesus connects to the promise of his presence: it is a gathering of people who seek God as they confess Jesus.

According to the Bible, faith derives from divine *promise*. Paul presents Abraham as an example of faith, precisely because Abraham believed in the promise of God to make him the father of many nations (Rom 4). When the church can be declared as an article of faith, this means that we trust in a promise such as Matthew 18:20: *to believe in the church is to believe in the promise that Jesus is present among those who are gathered in his name.*

---

14. In agreement with Volf, I believe to use Matthew 18:20 is not to base an entire understanding of the church on this verse alone, nor is it to derive an understanding of the content of the church from a detailed exegesis of this verse. Rather, the point being is to use this verse as a starting and focus point from which to build upon. Volf, *After Our Likeness*, 137 n. 37.

The Church: People Gathered in the Name of Jesus

To believe in the church cannot be put at the same level as believing in God. Only the triune God is the direct object of Christian faith, in the sense of trusting in and depending upon him. The church is not an object of belief in this primary sense. Faith in the church can, however, be *derived* from faith in God, or more specifically be described in the promise of the divine presence among those who seek God in the name of Jesus.

In one sense, the statement of the Augsburg Confession art. VII (cited above) can be understood as a commentary on Matthew 18:20. Both passages deal with people who gather together, and in both passages this gathering is qualified in more detail. Whereas Matthew 18:20 summarizes and specifies this by the statement "in Jesus name," the Augsburg Confession gives two qualifiers: First, it is about *who* is gathered, namely the saints, i.e. the Christians. Second, it is about *what* they are gathered around, namely the Word and sacraments.

A similar description of what it means to be gathered in the name of Jesus is found in Acts 2:42, which depicts the life of the congregation after Pentecost: "They devoted themselves to the apostles' teaching and fellowship, to the breaking of bread and the prayers." Out of these four aspects of church life, the prayers are also mentioned in the context of Matthew 18:20 as an aspect of being gathered in the name of Jesus. "The apostles' teaching" and the "breaking of bread" correspond then to the gospel and the sacrament of the eucharist[15] in the language of the Augsburg Confession. The gospel and the eucharist are simultaneously human activities (the Augsburg Confession speaks of "teaching" the gospel and "administering" the sacraments) and an outworking of the presence of Jesus. When the apostles' teaching is heard as the disciples of Jesus are gathered, this happens by faith in the promise that those who hear the apostles' message will also hear the voice of Jesus (Luke 10:16: "Whoever listens to you listens to me"). When Jesus' disciples share bread and wine together, this happens by faith in the promise that Jesus is made present in bread and wine (Matt 26:26, 28: "This is my body . . . This is my blood").

The fourth aspect in Acts 2:42 mentions the word *fellowship* (Greek: *koinonia*).[16] What is worth noting is that the fellowship itself is given

---

15. In the English language the meal instituted by Jesus is referred to by a variety of terms, e.g. the Lord's supper, holy communion, the mass, the divine liturgy, etc. In this book I have chosen to follow the example of the Lima Document (*Baptism, Eucharist and Ministry*) that refers to this meal as the *eucharist* or the *eucharistic meal*.

16. Cf. a more in-depth discussion of the New Testament concept of *koinonia* in chapter 5.

intrinsic value in and of itself. Fellowship is therefore, not merely a necessary means to *attain* the presence of Jesus. It is the place where Jesus *is* present. The church is not simply the place where people meet Jesus *individually*, but is a fellowship that seeks Jesus *together* and is as such, the place where Jesus is present. Fellowship is not only about an individual Christian who occasionally seeks fellowship in order to be inspired in his/her individual relationship with Jesus, rather it is only through being a member of this fellowship that the individual has fellowship with Jesus.

THE CONTINUING PRESENCE OF JESUS BY THE HOLY SPIRIT

During his earthly life, Jesus was present with his disciples physically and overtly: he was with them, spoke with them, listened to them, and ate with them. As such, his presence was also limited to certain times, places and persons. After the resurrection, his physical presence was temporarily reassumed, even if his corporeality was changed. It would also seem that his presence was only made manifest among his disciples, and not publicly as he had done before.

With the ascension, Jesus' physical presence among his disciples came to an end. This is not to say that his presence came to an end completely, however. In one of his final statements, Jesus assures his disciples that he will always be with them: "And remember, I am with you always, to the end of the age" (Matt 28:20). There is nothing in the New Testament that would indicate that his new presence was perceived as anything of less value than his physical presence. According to John 16:7, Jesus in fact states the exact opposite: "It is to your advantage that I go away." Nevertheless, it is clear the continuing presence of Jesus cannot be conceived of being disconnected to his earthly life. It is as the incarnated, crucified and risen Lord that Jesus is made present among his disciples.

The works and words of the earthly Jesus are, in a unique way, the norm and criterion for the latter experience of the presence of Jesus in the church. An essential aspect of the preaching of the church will always be the story of Jesus' life and words, as foretold in the four Gospels. This means the original *witnesses* of Jesus' life are of fundamental importance to the continued life of the church: these witnesses "declare to you what was from the beginning, what we have heard, what we have seen with our eyes, what we have looked at and touched with our hands, concerning the

The Church: People Gathered in the Name of Jesus

word of life" (1 John 1:1; cf. Acts 1:21–22). The first disciples were chosen by Jesus and given charge to pass on his message to others (Mark 3:14). These witnesses were sent by Jesus to speak on his behalf: "Whoever listens to you listens to me" (Luke 10:16). When the words of the Nicene Creed speak of the church being *apostolic*, this means that the church is a continuation of the church of the apostles which it is built upon their testimony about Jesus.

After the passing away of the first generation of disciples, their words of testimony were no longer available except through their (and their fellow workers') *writings* as collated in the New Testament. The apostolic character of the church, therefore, entails that the church is founded upon the witness of Jesus as testified and interpreted by the writings of the New Testament. The continuing presence of Jesus in the church does not mean any present experience of this presence can replace the memory of the Jesus' earthly life—the church is maintained through the apostolic witness. The church is therefore, "built upon the foundation of the apostles and prophets, with Christ Jesus himself as the cornerstone" (Eph 2:20).

It is not immediately clear whether Ephesians 2:20 refers to the prophets of the Old Testament or to the prophets in the early church. What is certain, however, is that those who wrote the New Testament understood themselves as continuing the story of God's dealings with Israel as witnessed by the Old Testament (Rom 1:2; Heb 1:1–2). For this reason, the church can also be seen as an analogy of, or in continuation with, the Old Testament people of God (Eph 1:14; Titus 2:14; 1 Pet 2:10).[17] This means the New Testament cannot be truly understood unless it is read in light of the Old Testament writings.

When the risen Jesus promises his disciples that he will be with them "to the end of the age" (Matt 28:20), this implies a promise that he will, once again, be directly and visibly present among them. Just as Jesus was taken up into heaven, he will return once again (Acts 1:11). When the kingdom of God comes, Jesus will be present in glory in the renewed earth (Rev 22:3). This means that the understanding of Jesus' presence in the church is oriented not only toward the *past*, toward the witness of Jesus' earthly life, but also toward the *future*, to his presence in the final

---

17. Küng, *Church*, 107–50; Dahl, *Das Volk Gottes*. The question of the relationship between the church and Israel/the Jewish people is, in itself, a comprehensive topic that will not be discussed in this book. Cf. Moltmann, *Church in the Power of the Spirit*, 136–50.

consummation. In the same way that it is important to give witness to Jesus' first advent, so the church too is to pray with expectation for Jesus' imminent return. An early Christian prayer that captures this sentiment, as transliterated from the original Aramaic, is *maranatha* meaning "Oh Lord, come!" (1 Cor 16:22; cf. Rev 22:20).

During the *in-between time* of the first to the second coming of Jesus in which the church now exists, the presence of Jesus is made manifest by the *Holy Spirit*.[18] The role of the Spirit in making present the continuing presence of Jesus is one of the central themes of Jesus' farewell discourses to his disciples. Describing the post-ascension time, Jesus promises the divine presence as being Trinitarian (John 14–16). Jesus has not acted on his own behalf but as an emissary sent by the Father: "I came from the Father and have come into the world" (John 16:28). What Jesus has received from his Father, he will pass on to his disciples: "As the Father has loved me, so I have loved you . . . I have made known to you everything that I have heard from my Father." (John 15:9, 15). By his work the "Father may be glorified in the Son" (John 14:13).

The relationship between Jesus and his Father means he provides access to fellowship with the Father in an exclusive manner: "No one comes to the Father except through me" (John 14:6); knowledge of Jesus is knowledge of the Father (John 14:7); those who see Jesus have also seen the Father (John 14:9); and through Jesus, the disciples have access to the Father, and he will hear them when they pray in his name (John 16:23).

In his farewell discourse, Jesus prepares his disciples for the fact that soon he will no longer be among them in the same way as he was before. This is not to say that the divine presence will cease, but rather it will continue in a different manner than before. When Jesus leaves the world to go to the Father (John 16:28), the Father will send the Spirit in his place (John 14:16–17, 26). When the Father sends the Spirit, he does so in the name of Jesus, and the task of the Spirit is to remind the disciples of what Jesus has already told them (John 14:26). The witness of the Spirit is consequently nothing other than the gospel of Jesus.

The advent of the Spirit does not *replace* Jesus and his significance for the disciples. On the contrary, the Spirit imparts the presence of Jesus. The overriding sin that the Spirit must convict is disbelief about Jesus (John 16:9). The task of the Spirit is to glorify Jesus by proclaiming the

18. Concerning the relationship between the church and the Spirit, see Küng, *Church*, 162–79.

message concerning him (John 16:14). At the same time, this message contains nothing more than what Jesus has received from the Father: "He will glorify me, because he will take what is mine and declare it to you. All that the Father has is mine. For this reason I said that he will take what is mine and declare it to you" (John 16:14–15).

The fact that the church's relationship with God is a relationship with the *triune* God is also articulated in other passages in the New Testament. In Ephesians 2:22, we read that the church, through Jesus, is "built together spiritually (Greek: in the Spirit) into a dwelling place for God." Similarly, Matthew 28:19 indicates that we become a part of the fellowship of the church through baptism "in the name of the Father and of the Son and of the Holy Spirit."

By taking John 17:11 as a starting point of the unity of the church as compared to the unity of the Father and the Son, the fellowship of the church too can be understood as reflecting the fellowship between Father, Son and Spirit. In this way, the fellowship between the persons of the Trinity, between people and God, and between people, can be seen as related and analogous. The fellowship of the church reflects the Trinitarian fellowship and provides access to this fellowship. This view of fellowship provides important perspective about the church as *koinonia*. Nevertheless, we must be careful not to draw too overt and conclusive parallels.[19] Not least, we must be careful not to draw too decisive outcomes about the relationship between the persons of the Trinity and groups within the church, for example, between clergy and laypersons.[20]

The fact that the Spirit replaces Jesus' earthly presence does not reduce, or neglect the significance of Jesus' relationship to his disciples. Jesus speaks of how he will go to the Father, yet he encourages his disciples to "abide" in him (John 15:4). When Jesus likens the relationship between him and the disciples, to the relationship between a vine and

---

19. Coming from the Greek Orthodox theological tradition, John Zizioulas has been drawn similar conclusions. Zizioulas, "Church as Communion," 105–6: "[W]hen we say that the church is koinonia, we mean no other kind of communion but the very personal communion between the Father, the Son and the Spirit . . . The church as a communion reflects God's being as communion in the way this communion will be revealed fully in the kingdom." Cf. Volf, *After Our Likeness*, see especially pp. 191–200, where the foundations and limits of this type of analogy are further discussed.

20. Volf, *After Our Likeness* is concerned with precisely this issue, of how varying understandings of the Trinity, based upon this type of analogy, can lead to varying ecclesiological consequences.

the branches (John 15:1–11), this clearly indicates that he will remain present amongst his disciples. At the same time, the image of the vine also indicates that the continuing presence of Jesus is not only in relation to the individual, but to the disciples as a fellowship: "I am the vine, you are the branches" (John 15:5).

Furthermore, in the other New Testament writings, the Spirit is understood as the one who represents the presence of God in the church. In the Acts of the Apostles, the gift of the Spirit is the elementary factor, both in the life of the individual believer, and in the life of the church. To "receive the gift of the Holy Spirit," and to receive salvation through Jesus, are two sides of the same coin (Acts 2:38). The Spirit is also active in the life of the church (Acts 5:32, 13:2, 15:28, 20:28). In Peter's speech on the day of Pentecost, the pouring out of the Spirit is seen from an eschatological point of view. The fact that the Spirit is now being given to ordinary men and women, and not only to selected individuals, is an indication that the end times have arrived (Acts 2:14–21). In this sense, the church is an end-times fellowship, specially equipped, and with a particular mandate to preach the gospel of God during the last days.

For Paul as well, the Spirit is the source of life, both the individual believer and the church. The Spirit is not understood as something *in addition* to faith in Jesus, but is because of faith in Jesus. The Spirit is the "Spirit of the Lord" (2 Cor 3:17) and the "Spirit of Jesus Christ" (Phil 1:19). Paul maintains that "anyone who does not have the Spirit of Christ does not belong to him" (Rom 8:9), and that "no one can say 'Jesus is Lord' except by the Holy Spirit" (1 Cor 12:3). In Paul's description of the church as the body of Christ, the Spirit is the power that binds the whole body together and coordinates the various gifts (1 Cor 12).

As it is the presence of Jesus what makes the church to be the church, this means it could not be a church without the presence of the Holy Spirit. The fact that the church presupposes the Spirit in order to be a church is not to say that the Spirit is a *part* of the church, or *the spirit of the church*. The Spirit is not someone the church *owns*. The church must *pray* for the presence of the Spirit and trust in the promise that Jesus will be present whenever two or more are gathered in his name.

After Jesus' ascension, his presence in the church through the Spirit also changes the relationship of the church regarding *places*. Before the ascension, the presence of Jesus meant his physical presence amongst his disciples. Fellowship with Jesus was thus, limited to a single place, Galilee,

Jerusalem, or wherever Jesus happened to be at any given time. When the presence of Jesus is conveyed by the Spirit, this limitation is removed: the Spirit can mediate the presence of Jesus in many places simultaneously. This does not mean that the church loses its relationship to places. Being church still means being *gathered* in the name of Jesus. Such a gathering presupposes a place where people come together. The church is still fundamentally connected to *places*. Through the Spirit, however, people can gather in the name of Jesus *concurrently* in various places. The church is still bound to places, but just not to one particular place. The church can exist at the same time in various places.

On the one hand, this means that congregations that gather in a given place are fully and wholly church—because the risen Jesus is among them. At the same time, the local congregation is never a church *alone*, but rather, it is the church together with other congregations who also gather in the name of Jesus. The fact that many individual congregations exist, does not mean, however, that the *real* church should be understood as an abstract, translocal entity.[21]

THE CHURCH AS THE BODY OF CHRIST

The intimate connection between Jesus and the church is expressed by Paul by the idea of the church as the body of Christ. In Romans 12 and 1 Corinthians 12, the fellowship of believers is likened to a body with many parts: "Now you are the body of Christ and individually members of it" (1 Cor 12:27; cf. Rom 12:4–5). On several occasions in the Letters to the Ephesians and Colossians, the church is also referred to as the body of Christ (Eph 1:23, 3:6; 4:4, 12; 5:23, 30; Col 1:18, 24, 2:17, 19, 3:15). In both letters, Jesus is identified as the *head* of this body (Eph 5:23; Col 1:18).

The idea of the church as the body of Christ has played a major role within ecclesiological thinking during the twentieth century. In many cases, this idea served to counterbalance a fairly institutional understanding of the church, which up until that point, had been the dominant view in many church traditions. Not least, this is true in Roman Catholic ecclesiology, where the idea of the church as the body of Christ has been an important motif, both for individual theologians and in official documents.[22]

---

21. Cf. the understanding of the universal church discussed in chapter 9.
22. Dulles, *Models of the Church*, 47–62.

The Real Church

In Protestant theology, this idea has also been a central ecclesiological motif, for example by such influential theologians as Dietrich Bonhoeffer and Karl Barth. In Bonhoeffer's early work on ecclesiology, *Sanctorum Communio*, the church is understood Christologically as the body of Christ. An underlining idea in this work is the church as a form of existence for Christ himself.[23] Although Bonhoeffer also emphasizes that the church is a concrete, empirical reality, his view of the church being the body of Christ leads to a dividing of the true church and the empirical church. As a social entity, the church is visible; as the body of Christ, it is invisible.[24] First and foremost, the sinfulness and imperfection of the empirical church makes it necessary to distinguish the empirical church from the true church beyond the empirical.[25] At the same time, Bonhoeffer attempts to show how there is still a close connection between the two, and how the sociology of the church is still of theological significance.

A similar line of thought can be detected with Karl Barth in his ecclesiological work in Volume IV of *Church Dogmatics*.[26] Apart from the fact that Barth is mostly unconcerned with the sociological aspects of the church, there remain certain similarities between his thinking to that of Bonhoeffer. First, is the fact that Barth is likewise initially interested in saying something about the visible and empirical church. He argues against an *ecclesiological docetism* that does not take seriously the visibility of the church. Arguing against this, Barth points out that, just as the individual Christian lives his or her life in space and time, the church too exists, not as an abstract entity, but as a concrete fellowship of human beings in space and time, visible to all.[27]

---

23. "Christ existing as church-community" (*"Christus als Gemeinde existierend"*). Bonhoeffer, *Sanctorum Communio*, 141, 199, 214. My references to Bonhoeffer in this book are limited to this early work and do not reflect his later theological development. For more on Bonhoeffer's understanding of the church in other works, see Green, *Bonhoeffer* and Nielsen, *Kirken, fællesskabet og teologien*.

24. "The church is visible as a corporate social body in worship and in working-for-each-other. It is invisible as an eschatological entity, as the 'body of Christ.'" Bonhoeffer, *Sanctorum Communio*, 141.

25. Cf. the parallel concepts of "the empirical and the essential church." Ibid., 217.

26. Barth, *Church Dogmatics* (hereafter cited as CD, followed by volume number). The passages on ecclesiology can be found in § 62 (CD IV/1), § 67 (CD IV/2), and § 72 (CD IV/3.2). Cf. the critical analysis in Healy, "Logic of Karl Barth's Ecclesiology."

27. "The individual Christian can exist only in time and space as a doer of the Word

The Church: People Gathered in the Name of Jesus

Second, Barth is similar to Bonhoeffer in the way he anchors ecclesiology to Christology. As synonymous with the New Testament idea of the church as the body of Christ, the church is *Jesus' earthly-historical form of existence*.[28] This means that the church is not only visible, but also *invisible*, just as the glorified Christ is visible only to the eyes of faith.[29] Barth uses the analogy of ecclesiology and Christology: just as Jesus as God's Son has assumed a human nature and entered the visible world, in the same manner the church has a visible and an invisible dimension.[30]

For both Bonhoeffer and Barth, the Christological anchoring of ecclesiology in the idea of the church as the body of Christ, leads to a conceptual duality about the church—making a distinction between the human, empirical church and the super-empirical, *true* church. The issue remains, whether this is an obvious and/or necessary outcome of seeing the church as the body of Christ.

In order to gain a clearer understanding of this standpoint, it is necessary to ascertain the *metaphorical* aspect beholden in this concept. The church *is* not a body in a literal, biological sense, although it has qualities that allow it to be *compared* to a biological body. This metaphorical way of seeing the church is one of many, which Paul uses to describe the church, for example the "temple of God" (2 Cor 6:14; Eph 2:20–22). To take these

---

(Jas 1.22) and therefore in a concrete human form and basically visible to everyone. Similarly the Christian community as such cannot exist as an ideal commune or universum, but—also in time and space—only in the relationship of its individual members as they are fused together by the common action of the Word which they have heard into a definite human fellowship; in concrete form, therefore, and visible to everyone." CD IV/1, 653. Cf. CD IV/3.2, 723–24.

28. "The community is the earthly-historical form of existence of Jesus Christ Himself." CD IV/1, 661.

29. CD IV/1, 660–61. Barth refers to the church's "spiritual character, this secret, which is hidden in its earthly and historical form and therefore invisible, or visible only to the special perception of faith."

30. CD IV/3.2, 722–30. Barth accepts that this analogy has limits: "Between its invisible being and that of Jesus Christ . . . there is indeed correspondence but no parity, let alone identity" (ibid., 729). In CD IV/2, Barth primarily makes the distinction between "the true church" (*"wirkliche Kirche"*) and "the mere semblance of a Church" (*"Scheinkirche"*). CD IV.2, 617. This distinction is not necessarily identical with the distinction between the visibility and invisibility of the church. Since he presupposes that the "true church" can present itself visibly when God acts through the church this would indicate that the visible church can only be called the "true church" under specific circumstances.

two concepts literally, would result in them cancelling each other out—the church cannot be both a body and a temple at the same time.[31]

Even though the concept of the body of Christ has a distinctive metaphorical aspect associated to it, it is important to stress that Paul undoubtedly wishes to say something about the reality this metaphor refers to. In other words, this is more than just an illustration. Of course, this raises the question of what kind of reality Paul is referring to in this concept, and what this implies about his understanding of the church.

The idea of the church as the body of Christ should be seen in correlation to other ideas Paul uses to depict the close relationship between Christ and believers. Such terms as Christ being *in* the believer (Rom 8:10; 2 Cor 13:5; Gal 2:20), and the believer being "in Christ" (2 Cor 5:17; Gal 3:27–28; Phil 3:9) are paramount in Paul's thinking. They display a deep and almost mystical identification of the believer with Christ. This is "a totally new form of existence, an existence of being fully controlled by Christ, of living through Christ living in the believer."[32] This close relationship between Christ and the believer does not suggest that the personal identity of the believer is negated, or that the believer becomes identical to Christ. At the same time, however, it suggests more than just having a *special relationship* with Christ—Christ is present in the life of the believer in a concrete way.[33]

From what I can discern, the relationship between Christ and the church (shown by the idea of the church as the body of Christ), and the relationship between Christ and the believer are understood in similar ways. In no sense does this negate one's humanity or the concrete and empirical nature of this humanity. In both cases, Christ is *present* in the life of the individual and the fellowship. The idea of the church as the body of Christ expresses, in a special way, the *closeness* of Jesus' relationship with the church. We can also say that there is a sort of mutual *identification* between Christ and the church, without speaking of an *identical reality*. According to Karl Olav Sandnes, the idea of the church as the body of

---

31. On the significance of metaphors in ecclesiology, see Rikhof, *Concept of Church*. Concerning the metaphorical aspect of concepts see Volf, *After Our Likeness*, 142–43. About the significance of the church as the body of Christ in the Pauline literature, cf. Roloff, *Die Kirche im Neuen Testament*, 100–10, 227–31; Banks, *Paul's Idea of Community*, 62–70.

32. Gert Pelser, quoted in Bassler, *Navigating Paul*, 43.

33. Cf. ibid., 35–47.

The Church: People Gathered in the Name of Jesus

Christ does not mean that "the existence of Christ after the resurrection is synonymous with the fellowship of the congregation. Even though the congregation can be said to be his body, according to the letters of the apostle, Christ stands above and outside the congregation."[34] At the same time, unity with Christ means that he identifies himself with the believer. According to 1 Corinthians 8:12, to sin against Christian brothers and sisters is to "sin against Christ" (cf. Acts 9:5).

The fact that the church is the body of Christ does not give grounds for regarding the church as divine. In and of itself, the church—as a fellowship of human beings—is entirely human. What makes the church special is its *relationship* with the divine, due to the fact that the glorified Christ has promised to be *present* in the church. It is questionable whether we should use the incarnation as a key to understanding the church, and to say humanity and the divine in the church have a similar relationship to each other as the two natures of Jesus have to each other as the incarnate son of God. The fact that Jesus is *present* in the church does not mean he is *identical* to the church as he is to his human nature.[35]

To interpret the language of the church being the body of Christ as an ontological identification could be understood as a very *high ecclesiology*: the church is not only human, but also has a divine aspect. However, by attributing all the weighty theological attributes to the *invisible* church, little is left to be said about the visible, empirical church. A high ecclesiology on behalf of the invisible church means a *low ecclesiology* on behalf of the visible church.[36]

It is not necessary to claim (as Bonhoeffer and Barth do) that there is a fundamental difference between the true church and the visible church. To say that the church is the body of Christ is not the same as saying the church hypostatically participates in divine nature, but it is to say that Christ is present in the church. Although it is true that the presence of Christ in the church is only available to those with faith (his presence has to be believed), the church where Christ is present is still fully visibly and empirically accessible for everyone. In contrast to Barth, it is crucial to claim that the *real church* is the concrete, visible church. When we see the church in this way, the idea of the church as the body of Christ can

---

34. Sandnes, *I tidens fylde*, 210 (our translation).

35. Such an incarnational analogy can be found in Karl Barth, for example (cf. above).

36. Healy, "Logic of Karl Barth's Ecclesiology," 265 points out that this is true of Barth's ecclesiology.

be understood as a profoundly meaningful metaphor of the continuing presence of Christ. This is not only as a super-empirical reality, but Christ present in the very midst of the tangible fellowship between people gathered in his name. The real meaning of this idea, however, is not to be exhausted by theological definitions, but belongs to the deeper aspects of the faith which we can never completely fathom. In the words of Paul, the relationship between Christ and the church is "a great mystery" (Eph 5:32).

UNDERSTANDING THE CHURCH FROM AN ESCHATOLOGICAL PERSPECTIVE

The promise of Matthew 18:20 means that Jesus will continually be present among his disciples after his resurrection and ascension. This entails both continuity and change—it is the same Jesus who is present, but in a different way. His presence is no longer conveyed through his earthly body, but through the presence of the Holy Spirit (cf. John 16:7).

This temporal perspective also has an *eschatological* dimension. Both the first advent of Jesus and his continuing presence in the church are anticipations of his return in glory. Central to the preaching of Jesus was the message about the *coming of the kingdom of God*:[37] "The time is fulfilled, and the kingdom of God has come near; repent, and believe in the good news" (Mark 1:15). Through the presence of Jesus, this kingdom was already in the process of being realized in the world, even if it remains to be fully realized. The fullness of the kingdom will take place when Jesus returns "with great power and glory" (Mark 13:26). The resurrection of Jesus is eschatological, because his victory over death anticipates the final victory over death in the last days (1 Cor 15).

The idea of the kingdom of God being *already and not yet* is characteristic of the New Testament's interpretation of the time between the first

---

37. The exact nature of the *kingdom of God* in the Synoptic Gospels is not immediately evident. The predominant theological view has been to interpret the kingdom of God theocentrically: *God as ruler* (the royal kingship of God). Sverre Aalen and Hans Kvalbein have challenged this view and are calling for a more soteriologically oriented interpretation of the kingdom of God understood as *the gift of salvation, the time of salvation, and the place of salvation*. For an overview of this research and arguments therein, see Kvalbein, "Kingdom of God" and *Jesus*, 75–181. Martin Synnes has given a critique of Aalen and Kvalbein's position, arguing I believe rather convincingly, for a more balanced interpretation which combines both the theocentric and the soteriological dimensions. Synnes, "Teosentrisk eller soteriologisk."

and second advent of Jesus. Believers are already partakers in the salvation of God, but this is not yet fully realized. The salvation which we have in the here and now is an *anticipation* and *foretaste* of the final salvation.[38]

To anchor the Christian faith in the *last things* also points to the *first things* of God's original creative will. The eschatological perspective has a corresponding protological perspective. The goodness and perfection of the final consummation reflects the goodness and perfection in God's original creation before the fall. This means salvation is a *restoration* and *renewal* of creation. Salvation does not mean we are saved from creation, but that creation is saved from the devastation caused by sin.

Furthermore, ecclesiology should be seen through the eschatological, *already and not yet* interpretative lens. On the one hand, the promise of Jesus that he would be present with those who gather in his name is a continuation of the earthly presence of Jesus among his disciples. On the other hand, it is also an anticipation that God is going to make his home among mortals: "He will dwell with them; they will be his peoples, and God himself will be with them" (Rev 21:3). A fellowship that gathers in Jesus' name, and dwells in his presence, is an anticipation of the perfected human fellowship that is to be realized in the forthcoming kingdom of God. A number of biblical references depict the kingdom of God as a feast "for all peoples" (Is 25:6; cf. 2:2–4). The people of God are going to be gathered from all ages and will share the banquet meal with "Abraham and Isaac and Jacob and all the prophets" (Luke 13:28).

There is both a close connection and a vital difference between the church and the coming kingdom of God. While the kingdom of God is an outworking of the sovereign work of God, the church is a fellowship made up of people. The goal for the salvation of God is the kingdom and not the church. This is why the church prays "your kingdom come" (Matt 6:10). At the same time, the forthcoming kingdom of God is the foundation for the church's existence. The people Jesus called were those who

---

38. This line of thought presupposes, what Kvalbein refers to as a certain consensus in post-war research, namely that Jesus sees the kingdom of God as being both present and future (already, but not yet). This understanding has replaced earlier interpretations of the kingdom of God as being either present or future. Kvalbein, *Jesus*, 80. Pioneers of this new interpretation were Oscar Cullmann (*Christ and Time* and *Salvation in History*) and Werner Georg Kümmel (*Promise and Fulfilment*). An eschatology determined by the relationship between anticipation and fulfillment has also influenced certain systematic theologians. Wolfhart Pannenberg, for example, has developed a salvation-historical hermeneutic that takes a more universal-historical slant, see e.g. *Revelation as History*.

accepted the message of the kingdom of God. The church is positioned in the world as a witness to the kingdom of God, and is the place where the forces of the kingdom are continually breaking through. The kingdom of God judges the church: judgment over its imperfection and sin, and its falsehood and betrayal. When the kingdom is ushered in, the wheat will be separated from the chaff (Matt 13:24-30) and the true and false disciples will be separated from each other (Matt 7:21-23).

While the expansion and decline of the church throughout history is partly dependent upon the faithfulness of people obeying God's call, the kingdom of God is not dependent on human efforts. This is a central point made in Jesus' parables about the kingdom. The seed sprouts and grows by its own accord without human intervention (Mark 4:26-29). When the fullness of the kingdom of God breaks in, this will not be the result of the efforts of the church, nor the final stage in the development of the church. The kingdom of God is not just the future for the church, it is the future for the entire world.[39]

The relationship between the church and the restored humanity of the last days also binds the church to *created* humanity. The renewal of creation is a realization of God's original intention for creation and the redemption of creation from the present world's character of sin and corruption. From an eschatological standpoint, the relationship between the church and the world must be understood dialectically. On the one hand, the church is something other than the world, something it must distinguish itself from. On the other hand, the created world (and created humanity) is something the church affirms and acknowledges. When the church seeks God in the name of Jesus, this is on behalf of the world, and for the sake of the world.[40]

The relationship between the church and the kingdom of God can be characterized by the two terms *sign* and *anticipation*. As a *sign*, the church points beyond itself to something else, something greater. The fact that the church is a *sign* does not mean that it is merely a *symbol* of something else. A symbol is a sign that points to something else without necessarily being part of that it points to. A road sign is an example of such a symbol. A road sign has little, or nothing in common with the reality to which

---

39. Concerning the question of the relationship between the church and the kingdom of God, see Pannenberg, *Systematic Theology*, vol. III, 27-38; Küng, *Church*, 54-55, 88-104.

40. This theme will be dealt with in greater detail in chapter 4.

it points: it is not the nature of the sign as a sheet of metal attached to a pole that allows it to function as a sign of a particular stretch of road. A sign, in the sense that I am referring to here, is portrayed by the fact that it includes the reality to which it points. An example might be the way a spring flower points to the truth that the season of spring is coming. The church is a sign in this sense of this meaning: It is more than a symbol and points to another reality by bearing a portion of this reality within itself. In the church, the reality of the kingdom of God is therefore *anticipated*.[41] The fellowship with God that humanity will participate in at the final consummation is anticipated in the church, through the presence of Jesus among those who are gathered in his name.[42]

The anticipation of the fellowship of the kingdom of God within the church is typified by contradiction and ambivalence. The church manifests by its fellowship, not only the fellowship of the kingdom, but also the fellowship of sinful humanity. Holiness and unholiness, belief and disbelief, will all exist side by side in the church until the final consummation. Although the church is the place through which the kingdom of God enters into the world, it is nevertheless not a *freed territory* where the kingdom is completely victorious. It is not possible to draw a line and say: inside this line the kingdom rules and the expansion of the kingdom means the extension of this line. On the contrary, the duality and struggle between old and new, between sin and holiness, faith and disbelief, is ever present wherever the gospel is preached. Through the gospel, the Christian is already pulled into the realm of the kingdom of God, but cannot claim to be completely yet free from the powers of sin and corruption. This means that the call of the gospel to repentance must apply, not only to those who are *outside* the church in some way or another, but also to those who see themselves as being inside the Christian fellowship.

The fact that the church has the quality of an anticipatory *sign* means the reality anticipated is greater than the anticipation itself. The reality of the kingdom of God is present, but is not yet finally and fully realized. As

41. Pannenberg sums this up in the following manner: "The church, then, is not identical with the kingdom of God. It is a sign of the kingdom's future of salvation. It is so in such a way that this future of God is already present in it and is accessible to people through the church, through its proclamation and its liturgical life." *Systematic Theology*, vol. III, 37.

42. "As an anticipation of this future fellowship in God's kingdom, the elect community also exists in its particularity as a sign of our human destiny in the counsel of our Creator." Ibid., 502.

anticipation the church points beyond itself towards the final realization. The church exists in a continual tension between what it is presently and what it is a sign of—pointing towards the future. The church exists in the tension between *already* and *not yet*. It is important to remember, however, that it is precisely by anticipating the reality of the kingdom that the church points toward the final realization. The church cannot content itself by *talking* about the final realization if it does not anticipate something of this realization in its existence in the here and now. The church cannot content itself by talking about the fellowship that will be realized in redeemed humanity, but should seek to anticipate this fellowship in the present, even in a preliminary and imperfect manner. As anticipation, this fellowship points beyond itself, and is a sign of the final realization of the kingdom.

THE HOLINESS OF THE CHURCH

To see the church from the eschatological perspective provides the key to a renewed understanding of the various aspects of the church's existence as encapsulated by the Nicene Creed of the church being "one holy catholic and apostolic church."[43] The dilemma that immediately comes to mind, is how these attributes of the church can match up to the actual experience of the church that does not always appear to be one, holy, etc. One solution to this dilemma is to postulate the idea that the church's true nature is *beyond* the church as we experience it. According to such a mindset, it is the invisible church that is one and holy, because the visible does not seem to be neither one nor holy. An eschatological understanding of the church provides an alternative model for understanding the mismatch between such attributes and the actual experience of the church. Instead of seeing this as a polarity between the inner and outer, invisible and visible, it is possible to see the church as an expression of its eschatological destiny—which it already partakes in, but has not reached its full realization.

In the following section, I will show how an eschatological model can be applied to the idea of the holiness of the church.[44] The attribute

---

43. For a more in-depth study concerning these foundational ecclesial attributes see Küng, *Church*, 263–359. In contrast to many works of ecclesiology, I will not give a detailed presentation of the church as ascribed in the Nicene Creed. I will only refer to the Nicene statements as they arise in line with the arguments presented in this book.

44. For further study about the church's holiness see Johnson and Brower, *Holiness*

The Church: People Gathered in the Name of Jesus

of the church's holiness is one example that necessitates some kind of discernment between the church we believe in and the church we experience. To separate the church's holiness from the actual church is not in accordance with a New Testament understanding. In addition, the expression *holy church* is not in the New Testament. The only place where holiness is linked directly to the church as such, is in Ephesians 5:26–27, which states that Christ gave Himself for the church to "make her holy" so that it could be "holy and without blemish." First and foremost, the concept of holiness is related to the people who constitute the church. Often we see the term "holy" applied to church members (for example, 2 Cor 13:12; Eph 1:1; Phil 1:1; Col 1:2; and Heb 13:24).[45]

From a biblical point of view, to say that someone or something is holy refers principally to the relationship with God himself. In the Old Testament, holiness is a cultic concept used about people or objects that are set apart for use in the cult of worship. In this context, the opposite of holy is profane or secular. While the primary reference to holiness was related to the sanctuary and those who served there, holiness was also used in a more general sense to include the whole people of Israel: "Sanctify yourselves therefore, and be holy, for I am holy" (Lev 11:44). Israel is called a "priestly kingdom and a holy nation" (Exod 19:6). They were called to be separated unto the Lord and be bearers of his presence. The call to holiness includes the demands of cultic purity, as well as the call to keeping the Lord's commandments in all aspects of life (Deut 28:9).

The New Testament refers to the notion of holiness as being a characteristic of people in relationship to God, for example, in 1 Peter 2:9 the term "holy people" is used about the church. The New Testament also associates holiness with the presence of God. However, this presence is not related to a particular physical location, but to the Holy Spirit in the believer. According to 1 Corinthians 6:19, the the body of a Christian is perceived as being the temple of the Holy Spirit. Also, in Ephesians 2:21–22 the faithful community is referred to as a temple for God.

Holiness is not an inert reality, but something that is in constant motion—something to be constantly realized. The church's holiness is, therefore, an expression of its *sanctification*,[46] where the subject of this

---

and *Ecclesiology*; Küng, *Church*, 319–44.

45. The Augsburg Confession interprets the church in a similar and personal way as the *congregatio sanctorum*, "the assembly of saints" (article VII).

46. Aagaard, *Identifikation af kirken*, 21–23, points out that the church's holiness ac-

sanctification is God himself. In the Lord's Prayer Jesus taught his disciples to pray for the name of the Father to be hallowed and ask for his kingdom to come (Matt 6:9–10). The notion of God's kingdom is used in a similar way to the notion of sanctification, indicating that holiness already exists in the world, yet is not fully realized. To be holy, is not a state of being once and for all, but something you constantly have to partake in—to have become holy and increasingly becoming holy (1 Cor 1:2; 1 Thess 5:23). The call to holiness and transforming sanctification is necessary because God is holy: "He who called you is holy, be holy yourselves in all your conduct" (1 Pet 1:15). Thus holiness does have an intrinsic ethical dimension. It is the will of God that Christians "be holy and blameless before him in love" (Eph 1:4).

Compared to the Old Testament, it is interesting to see how holiness in the New Testament is almost exclusively associated with people in relationship with the holy God. There is no evidence in the New Testament of speaking of holy times, holy places, or holy actions.[47] Baptism and the eucharist are even not described as being holy. This does not mean that we cannot describe these actions as *holy acts*, as later church history bears witness. The point being is we cannot ascribe these actions as holy independent of God's action, and people being made holy through his actions. The church's holiness is not about holy places, offices, times or actions, but about people who, through the Holy Spirit's work have been called to be part of the communion of saints.

The believer's holiness is to be understood from an eschatological perspective, which means that the holiness of the church's life co-exists side by side with its sinfulness. *Communio sanctorum* (community of saints) is also *communio peccatorum* (community of sinners). Jesus' disciples should pray daily: "Forgive us our trespasses" (Matt 6:12). In the face of holiness in the temple, the Israelites had to purify themselves through various cultic purification rites. In the Old Testament, the focus gradually moved more and more toward *sin* as being the real problem when standing before the presence of the holy God. In Isaiah's vision of God in the temple, it was precisely sin that had to be removed before he could come into God's presence (Isa 6:5–7). Jesus' preaching about the

---

cording to Luther is synonymous with its continual sanctification and struggle against sin.

47. The exception being the "holy kiss" (Rom 16:16; 1 Cor 16:20; 2 Cor 13,12; 1 Thess 5:26).

kingdom of God goes hand in hand with his forgiveness of sins (e.g. Matt 9:2). For the early church, it was clear that Jesus' own death was the basis for the forgiveness of sin. The foundation for receiving of the forgiveness of sin is through baptism in Jesus' name (Acts 2:38). Baptism does not mean complete freedom from sin, however. Followers of Jesus still continue to sin and need to confess their sins to receive, by faith, the promise of forgiveness of sins in the name of Jesus (1 John 1:8–9).

The fact that the church is a *communio peccatorum* means that the reality of sin is always part of the church's life. The battle between holiness and sin is not just something that occurs in the relationship between the church and a sinful world, it is a struggle the church battles within itself. Neither the individual, nor the Christian community will be free from the need to confess sin. True holiness requires confession and forgiveness of sins. The church is a fellowship of forgiveness where believers continually confesses their sin and pronounce forgiveness—as believers are forgiven by God, so they too forgive others (Matt 6:12; Eph 4:32; Col 3:13).

It is important to stress that it is not only church members who are sinful, but also the *church itself*. In Roman Catholic ecclesiology, while acknowledging that its members are sinful, there is a tendency to perceive the church as being sinless. The church is not just a fellowship of sinners, but also a fellowship that sins. Seen from the eschatological perspective there is an insoluble simultaneity of holiness and sin, which not only affects the individual Christian, but also the Christian fellowship. An understanding of the church as sinless does not correspond with the evidence: Throughout history the church has often failed to live according to the will of God. It has not always been there for the weak, or stood up for human dignity, but instead it has often taken the side of the powerful and strong for its own gain. Time and again, the church has compromised the radical nature of its call. All too often, it has endured injustice and discord within his its own community. Perhaps one of the church's worse sins is when it sees itself as being above the imperfection and sin of the world. Thus, the church is characterized by arrogance and pride. The only thing the individual and church can boast of is the remission of sin through the death of Jesus: "May I never boast of anything except the cross of our Lord Jesus Christ" (Gal 6:14).[48]

---

48. The sinfulness of the church is stressed in the writings of Küng and Healy for example. Küng, *Church*, 319–30; Healy, *Church, World, and the Christian Life*, 7–14.

The ecclesiological *simul justus et peccator* (at at the same time justified and sinner) does not mean these are two equal sides of the church's existence. What makes the church to be the church and gives it its essential identity is holiness, not sin. While Christians share the same propensity to sin as other people, it is *holiness* that marks the church to be church—to be part of the church is to be holy. While sin is something you confess and turn from, it is holiness that remains the goal. It is the church's holiness as fulfilled in the end of the age that is confessed by the declaration of faith ("I believe in the holy catholic church . . .").

This does not mean that sin and holiness can be assigned to the visible and invisible dimensions of the church respectively. Bonhoeffer, for example makes this distinction: "Here we still walk in faith, which means we can see nothing but our sin, and accept our holiness in faith."[49] On the one hand, sin has aspects that are not directly experienced, especially when it comes to the relationship with God. On the other hand, holiness should also be experienced. In the life of the church, holiness should be visible: Christians should live in such a way that shows they belong to Christ and have turned away from their sin (cf. Rom 6).

As an embodiment of God's eschatological gift of salvation, holiness is not something the church *owns*, but something God continually *provides* through the sanctification of the church. Holiness can never be separated from the action of God within the church, and it can never be made into something that the church can take credit for. As Luther writes in his explanation of the first petition of the Lord's Prayer in his Small Cathechism, the church is to pray to God to sanctify his holy name: "It is true that God's name is holy in itself, but we ask in this prayer that it may also become holy in and among us."[50]

THE ESCHATOLOGICAL RESERVATION: "NOT EVERYONE WHO SAYS LORD, LORD . . ."

The fact that the church is not identical to the forthcoming kingdom of God shows the necessity of endorsing a fundamental *eschatological reservation* when it comes to the church as it exists now: Not everything or everyone in the church will be part of the final consummation. Between the church and the final consummation is the inevitability of judgment

---

49. Bonhoeffer, *Sanctorum Communio*, 212.
50. Kolb and Wengert, *Book of Concord*, 356.

day. This judgment is not only an indicative of the *world*—of everything *not* being church—but also indicative of the *church itself*. Many of the passages in the New Testament that refer to judgment day stress that a judgment will be for those, not only outside of the church, but also for those who believe they are safe within the church. According to 1 Peter 4:17 judgment will "begin with the household of God." To have followed Jesus, or have had fellowship with him, is no guarantee of being part of the forthcoming consummation of the kingdom of God. On the contrary, Jesus says in Matthew 7:21–23:

> Not everyone who says to me, "Lord, Lord," will enter the kingdom of heaven, but only one who does the will of my Father in heaven. On that day many will say to me, "Lord, Lord, did we not prophesy in your name, and cast out demons in your name, and do many deeds of power in your name?" Then I will declare to them, "I never knew you; go away from me, you evildoers."

According to Luke 13:24–30, some of those who "ate and drank" with Jesus, will be shut out when people from all corners of the world are sat at the table in the kingdom of God. Applying this to the church, this means that after the promises of Jesus are fulfilled, not all who were gathered in his name will be included at the feast of the eschatological kingdom of God. Not all who share in Jesus' eucharistic fellowship and call themselves believers, will be part of the final community with God.

In a similar way there are a number of references about judgment day that have a surprise element: some will be amazed that they will be part of the kingdom of God, while others will be shocked that they are left outside. As exemplified in Matthew 25:31–46, this is a double surprise, where both those who are welcomed indoors and those who are excluded will be astonished by the judgment and its justification. As captured by Luke 13:30, this is a reverse of what is expected: "Indeed, some are last who will be first, and some are first who will be last."

The passages about judgment day accentuate that it is not simply an arbitrary decision between those who are accepted, and those who are not accepted. There is a connection between the life we live and the sentence passed. In Matthew 7:21–23 Jesus makes clear that *injustice* is incompatible with getting into the kingdom of heaven, despite any manifestation of works of power. There is not necessarily a connection between visible and revelatory, and the hidden life of the person concerned. The function of judgment day is precisely to make the hidden visible: "The Lord . . . will bring to light the things now hidden in darkness and will disclose the purposes of the heart" (1 Cor 4:5).

Judgment is determined, not only by the situation here and now, but also by what will happen in the future. The ability to turn from sin and have sins forgiven, is always available in the present (Jas 5:20). To fall away remains a possibility that threatens the salvation of the believer, for example, due to false doctrine (1 Tim 4:1) or persecution (Matt 24:10). It is important to persevere until the end: "Hold fast to what you have, so that no one may seize your crown" (Rev 3:11).

An example of one of the church fathers who endorsed this understanding of the church is Augustine. In his seminal work *De Civitate Dei,* Augustine argues that it is possible to understand the church in two ways: the present church is both good and evil, but the future church will be perfected without any trace of evil.[51] In the same way, the church has within it both false Christians as well as its enemies who are destined to come to faith.[52] False Christians do not appear to be different from true Christians, and true Christians can appear to be false Christians.

Augustine believes that the "City of God" is not identical with the church, but is the goal of the church on a journey towards this destiny. When the city of God is present in the world, it is intertwined with the earthly city. Only on judgment day will they finally be separated from each other.[53]

Following Augustine, the Reformation theologians also emphasized that church consists of both true and false Christians. For the reformers this insight was developed as a response to two challenges. Firstly, the challenge of the Roman Catholic tendency of identifying the church as an institution—the reformers responded by stressing the church as a fellowship of believers. Secondly, the challenge of the radical reformers who

---

51. Augustine, *City of God*, book XX, chapter 9.

52. "She must bear in mind that among these very enemies are hidden her future citizens; and when confronted with them she must not think it a fruitless task to bear with their hostility until she finds them confessing the faith. In the same way, while the City of God is on pilgrimage in this world, she has in her midst some who are united with her in participation in the sacraments, but who will not join with her in the eternal destiny of the saints." Ibid., book I, chapter 35, p. 45.

53. "In truth, those two cities are interwoven and intermixed in this era, and await separation at the last judgment." Ibid., 46. Cf. Healy, *Church, World, and the Christian Life*, 55–56.

wanted to establish a *pure church*—the reformers responded by stressing that the church consists of both true and false Christians.

One of the classic texts dealing with this theme is found in the Augsburg Confession, article VIII:

> Although the church is, properly speaking, the assembly of saints and those who truly believe, nevertheless, because in this life many hypocrites and evil people are mixed in with them, a person may use the sacraments even when they are administered by evil people . . . Both the sacraments and the Word are efficacious because of the ordinance and command of Christ, even when offered by evil people.[54]

The underlining aim of this article is to confront the Donatist misconception, namely that the effectiveness of the sacraments is dependent on the personal holiness of the minister. At the same time the article reveals an understanding of the church as being a *mixed assembly* of both true and false believers. The church is a gathered fellowship through Word and sacrament and is understood to consist of both those who have true faith in their hearts and those who have not. Moreover, it is these *saints and true believers* who are according to the article, strictly speaking, the church. This implies a certain dualism in the concept of the church: between the *real church* of the true believers, and the church as a mixed congregation *in this life* of true and false Christians.

This leaves us with the question of how the church "properly speaking" should be interpreted. One possibility is to understand it as the eschatological tension between what the church is ("in this life") and what it will be at the final consummation. This means that the two sides of the church's existence are presently inseparable, and what the church *really* is can therefore only be understood from the eschatological point of view. It is from this perspective that the church can be viewed as holy. Even if the church is characterized by both holiness and sin, holiness stills marks the church's true identity.

An alternative interpretation of this notion of the church "properly speaking" is to understand this as a distinction between the outer and an inner church, the visible and an invisible church. According to this point

---

54. Kolb and Wengert, *Book of Concord*, 43. For an overview of ecclesiology in the Lutheran confessions see Austad, "Kirche."

The Real Church

of view, the true church has an inner and invisible quality, whereas the visible church is a kind of outward manifestation of the true church.

The possibility of such an understanding is confirmed by Philipp Melanchthon in the Apology of the Augsburg Confession. Here he refers to the allegation made against the reformers that they understood the church as a "platonic republic" rather than as a reality. Arguing against this allegation, Melanchthon states that the reformers believe "this church truly exists, consisting of true believers and righteous people scattered through the entire world" (Apol VII–VIII, 20). The church consists of specific people. In reality, however, these people do not exist as a set apart group—their identity is hidden. The church is "principally an association of faith and the Holy Spirit in the hearts of persons. It nevertheless has its external marks so that it can be recognized, namely, the pure teaching of the gospel and the administration of the sacraments in harmony with the gospel of Christ" (5). However, "in this life hypocrites and wicked people, who are mixed in with these, participate in the outward signs. They are members of the church according to their participation in the outward signs and even hold offices in the church" (28). It would seem that Melanchthon still assumes the outer-inner hermeneutic.[55]

A similar outer-inner distinction can be found in Luther's theology. Rather than talk of an invisible church, Luther seems to want to describe the true church as *hidden*. According to Paul Althaus, Luther does not make any absolute distinction between the hidden and visible church, but rather these two are qualities of the same church.[56]

Even beyond the special ecclesial context of the Reformation, the distinction between the hidden and visible church is still widely used in Lutheran theology. For example, Regin Prenter in his dogmatics bases his understanding of the church upon the Augsburg Confession formulation of the church as a gathering of *true believers* as constituted by the Word and faith.[57] While the Word is outward and visible, a believer's faith remains invisible. This duality between the visible word and invisible faith makes the church simultaneously visible and hidden—visible because

---

55. Kolb and Wengert, *Book of Concord*, 174–78.

56. Althaus, *Theology of Martin Luther*, 293. Cf. Neebe, *Apostolische Kirche*, 215–44.

57. Prenter, *Creation and Redemption*. This is with reference to pp. 515–45: § 39 "The Church of the Word and of Faith." In *Kirkens lutherske bekendelse*, 85–93, Prenter places greater emphasis upon the assembly of believers as the bearer of the visible character of the church.

the church is constituted by the Word, and hidden because the church is a community of the faithful: "When we move from the word to faith, we move from God's visible sign to man's invisible faith."[58] Granted, the fruits of faith are visible, but faith itself remains invisible. The reason for this is that faith not only adheres to the visible sign, but to invisible grace witnessed in the sign.

An outcome of Prenter's distinction between the church visible and hidden means, to a large extent, that the church as a community remains a hidden reality. The church's visibility is associated with the Word and sacrament as the visible sign of God's grace: "It is manifest through the preaching of the word and the administration of the sacraments."[59] From Prenter's point of view, the church becomes primarily visible by the administration of Word and sacrament through the ordained ministry.

In contrast to Melanchthon apology, the church as visible and concrete fellowship almost disappears in Prenter's interpretation. While Melanchthon distinguishes between an outer and inner community, there seems to be only an inner community with Prenter—where the church's outer reality is reduced to an institutionally embedded facilitator of grace.

I believe such an understanding of the relationship between the church visible and hidden falls short of a New Testament understanding of church as a concrete fellowship. Furthermore, one of Prenter's reasons for understanding the church as hidden, namely that faith is invisible creates difficulties.[60] Although faith is not directly accessible to anyone other than the believer, it is indirectly available to others through the believer's statements about his faith, and through the impact of faith through word and action. Paul assumes as such, that there is a clear connection between faith in the heart and confession of the mouth: "For one believes with the heart and so is justified, and one confesses with the mouth and so is saved" (Rom 10:10). In the New Testament, faith is also expressed by specific attitudes and actions. For example, Jesus saw the faith of the people when they lowered a paralyzed down to him through a hole in the roof

---

58. Prenter, *Creation and Redemption*, 528.

59. Ibid., 527.

60. It is unclear whether Prenter's argument about the invisibility of faith primarily refers to the character of faith as an inner, psychological phenomenon, or whether he imagines faith as hidden in more ontological sense. An understanding of faith as supra-empirical reality prior to any experience we can have is not uncommon in Protestant theology during the twentieth century.

(Mark 2:5). *The believers* or *those who came to faith* are mentioned in several places concerning a specific group of people (John 11:45, 12:42; Acts 4:32, 5:12, 9:42). According to Romans 1:8, the faith of the Roman church was proclaimed throughout the world. Faith is not an isolated inner state, but something that shows itself in deed (Heb 11).

From a New Testament reading, the hidden aspect of faith is whether it will pass its test at the day of judgment. The difference between false and true faith is thus hidden, even for the believer. However, this does not prevent constant self-examination: "Examine yourselves to see whether you are living in the faith. Test yourselves" (2 Cor 13:5). Paradoxically, it is the *not visible* faith that is dead: "For just as the body without the spirit is dead, so faith without works is also dead" (Jas 2:26).

The difficulty of talking about the true church as consisting of the true believers is that such a church can never be experienced as a *fellowship*. Being a fellowship means people must *be known* to each other. This will surely be the case after judgment day when the true believers will appear to each other as a fellowship in the kingdom of God. As the true believers cannot be identified before judgment day, the fellowship of the church in the here and now is a fellowship of both true and false believers and as such serves as an anticipation of the fellowship in the kingdom of God.

The *eschatological reservation* which applies to the church until judgment day should not lead to a dichotomy of meaning between the church as visible and invisible, but should be understood as a tension between the church in its present reality, and as an anticipation of God's kingdom fellowship. The point is not a difference between the idealized fellowship and the real fellowship, but between the fellowship of the church as it is experienced here and now, and the fellowship that will one day be experienced in the perfect kingdom of God.

A HEAVENLY CHURCH?

The fact that the church is oriented toward the coming kingdom of God means Christian hope and faith needs to be radically connected to this world. In the history of the church the future-perspective has often been replaced by an upward-perspective. Most notably, Greek philosophical thought has contributed to this paradigm shift.

The Church: People Gathered in the Name of Jesus

According to the upward-perspective, hope is not something that is primarily in the future, but found in the transcendent heavenly reality. Rather than being linked to the kingdom of God which shall be revealed in the world, hope is anchored in a reality *beyond* and *above* the world. Hope is thus linked to *getting to heaven*, and not so much to the bodily resurrection. One consequence of this shift is an individualized eschatology. The final salvation is something that happens to the individual after death, and not the salvation of the world to which humanity is part of. Another consequence is salvation is conceived as the manifestation of an *invisible* and *spiritual* reality, somewhat remote from human life in the world. Although theology has rarely denied the biblical view about the last days and the resurrection of the dead, this view has often been overshadowed by the heavenly and has become an appendix, rather than a main theme. In keeping with a more historical and eschatological move in recent theology, the upward-perspective thinking has become more and more problematic.[61]

This orientation towards the heavenly and invisible also has had consequences for ecclesiology: those that are saved reside in the perfect heavenly church, while those in the imperfect earthly church are on a journey toward salvation.[62]

If hope is linked to history and the future, this is not to deny heaven as a theological notion. Heaven conveys the idea that life has another dimension other than the world we immediately experience (Col 1:16). It also says something about the distance between God and the world. God's "place" is heaven (see for example the wording of "Our Father in heaven," Matt 6:9). Even though God is beyond the world, this does not mean he is not close to the world or that he does not draw close to it. Moreover, the biblical witness narrates how God, in different ways, makes himself known to people, most markedly through words (Heb 1:1). The climax of this revelation is the Word becoming the man Jesus (John 1:14). He, who was not part of this world, "descended from heaven" (John 3:13) and

---

61. A classic statement for such a concept can be found in Althaus, *Die letzten Dinge*.

62. Healy, who is otherwise concerned that ecclesiology should be about the concrete and real church, believes that alongside the church in the world ("the pilgrim church") there is *another* church, namely the *heavenly* church that he identifies as the eschatological church. He even gives the heavenly church an independent status and claims that those who do not belong to the pilgrim church can be saved through the heavenly orientated church instead. Healy, *Church, World, and the Christian Life*, 37, 150–51.

became part of the world. Forty days after his resurrection he was "taken up to heaven" (Luke 24:51) and was seated at the right-hand of God (Eph 1:20). The church is waiting for the return of Jesus "from heaven" (1 Thess 1:10, 4:16). The fact that Jesus ascended to heaven, does not mean God is absent in the world, rather his presence is communicated when "the heavenly Father give[s] the Holy Spirit to those who ask him" (Luke 11:13).

Salvation can be said to be associated with heaven as a place when meaning this is where salvation *comes from* rather than the place it will be *realized*. Salvation is complete in heaven, but we do not go there to receive salvation, it comes to us (Phil 3:20; 2 Cor 5:2; Col 1:5; 1 Pet 1:4–5). In the Book of Revelation the final vision of the fullness of salvation is described by John as "the holy city, the new Jerusalem, coming down out of heaven from God, prepared as a bride adorned for her husband" (Rev 21:2).

First and foremost, what binds Christians to heaven is that is the place where the Lord resides until his return. Jesus' exaltation to the Father's right hand, therefore, implies a new kind of proximity to the heavenly reality. Not least, this is an important viewpoint in the Letters to the Colossians and Ephesians, which emphasize the cosmic significance of Jesus' saving action. For example, in Ephesians it is written that God "has blessed us in Christ with every spiritual blessing in the heavenly places" (Eph 1:3). Fellowship in Christ means that God has "raised us up with him and seated us with him in the heavenly places in Christ Jesus" (Eph 2:6). Christians should therefore, have their minds focused on the heavenly reality as the place where the exalted Christ abides (Col 3:1–2).[63]

The idea that such a fellowship is a meeting place between heaven and earth is also expressed by notion of the interconnection between the church's worship and the praise of angels. According to the Old Testament, one of the angels' foremost tasks is to praise God (Isa 6; Ps 103:20–21, 148:1–2). The purpose of the angels is also confirmed in the New Testament (Luke 2:13–14; Rev 4–5). In the Byzantine tradition, this idea was further developed, where it was believed that angles take part in the church's worship. According to Otfried Hofius, the idea that the angels are present in the church's worship is rooted in the New Testament witness, for example, 1 Corinthians 11:10. Hofius also suggests it refers to angels when it states that God has given Christians a "share in the inheri-

---

63. For an analysis of the meaning of heaven in Paul's theology, see Lincoln, *Paradise Now and Not Yet*.

The Church: People Gathered in the Name of Jesus

tance of the saints in the light" (Col 1:12) and "you are citizens with the saints and also members of the household of God" (Eph 2:19).[64]

As Christ is in heaven, it is also possible to think of heaven as a place where Christians will go to after death. Paul refers to death being "away from the body and at home with the Lord" (2 Cor 5:8) and "to depart and be with Christ" (Phil 1:23).[65] This state of being in Jesus' presence is not the ultimate goal for the Christian, but an in-between state that anticipates the resurrection on the last day (cf. 1 Thess 4:16).

Some biblical references describe this in-between state as a collective assembly. For example, in Hebrews 12:23 the heavenly Jerusalem is described as "the assembly of the firstborn who are enrolled in heaven" where "the spirits of the righteous [are] made perfect." The first clause probably refers to Christians who have passed away, and the second clause probably to the believers from the Old Testament times.[66] In the Book of Revelation, the worshippers at God's throne in heaven are not only the angels and the heavenly beings, but also the deceased Christians (Rev 7:9–17, 15:1–4, 19:1–8), who have remained steadfast in their faith (many having died for their faith) and overcome evil (Rev 12:11, 15:2).[67]

The idea of those who have been victorious probably came about to distinguish between *ecclesia militans* (the church militant) and *ecclesia triumphans* (the church triumphant). The term *ecclesia triumphans* can rightly be understood as those who have gone before and are now at home with God. However, this becomes problematic if the notion of *the heavenly church* is identified as the *eschatological* community, or the pilgrim church that is already perfected. Such a view ignores the victory of the kingdom of God that will take place upon Christ's return and the resurrection of the dead. Furthermore, *the heavenly church* partakes in the reality of salvation *already and not yet*. Admittedly, they "will hunger no more, and thirst no more" and "God will wipe away every tear from their eyes" (Rev 7:16–17). At the same time they wait—with their brothers and sisters on earth—for the day of the Lord to come. In John's vision

---

64. Hofius, "Gemeinschaft mit den Engeln," 186–90.
65. A similar concept is expressed in Luke 16:19–31, 23:43; John 14:3.
66. Hofius, "Gemeinschaft mit den Engeln," 192.
67. It is important to shed some light of caution when using Revelation in a doctrinal context. This is partly due to the book's use of figurative language, and partly due to the vague nature and uncertain timeframe of events the book describes. For example, it is uncertain whether descriptions of *heaven* refer to a reality above this world, or whether they should be understood as (symbolic) descriptions of the eschatological fulfillment.

it is precisely the martyrs' souls who represent the impatience for justice and redemption: "Sovereign Lord, holy and true, how long will it be before you judge and avenge our blood on the inhabitants of the earth?" (Rev 6:10).

To speak of a church in heaven is only reasonable if we consider this church is neither the goal of the church, nor the real or true church. In some ways, this church is subsidiary compared to the earthly church. It is in an in-between state and characterized primarily by *what it has been* (on earth) and of *what it shall be* (the final consummation).

The overriding point of the idea of a heavenly church is to maintain the comprehensiveness of the church of Christ as, not only being in *all places*, but also being at *all times*. First and foremost, this implies an intrinsic link to the church of the past as a *historic* reality. The present church is in communion with those that have gathered in the name of Jesus from earlier times. In order to understand and shape the church of today, we have to take the church of the past into account.

This perspective implies that these people and these communities are not *just* history, but are in the eyes of God, also present and future. This is emphasized by Jesus when he spoke of the "God of Abraham, Isaac, and Jacob" as a reference point when talking about the resurrection of the dead. To say God is not a God of the dead, but of the living, implies that the dead will be raised (Matt 22:31–32). The understanding of Abraham, Isaac, and Jacob as being more than just historical figures is not primarily a reference to their possible existence in a heavenly reality parallel to our world. Rather, it alludes to the eschatological resurrection of the dead in the last days. The eschatological perspective keeps the past, present, and future in paradoxical unity. The fact that we praise God with those who have gone before us means our worship flows with the praise which sounded in the past, without necessarily postulating a type of simultaneity between our worship and praise of the dead in the in-between state.

This also means that our *relationship* to Christians of the past is primarily to remember them as historical examples figures, and to share with them the hope we will come together as the people of God at the final consummation of the kingdom of God. Therefore, to pray to the dead, as if they are able to take part in our life here and now, is to miss the point and has no biblical warranty.[68]

---

68. This point is also made in the Augsburg Confession article XXI concerning the saints. We are not to be "calling on the saints or pleading for help from them," however

The Church: People Gathered in the Name of Jesus

THE PRESENCE OF JESUS IN WORD AND SACRAMENT

What constitutes the church as church is the presence of Jesus as mediated through the Holy Spirit. According to the Augsburg Confession this takes place through Word and sacrament as stated in article VII: "The church is the assembly of saints in which the gospel is taught purely and the sacraments are administered rightly." In the following section we will look closely at the biblical basis for such an understanding, and consider how the presence of Jesus is mediated is interpreted by this statement.

God's presence, as conveyed through *words from God*, is a central theme of the Old Testament. People are brought close to God by God *speaking* to them. The biblical story of salvation begins with God speaking to Abraham: "The Lord said to Abram . . ." (Gen 12:1). The highpoint of the story of revelation is God's announcement of the law to Moses on Mount Sinai. As illustrated by the account of Moses' encounter with God on the mountain, to see God face to face is something humans are not allowed to do (Exod 33). The people of Israel are prohibited to make themselves any graven image, neither of the Lord, nor of some other god (Exod 20:4). Instead, the people are called to *hear* the word of the Lord. In the exhortation in Deuteronomy 6 God charged Israel to *hear* (v. 4: "Hear O Israel"), *recite* and *write down* (vv. 7–9), and *keep* the Word of God (vv. 17–18).

The emphasis that God's word as the main medium of revelation must not obscure the fact that the God of the Old Testament also reveals himself through his *works*. Revelation is not just a collection of timeless truths, but is related to what God has done, what God does, and what God will do in the history of the world and with Israel in particular. The revelation of God, through word and action, is a revelation of God himself—an outworking of his *self-revelation*.[69]

---

we may remember them "in order that we may imitate their faith and good works, according to our calling." The only place in the Bible where the dead are evoked is when Saul calls upon the dead Samuel (1 Sam 28). This action is understood as a mistake and against the will of God (see also Lev 19:31).

69. The fact that God reveals himself through his acts in history is particularly emphasized by Wolfhart Pannenberg (e.g., in his early work *Revelation as History*). In his early work Pannenberg's emphasis of God's *acts* leads to a weakening of God's self-revelation by his *word*. In later work, he presents a more balanced view of the interconnection between the revelatory nature of both word and acts. *Systematic Theology*, vol. I, 230–57.

The New Testament sees Jesus as a continuation and fulfillment of the Old Testament revelation of God (Heb 1:1–2). The major difference between Jesus, Moses, and the prophets, is Jesus is not only God's messenger, but the Word of God *in persona* (John 1:1–18). Jesus integrates in his person the Old Testament duality of being both God's voice and God's work. This means Jesus, not only brings the message of God, but *is the message*. We see this evidenced by Jesus' works, where he combined the preaching of the kingdom of God with the miracles of the kingdom of God.[70] Moreover, we see this through God's principle act of salvation: the death and resurrection of Jesus and the sending of the Spirit. These events signal the beginning of the anticipated judgment and new creation in the last days. The message that the apostles preached, was not only a passing on of *Jesus' message*, but also a message *about* Jesus as the crucified and risen Messiah.

The key term in the New Testament that encapsulates this message is *gospel*.[71] This term is referred to for both Jesus' proclamation of the kingdom of God (Mark 1:14–15) and the latter preaching of the crucified and risen Jesus. Paul summarizes the message of God's saving action: "The gospel concerning his Son, who was descended from David according to the flesh and was declared to be Son of God with power according to the spirit of holiness by resurrection from the dead, Jesus Christ our Lord" (Rom 1:3–4). According to Paul, the gospel is more than a summary of information—it is also a message of transforming power to those who believe: "It is the power of God for salvation to everyone who has faith . . ." (Rom 1:16). Therefore, Paul points out that faith comes by hearing the message of Jesus (Rom 10:17). It is by faith in Christ that people can come into the living relationship with God and thereby share in the reality of God's kingdom. As Paul rhetorically asks the Galatians: "Did you receive the Spirit by doing the works of the law or by believing what you heard?" (Gal 3:2).

It is, therefore, the gospel that creates the church by making present the risen Lord and calling people to faith in Jesus. It was by hearing Jesus' message about God's kingdom that the first disciples were summoned and

---

70. See chapter 4.

71. In the Lutheran tradition the term *gospel* is both used in a more extensive way to denote the totality of the Christian message, and also more specifically to illustrate the contrast between the gospel and law (cf. the expression "law and gospel"). See the Formula of Concord, Epitome, article V. Kolb and Wengert, *Book of Concord*, 500.

formed. On the day of Pentecost it was Peter's preaching of the crucified and risen Jesus that brought 3,000 people to faith and incorporated them into the church (Acts 2). Further on in the Acts of the Apostles, we see the same pattern employed: the gospel is preached, people come to faith, and churches formed: "Come, let us return and visit the believers in every city where we proclaimed the word of the Lord and see how they are doing" (Acts 15:36). According to 1 John 1:3, it is the preaching of the gospel that is the basis for fellowship with God and other Christians: "We declare to you what we have seen and heard so that you also may have fellowship with us; and truly our fellowship (*koinonia*) is with the Father and with his Son Jesus Christ." As documented in Acts 2:42, one of the essential components of the first Christian communities was to gather around the "apostles' teaching."

The gospel, which forms the foundation for fellowship with God and one another in the church, is not any message, but the message which the apostles preached. Paul's fervent reaction in the Letter to the Galatians against those who preached "another gospel" (Gal 1:6) testifies against any distortion of the message. The true gospel is marked by its *content*: Jesus Christ as the only means of salvation, and its *source*: the apostles' testimony of Jesus. After the apostles had passed away, the biblical writings become the means by which the gospel was passed on and the source where the church continually finds its life. Being founded on the gospel, not only refers to the church's historical origin, but also means that the gospel makes Christ present amongst those gathered in his name.

The witness about the events at Pentecost (Acts 2) points to another aspect of what it means to be part of the church, namely *baptism*.[72] The crowd that became convinced by the gospel asked Peter what they must do now. Peter replied: "Repent, and be baptized every one of you in the name of Jesus Christ so that your sins may be forgiven; and you will receive the gift of the Holy Spirit" (Acts 2:38). Baptism is not only salvation for the individual, but also includes a participating in the fellowship of those who are saved: "Those who welcomed his message were baptized, and that day about three thousand persons were added" (Acts 2:41).

Through baptism we are brought into fellowship with Jesus—baptized into his death and resurrection (Rom 6:1–14; Col 2:12). Baptism

---

72. For further study about the relationship between baptism and ecclesiology see Pannenberg, *Systematic Theology*, vol. III, 239–83; Küng, *Church*, 203–11; Schlink, *Doctrine of Baptism*, 72–81.

establishes, not only a relationship between Jesus and the individual, but also brings us into fellowship with one another as one body: "For in the one Spirit we were all baptized into one body" (1 Cor 12:13). Baptism constitutes the fundamental unity between Christians as the church, for there is only one baptism in the name of Jesus. The church is thus the fellowship of the baptized. As the baptized community, baptism relativizes differences among the Christians: "As many of you as were baptized into Christ have clothed yourselves with Christ. There is no longer Jew or Greek, there is no longer slave or free, there is no longer male and female; for all of you are one in Christ Jesus" (Gal 3:27–28).

Through the use of water, baptism is a *sign* of the baptismal union with Christ in his life and death. This sign is more than symbolic, but an efficacious sign that signifies what it is. Baptism not only *symbolizes* that the baptized is united with Christ, but brings about this union *in reality*. At the same time, it is important to emphasize, that baptism—as sign—also points to the future. It points towards the baptismal life of the Christian life, and life in the church as a whole (cf. Rom 6), as well as forward towards the fullness of resurrection reality. Such an efficacious sign has in the ecclesial tradition been described as a *sacrament*.[73]

While baptism is something that occurs only once in life (although it happens repeatedly in the life of the church, when new members are added), the *eucharist* is reoccurring event. As baptism is a sacrament, so is the eucharist—an efficacious sign giving what it signifies. The eucharist is closely connected to the fellowship character of the church. It is no coincidence that the eucharist is in form of a *meal*. A distinctive feature of Jesus' ministry was that he ate together with different people. As Wolfhart Pannenberg points out, the eucharistic meal not only reflects Jesus' *last* meal with his disciples, but it also reflects the many other meals he ate with people.[74] As the Gospels narrate, this aspect of Jesus' ministry is reflected in the charges made against him that he was a "glutton and a drunkard, a friend of tax collectors and sinners" (Luke 7:34). By using the Old Testament comparison of the Messianic era symbolized by a meal (Isa 25:6; Luke 13:29), Jesus shows that he understood his own fellowship

---

73. Regarding the concept of sacrament, see Pannenberg, *Systematic Theology*, vol. III, 238, 336–45.

74. Ibid., 283ff. Concerning the eucharist see also Küng, *Church*, 211–24; Welker, *What Happens in Holy Communion?*

meal with sinners as an anticipation of the community in the kingdom of God.

During his last meal with his disciples before his death, Jesus specifically makes reference to the correlation between this meal and the forthcoming kingdom of God: "I have eagerly desired to eat this Passover with you before I suffer, for I tell you, I will not eat it until it is fulfilled in the kingdom of God . . . For I tell you that from now on I will not drink of the fruit of the vine until the kingdom of God come" (Luke 22:15–16, 18). Even though Jesus is aware that he will not be able to have another meal together with his disciples until God's kingdom has come, he charges his disciples continue to keep the meal—to eat it in remembrance of what relationship they had with him: "Do this in remembrance of me" (Luke 22:19). Paul argues that remembrance is something far more than a passive memory, but rather it is an *active proclamation* of Jesus' death: "For as often as you eat this bread and drink the cup, you proclaim the Lord's death until he comes" (1 Cor 11:26). Celebrating eucharist is therefore, something that takes place *until further notice* and acts as a sign until it is replaced by the feast of the kingdom of God.

The eucharist is not only remembrance of the past, but also an anticipation of the future. Based upon Jesus' own words, we see how the early church understood Jesus to be *present*, in a special way in the eucharistic meal: "This is my body . . . this is my blood of the covenant, which is poured out for many for the forgiveness of sins" (Matt 26:26, 28).

The reference to his body and his blood is not to be understood as referring to two different aspects, or parts, of Jesus, rather they point to his whole being. When the bread is eaten (Jesus' body) and wine drunk (Jesus' blood), we share in Christ himself and partake in his redemptive work: "The cup of blessing that we bless, is it not a sharing in (*koinonia*) the blood of Christ? The bread that we break, is it not a sharing in the body of Christ?" (1 Cor 10:16).

As summarized by many ecumenical documents, the concept of remembrance in the eucharist unites past, present and future. For example, the Lima Document states:

> Christ himself with all that he has accomplished for us and for all creation (in his incarnation, servant-hood, ministry, teaching, suffering, sacrifice, resurrection, ascension and sending of the Spirit) is present in this *anamnesis*, granting us communion with himself. The eucharist is also the foretaste of his *parousia* and of

the final kingdom. The *anamnesis* in which Christ acts through the joyful celebration of his Church is thus both representation and anticipation.[75]

The eucharist involves, not only fellowship with Jesus, but also with everyone who is part of the same church. It is not a solitary meal between the individual and Jesus, but is shared with all those who take part in the eucharist. As all share in the one Christ, all have fellowship with one another: "Because there is one bread, we who are many are one body, for we all partake of the one bread" (1 Cor 10:17). More than anything else, the eucharist demonstrates to the world what the church is: People who have fellowship with Jesus Christ and each other. This community is primarily not of human initiative or merit, but a giving of Jesus himself to his people.

An important question to ask is, what is the *relationship* between the presence of Jesus in the eucharist and his presence in general? To say that Jesus is *only* present in the eucharist is clearly too narrow of a view. From what I have shown above, Jesus is also present in his word and through baptism. The eucharist is, therefore, not the only way Jesus is made present in the church. Although the eucharist should have a central role in church life, it is in my opinion, an overemphasis to say that it is the eucharist that makes the church to be church.[76] There is no basis for asserting that Jesus is only present in worship when the eucharist is celebrated, or that the eucharist must be celebrated in order for church service to be a real service. It is the same Jesus Christ who is present both in the Word proclaimed and when the eucharist is celebrated—it is the same Spirit that makes Jesus present in both.[77] For the eucharist to be the eucharist, it is necessary for the Word to be proclaimed over the elements, not least by the words of institution. The eucharist does not convey something or somebody else than the Word, even if this is in another *form*. While Jesus

---

75. *Baptism, Eucharist and Ministry*, II Eucharist, para. 6–7, p. 11.

76. In my opinion Pannenberg has taken this analogy too far when says: "The Lord's Supper constitutes the church as the body of Christ and consequently as the fellowship of believers." *Systematic Theology*, vol. III, 431; cf. p. 292. The difficulty with this view is that it logically *de-churches* those churches that do not celebrate the eucharist, such as the Quakers and the Salvation Army. Even if we acknowledge that the eucharist is an important aspect of what it means to be a church, it is unfounded to say that these churches that do not celebrate the eucharist cease to become churches.

77. The real presence of Jesus is mediated through the Holy Spirit, see ibid., 320–24.

is received through *listening* to the Word, in the eucharist he is received by *eating*. Jesus' presence is not limited to receiving only by understanding a message, but is also disseminated through specific physical elements. He is made present, not only in our minds, but also in our bodies. As sacramental sign the eucharist embodies, in a unique way, the church as fellowship with Jesus and with each other. Although the eucharist is not the only medium for the presence of Jesus, it should have a central place in life of the church and be celebrated regularly. As Paul describes in 1 Corinthians 11:17–34 and as described in Acts 2:42 "the breaking of bread" was a regular event in the life of the early church.

To celebrate the eucharist is a central aspect of what it means for the church to be gathered in the name of Jesus. In a distinctive way, Jesus has promised to be present in the eucharist. The eucharist, therefore, remains the primary expression of what the church is: Jesus as present in the midst of his people.

3

Sociological and Theological Perspectives

NOT ONLY CAN THE church as empirical reality be analyzed theologically, but it can also be analyzed by other sciences. As social reality, the church can be interpreted through social sciences, and not least through sociology. The question of the relationship between theology and sociology is itself a complex subject that is outside the scope of this book. I will, therefore, limit myself to comment on two questions, each in its own way is relevant to a theological understanding of the church. The first question is about how sociology understands the nature of social reality and how this can potentially impact the theological understanding of the church. The second question concerns the relationship between sociological understanding of the human community as created by humans, and the theological notion that the church is an expression of God's work.

THE NATURE OF SOCIAL REALITY

Unlike other sciences, sociology has no particular monopoly on any area of reality. Social science, like other human sciences, is the study of humanity and the human reality. What is characteristic of sociology, however, is that it examines the human reality in a particular *perspective*, namely understood as *social reality*. Sociologists study how people interact and respond to each other, and how this interaction takes place within the framework of social groups or society as a whole.[1]

What is of interest in the context of this research is how sociologists understand the nature of social reality: what *is* society? This kind of ontological question is not, it seems, addressed by sociologists in general. Nevertheless, it is an interesting question from a theological point of

---

1. Cf. a standard textbook definition of sociology as "the study of human social life, groups and societies." Giddens, *Sociology*, 7.

Sociological and Theological Perspectives

view, as theology asks similar ontological questions about the nature of the church. There are certain parallels: Theologians have often spoken of the *invisible* church to express certain aspects of the church. Actually even the object of sociology: *society*, is not accessible for direct observation in its totality. People's actions, individually or as a whole, are observable, as are material aspects of society, such as buildings, objects and documents. Society *as such*, however, is not possible to observe directly—it remains "invisible."

So is there a societal reality, or is it just an illusion? One of the early sociologists who argued for society's objective existence was Emile Durkheim. Although society consists of individuals, it is more than the sum of its parts. Society can therefore be examined as an independent object, as a system with its own mechanisms and laws. These are mechanisms that seem to be relatively independent of the individual's own motivations and beliefs. Durkheim believes society can be studied "from the outside," "as things." At the same time society can be represented as a *collective consciousness*. This consciousness keeps the society together and enables the individual to act according to society's norms. In the collective consciousness religion plays a vital role. According to Durkheim, God is nothing but a symbolic expression of society itself.[2]

In contrast to Durkheim's analysis, Max Weber places greater emphasis upon the *meaning* that individuals ascribe to their actions. Rather than *explain* the societal phenomena according to certain laws, it is important to *understand* these laws. The object for the sociologist according to Weber is, not society as such, but *social action* and its meaning for individuals. Since different individuals usually have similar motives and act in similar ways, sociologists are able to *classify* and describe typical forms of social action. Social groups are not independent objects, but the result of intentional interactions between individuals. Interpreted from this point of view, the sociological task is to look for the motives that make individuals act in a certain way as constituting the group. Weber acknowledges that the individual can be guided by notions of collective entities (society, state, nation, family, etc.). For the sociologist, such concepts are only important insofar that they affect the individual's action, and cannot be perceived as objective reality.[3]

---

2. Frisby and Sayer, *Society*, 34–51.

3. Ibid., 54–55; 67–72. The difference between Durkheim and Weber corresponds to the general distinction in sociology between structural and agency-oriented theories.

While the weakness of Durkheim's thesis can be seen as the overshadowing of the individual, Weber runs the risk of making too little room for the structural and collective. In modern sociology, there have been various attempts to reconcile these two perspectives. An example of the uniting of the perspectives of Durkheim and Weber can be found in Peter Berger and Thomas Luckmann's work *The Social Construction of Reality*.[4] They believe the solution lies in avoiding making the choice between an understanding of society as objective reality and society as a subjective idea. Society is characterized precisely by the fact that it is both. According to Berger and Luckmann the key to understanding this relationship is given by the sociology of knowledge, i.e. the sociological sub-discipline that deals with the social function of knowledge. In this context, *knowledge* is a broad term that includes all forms of explicit and implicit ideas about life. Such knowledge is of societal significance to the extent that we share it with other people. In fact, it is shared knowledge that makes society possible. Society exists only because people share the idea that society exists. Being a part of society is to share in the knowledge of society.[5]

The fact that society is based on the idea about society does not mean that society has no objective reality. This reality is experienced by those who would try to challenge the norms of society through a wide range of measures, from mild forms of social control, to law enforcement through the police and penal system.

A pivotal concern of Berger and Luckmann is to highlight society's human character—as a product of human activity past and present. Society is, in fact, not given once and for all, but is constantly changing through human creative activity. The basic social nature of humanity

---

Beside Durkheim, Karl Marx, Talcott Parsons, Jürgen Habermas, and Niclas Luhmann are examples of structure-oriented theorists. Beside Weber, Georg Simmel, and George Herbert Mead are examples of agency-oriented theorists. Furseth and Repstad, *Introduction to the Sociology of Religion*, 47–49.

4. Berger and Luckmann position themselves as part of a group of sociologists who want to understand the relationship between the individual and structure, combining insights from a structural and agency-oriented theories (see previous footnote). Other sociologists with similar concerns include Pierre Bourdieu, Michel Foucault, Anthony Giddens, and Zygmunt Bauman. Furseth and Repstad, *Introduction to the Sociology of Religion*, 49-74.

5. For this and the following, see Berger and Luckmann, *Social Construction of Reality*. Cf. Berger, *Sacred Canopy*.

means people cannot live without being in interaction with other people. The *forms* of this interaction are not a given once and for all, but are something we constantly create. The forms of society will, therefore, vary greatly between different cultures and generations.

According to Berger and Luckmann society is thus an objective human reality:

> Social order exists *only* as a product of human activity. No other ontological status may be ascribed to it without hopelessly obfuscating its empirical manifestations. Both in its genesis (social order is the result of past human activity) and its existence in any instant of time (social order exists only and insofar as human activity continues to produce it) it is a human product.[6]

This means that any conception that society has an existence prior to, or independent of human activity, is false. Admittedly, this kind of objectification (reification) of society is very widespread. Berger and Luckmann call this kind of knowledge about society *legitimation*. These are notions that serve to justify society, social relations, and norms. Most notably religious knowledge serves such a function of legitimation. By presenting specific institutions or norms as rooted in the divine or the sacred, they are given a different authority than being just as a result of human activity. A classic example is the view of the king or ruler as appointed by God who exercises authority over his subjects on God's behalf.

Roy Bhaskar proposes an understanding of the relationship between the individual and society that has much in common with Berger and Luckmann's model. However, he disagrees with them on one important point. It is not true, he contends, that society is created by people as if there was nothing that existed before. For those who are part of society, society is experienced as a given. From this standpoint, human activity serves to reproduce and transform the given societal forms. Society is something that is given prior to the individual, yet it can also be changed through human practice. Like Berger and Luckmann, Bhaskar rejects the reification of society: while society is an objective reality, it remains dependent upon human activity.[7]

We can see that these fundamental sociological issues can also be applied to the theological context. Different sociological positions can in-

---

6. Berger and Luckmann, *Social Construction of Reality*, 70.
7. Bhaskar, "Critical Realism," 212–15.

fluence theological and ecclesiological understanding. A notable example of this is found in Dietrich Bonheoffer's *Sanctorum Communio*.[8] In this work, Bonhoeffer draws upon a sociological and philosophical tradition that is not so concerned about concrete historical circumstances, but more about the constituting societal features *in* the empirical reality. This view places emphasis upon the autonomous character of society in relation to the people that belong to it. Following this line of thought, Bonhoeffer introduces the notion of a "collective person" to understand social groups in general, and the church in particular. A collective person is a group entity that functions as an individual and is therefore ontologically independent. This means, like the individual, the collective person can stand in an *I-you* relationship to another group, an individual, and to God. As an objective reality, the collective person is described by Bonheoffer as having an "objective spirit."[9]

By introducing such concepts as the collective person and objective spirit, Bonheoffer has established an ontological basis for his ecclesiology. The church differs from other societies, in so much as the collective person is Christ, and the objective spirit is the Holy Spirit. Such an ontological identification with Christ and with the Spirit makes (as I have pointed out in chapter 2) any identification with the empirical church complicated. In this case, the idea of a real church as not being identical with the empirical church, is therefore founded not only upon theological reasons, but can also be justified by a certain sociological reasoning where social reality *is reified* and is given an independent ontological status—in this case as something that is beyond experience.

Peter Berger has given a detailed analysis about the possibilities and limitations of Bonheoffer's early work. As a sociologist he criticizes Bonheoffer for taking advantage of a type of sociology that is abstract and non-empirical, by using terms such as collective person and objective spirit. Such concepts are, argues Berger, an expression of an extreme social realism, which can easily lead to a social mythology. From a sociological and empirical point of view, such concepts are unnecessary and unfounded, and do not take into account of the fact that all social phenomena are subjective and human-shaped in nature. In addition, Berger raises an important *ethical* argument against this kind of social ontology.

---

8. Bonhoeffer, *Sanctorum Communio*. See chapter 2.
9. Ibid., 76–80, 97–106.

Sociological and Theological Perspectives

To understand institutions as analogous to persons attributes to them a value in their own right. Arguing against this claim, Berger believes institutions only have ethical value as long as they serve and protect real persons.[10] Implicitly, Berger assumes this is a warning against placing the interests of institutions over the concerns of people and as such should be applied to the church as well.

Berger argues, convincingly in my opinion, that the kind of social ontology proposed by Bonheoffer is sociologically questionable. This is true on a more general basis and specifically in relationship to the church as a social reality. Theological attempts to make the church an objective reality without reference to human experience and activity cannot be justified sociologically. Furthermore, I believe there are no independent theological reasons for such an understanding. To interpret the church in its empirical reality as a concrete human community should be sufficient.

The sociological perspective of society contributes at the same time to a theological understanding of the church as being a human community. That fact that the church is, in a certain sense, *invisible* is not something only applicable to the church, but for all human societies. There are often aspects of the church that theologians give a certain theological weight to, which from a sociological perspective it shares with other social sciences.

Another sociological point is the role that knowledge plays (in the widest sense) in maintaining society. From the viewpoint of the church, it points to *faith* as essential for the church's existence. Part of the role of theology is to interpret this faith. Belief in the church is therefore crucial for the church's (objective) existence.

A sociological perspective that is applicable to the church, as it is for society, is based upon the role of human activity. We inherit society as a given reality, whereupon we assimilate the social formations from those who have gone before us. This gives sociological meaning to the theological idea that the church exists before the faith of the individual. Such a view does not necessitate the idea of the church as a reality pre-existent to experience. Rather it points back in time to those who have gone before us, even all the way back to the first disciples who were first called by Jesus. At the same time the church has to be maintained and upheld as an ever changing reality of those who live today.

---

10. Berger, "Sociology and Ecclesiology," in particular pp. 76–78.

IS THE CHURCH A RESULT OF HUMAN WORK OR THE WORK OF GOD?

The claim that the church as human community is the result of human work seems to be in conflict with a theological understanding of church as an expression of God's action. Such a potential conflict is not peculiar to ecclesiology, but is related to the theological challenges innate in sociology's perspective on reality.

This apparent conflict between sociology and theology is discussed by Peter Berger, who besides being a sociologist also considers theological issues in his writings. Even though Berger does not discuss the issue as related directly to ecclesiology, the questions he raises are relevant to our discussion. According to Berger, sociology is an empirical science, and as such must work from what he calls a *methodological atheism*. Therefore, the sociologist *qua* sociologist has no interest in the question of God and God's relationship to the world—the fact that a sociologist might believe in God or not, should not play any role in his sociological analysis. However, the sociologist cannot exclude the possibility that the empirical data researched can in some way correspond to transcendent realities.[11]

An interesting aspect of Berger's position is it not only presupposes a certain conception of sociology, but it also presupposes a certain theological point of view as well. It is worth noting what reality status Berger assigns to theological statements, or to put this another way, how he perceives the *object* for theology. Berger thus appears to assume that theological statements refer to a transcendent, supernatural reality *beyond* the empirical reality.[12] He claims that, although religion from a sociological perspective is understood as a projection of human relationships based upon the human reality, we cannot exclude the possibility that these projections match reality "out there."[13]

From a theological point of view, I believe it is reasonable to question the claim of theology as exclusively confined to the transcendent and trans-empirical world. The idea of God's transcendence is indeed an im-

---

11. *Sacred Canopy*, 100, 179–85. Pål Repstad believes *methodological atheism* is too absolute and proposes instead the less provocative term *methodological agnosticism*. "Between Idealism and Reductionism," 94.

12. See also Berger, *A Rumour of Angels*. Underlining this point of view are certain theological concepts taken from neo-orthodox theology (Berger openly admits to Barth's influence).

13. *Sacred Canopy*, 181.

portant part of a Christian understanding of God. As creator of the world, God himself is not part of the world. However, this does not exclude the fact that God works in and for the world by his creative and saving work. The fact that God's saving grace is something that takes place in the world is made explicit by the incarnation of the Son and by the outpouring of the Spirit. A true theological understanding of reality is to see God's ongoing work as both creator and savior of the world in the present and the world as an expression of God's handiwork. This is a central aspect of the Christian understanding of God even if it is being challenged by a closed, positivistic worldview that wants to banish God to the transcendence or the innermost depths of the soul.

It is somewhat unclear how extensive are the consequences of Berger's methodological atheism. The question is whether it is only methodological, or whether it also contains ontological implications. The fact that Berger's perspective does not exclude the possibility of a God *beyond* the world is clear. More questionable is whether this viewpoint allows for the notion of a God *in* the world.

As Robin Gill points out, Berger's sociological position is potentially, not only in conflict with theology, but also to other empirical sciences, such as psychology. By treating all phenomena as fundamentally social phenomena, makes it difficult to have a specific psychological angle about the same phenomena.[14] To get to grips with these difficulties (in terms of both theology and psychology) Gill introduces what he calls an *as if* methodology as a replacement for Berger's methodological atheism. Applying such a methodology enables the sociologist to work *as if* all human actions are socially conditioned, including religious phenomena. By appropriating a methodological and not an ontological perspective, allows for a sociological *as if* perspective, while not excluding other *as if* points of view in either psychology or theology. Theology could methodologically operate with its own *as if* outlook by examining the world *as if* God really exists.[15] Applying this to ecclesiology would mean you

14. Gill, *Social Context of Theology*, 32–33.

15. Ibid., 37–40. A similar complementary understanding of the relationship between theology and sociology is found in work of the sociologist of religion, David Martin (e.g., in *Reflections on Sociology and Theology*). It is important to say, that the relatively harmonious coexistence between sociology and theology remains controversial in theology. One notable proponent is John Milbank (*Theology and Social Theory*), who wants to make the *contradiction* between sociology and theology succinct. Milbank believes sociology is not only methodologically atheistic, but overtly atheistic. The meta-

can both examine the church sociologically (as if it is a result of human activity) and theologically (as if God works in and through the church). It would thus be possible to work from two and not necessarily mutually exclusive, different perspectives.[16]

Whether it is possible or desirable to work from these two different perspectives largely depends upon our theological understanding of how God acts in the world and how we can experience God's acts. From a creational and incarnational theological point of view, there is reason to assert that God is not only *outside* the world (or that God only in exceptional cases intervenes through supernatural events), but is also actively present *in* the world. It does not necessarily mean God is directly accessible by experience: to recognize something as an act of God requires it being interpreted and experienced as such. In the light of faith we can, what Eberhard Jüngel calls, have an "experience with the experience."[17] This opens us up to experience God's works in the world through human activity, meaning human activity can be understood as an outworking of the work of God. Applied to the church, this means it can be understood at the same time as a result of human actions (such as sociology assumes) and as an expression of the work of God (as a theological perspective assumes). I concur with the words of Nicholas Healy, who based upon Hans Urs von Balthasar's theodramatic theory, formulates this view as follows:

> Both divine and human agency, moreover, must be understood, as in premodern theology generally, without any kind of division of labor. It is not the case, as has sometimes been assumed in modern theology, that God acts in certain areas while humans are left to act in other areas more or less alone. Human agency is *fully* constitutive of *all* human institutions and bodies, including the church.

---

narrative that sociology operates from is completely different from that of the Christian meta-narrative. Milbank would like what he calls a "Christian sociology" to replace secular sociology. Cf. Furseth and Repstad, *Introduction to the Sociology of Religion*, 203–4. Healy, in a similar fashion, would like to see an ecclesiological method based upon what he calls "a theological form of sociology." *Church, World, and the Christian Life*, 166–67.

16. For example, we can find this in the work of Zygmunt Bauman (who admittedly does not mention theology in this context): "Sociology, we may conclude, is first and foremost a way of thinking about the human world; in principle one can also think about the same world in different ways" (*Thinking Sociologically*, 8). Johannes van der Ven believes sociology and theology have the same material object, but different formal objects (theology sees the church from its future in the perspective of the gospel) (*Ecclesiology in Context*, x).

17. Jüngel, *God as the Mystery of the World*, 182.

Sociological and Theological Perspectives

At the same time, divine agency is *fully* constitutive of all such bodies, including those that are non-ecclesial and non-religious.[18]

The result of such a view means theology is able to incorporate experience. While sociology is limited to understanding this reality as only an expression of human action, theology is able to reflect upon how this can be an expression of the work of God in the world. This means that theology should not leave experience to sociology, but rather it should seek to understand it as a possible manifestation of God's work in the world.

The fact that theology can see human activity as an expression of God's work does not mean that *all* human activity is an expression of God's work. For example, human activity can also be a manifestation of that which is contrary to God's will (sin). When trying to identify and interpret God's works in the world, the church is dependent upon theological criteria as given by biblical revelation.

This brings us unto another point where sociology and theology differ, namely with regards to how the object of research is defined and delineated. The use of concepts and definitions in the sociological context is a question of what is most *suitable*. Concepts are nothing more than attempts to systematize various empirical phenomena as based upon their mutual similarities and differences. As such, there are no right or wrong concepts, only ones that are more or less applicable. When it comes to the term *church* for example, this is used in various ways without one meaning being more correct than another.

A common sociological usage of the term church is given in the well known *church-sect typology* as developed in the work of Max Weber and Ernst Troeltsch. They define *church* as one of several different social forms of Christian groups, namely a religious institution which is open to, and seeks to dominate the wider society, whereas a *sect* is defined as a small group that cuts itself off from the local community.[19] In applying this definition to the first century Christian fellowship would mean the church would probably have to be understood as a sect and not a church. Whether or not we use such concepts is, in a sociological context, a matter

---

18. Healy, *Church, World, and the Christian Life*, 66–67. Van der Ven articulates this as "the principle of noncompetition," i.e. God and human actions do not exclude or replace one another: "God does not cancel out the activities of people in the church, but inspires, intensifies, and orients them. God gives to the people to form the church themselves, to do the church themselves" (*Ecclesiology in Context*, xiv).

19. Cf. Furseth and Repstad, *Introduction to the Sociology of Religion*, 133–40.

of preference. There is, for example, nothing in the way of constructing a sociological term *church* which includes both *church* and *sect* as defined by Weber and Troeltsch. For the interdisciplinary cooperation between sociology and theology it may even be suitable to refer to the same phenomenon using the same term. However, the use of shared terminology is no precondition for this type of cooperation, as theological and sociological concepts will never be fully compatible.

Sociologically speaking, it is of equal importance to *differentiate* as it is to *define* concepts. For sociology, it is important to examine the various variants of the phenomenon of the church, rather than make sharp demarcations of what is church, and what is not. It may also be of interest to show how some Christian groups have similarities with non-Christian groups, as they do with other Christian groups.

From a theological point of view, to define the concept *church* is not just a matter of preference. Theologically, it is necessary to talk about the church in the singular: *the* church. As God is one, it follows that there is only one church of God. The question is how this notion of the one church can relate to the empirical diversity of Christian churches and groups. The theological concept of the church, in this context, means *more* than a particular classification or definition of specific empirical phenomena. Such an appraisal is based upon the idea that the church has a certain real character beyond such classifications, namely the church as a fellowship where Jesus is present. Theology cannot, therefore, be restricted to the classification of empirical data, as it needs a criterion to distinguish between church and non-church. The need for such a criterion is also used for traditional theological discussions about the *marks of the church* (*notae ecclesiae*). According to a Lutheran understanding, the Word and sacrament are the primary marks of the church, and thus the bearer of the presence of Jesus.[20] While from a sociological perspective there will be no fundamental difference between the church and any other religious community, whereas from a theological perspective, gathering in the name of Jesus marks the church as a unique expression of God's saving presence in the world.

---

20. For further discussion about this issue within the context of Lutheranism see Lathrop and Wengert, *Christian Assembly*.

4

Sent Out into the World

An important issue for ecclesiology is the relationship between church and that which is *not* church. The central contrasting term to church in this context is *the world*. The issue is thus a question about the relationship between the church and the world.

This is an issue which has many aspects to it. First, it is necessary to ask what the church's identity is in regard to the world. This applies to both how the church is *opposed* to the world, and what the church has in *common* with the world. In other words, what does it mean to be *in the world* but *not of the world*?[1] Second, it is necessary to ask what the church's *task* is in relation to the world. Being a church is not only to be *gathered* in Jesus' name, but also to be *sent out* in Jesus' name.

CHURCH AND CREATION

The understanding of the relationship between the church and the world is not a unique issue in ecclesiology, but is closely related to a general theological understanding of the relationship between creation and redemption. Ecclesiology cannot just have an affiliation with soteriology in a narrow sense, but should be rooted in creation theology. This does not mean, of course, that the church can only be understood as part of the created order, or that ecclesiology should be completely incorporated into creation theology. Just as creation and redemption cannot be mutually identified with each other, or separated from each other, the same is true of the church and the world.

The key to a proper understanding of the relationship between creation and redemption and the relationship between the church and the world lies in the *eschatological perspective* (as I have pointed out before in

1. John 17:11, 14 ESV. In the NRSV this is translated as "do not belong to the world."

chapter 2). According to this insight, there is a bond between this world and God's new creation as characterized by continuity and discontinuity. God will create the world *anew,* which means the *world* will be created anew.

The biblical understanding of reality brings together the three aspects of creation, sin and redemption. The world in which we live displays the original created order and the will of God, as well as the reality of sin and evil forces. The reality of sin and evil does not negate the reality of the world being created, but implies what is created is *fallen.* The reality in which we live is at the same time a world created by God and tainted by evil.[2]

God's initiative to free creation from sin and evil is encapsulated by the notion of redemption. While the new creation is a realization of God's original plan for creation, it is not only a recovery of the original creation. The new creation is something *more* than a restoration of creation—it is the *fulfillment* of creation. The new world will be even more glorious than the first. This insight has classically been articulated by Irenaeus as the theology of *recapitulatio.*[3]

The correlation between the reality as we experience it now and God's new creation can be described as both *continuity* and *discontinuity.* It is continuity in so far as the new creation will be a restoration and fulfillment of the world as constituted by the will of God. The new creation implies an affirmation of everything good, beautiful and true in life. It is discontinuity in so far as the new creation will be the liberation from all that corrupts God's creation—sin and evil. The new creation is a confirmation of the human protest against sin and evil as well as an indictment of humanity's propensity to evil. Because good and evil are so interwoven and not easily separated, continuity and discontinuity are connected to each other in a complex and dialectical relationship. In the existence of life, good and evil are often woven tightly together. Therefore, any attempt at trying to identify the goodness of creation as distinguished from the depravity of creation remains an ambiguous task.

The promise of God's new creation does not mean that God has withdrawn from the world and left it to its own devices. On the contrary,

---

2. This duality is illustrated by the classical Lutheran doctrine of original sin as found in the Formula of Concord's understanding of humanity as being at the same time created and fallen, see Epitome, article I. Kolb and Wengert, *Book of Concord,* 487–91.

3. Wingren, *Man and the Incarnation.*

Sent Out into the World

God is active in the world, both as creator and savior. As creator God still holds the world in his hands and creatively interacts in the world. Even as a *fallen* world, God still interacts as creator and as judge, and seeks to set boundaries to limit the effects of evil. Furthermore, through his act of salvation God is savior *of the world*.

When the New Testament refers to the world, there is an innate tension between the world as the object of God's salvation and as the object of God's judgment. In John's Gospel and in his first letter, "the world" (in Greek: *kosmos*) is a key word which describes the created and fallen reality. The starting point for understanding the world is that it is created by God: "The world came into being through him" (John 1:10). God's saving work in Jesus is for the world's sake and flows from God's love for the world that he has created: "For God so loved the world that he gave his only Son . . ." (John 3:16). The economy of salvation is not only for Christians, but the entire world: "He is the atoning sacrifice for our sins, and not for ours only but also for the sins of the whole world" (1 John 2:2; cf. John 1:29). Jesus was sent to the world "in order that the world might be saved through him" (John 3:17).

The tragic outcome of God's saving work for the world is that not everyone accepts his salvation, but just a few: "He was in the world, and the world came into being through him; yet the world did not know him" (John 1:10). Thus, the "world" is not only a name for the created and fallen world that God will save, but also refers to those in the world who have rejected God's offer of salvation. As such, they come under God's judgment: "And this is the judgment, that the light has come into the world, and people loved darkness rather than light because their deeds were evil" (John 3:19).

Based upon this understanding, we can see that the love for the world and the love for God contradict and exclude each other: "Do not love the world or the things in the world. The love of the Father is not in those who love the world" (1 John 2:15; cf. 16–17; cf. Jas 4:4). Christians are not to expect anything but hatred from the world's side (John 15:18–27; 1 John 3:13).

The same twofold view of the created world is also found in the other New Testament writings. For Paul, *this world* is in contrast to the forthcoming world that Christians will be a part of. Christians receive, not the spirit of the world, but the Spirit of God (1 Cor 2:12); the world's wisdom is opposition to the wisdom of God (1 Cor 1:20–21, 3:19); and the world in its present form will therefore pass away (1 Cor 7:31).

At the same time, salvation is understood as something that happens for the sake of the world. As Paul writes: "In Christ God was reconciling the world to himself" (2 Cor 5:19). Furthermore, Paul outlines in Romans 8:19–22, that salvation has consequences not only for humanity but also for the whole created reality:

> For the creation waits with eager longing for the revealing of the children of God; for the creation was subjected to futility, not of its own will but by the will of the one who subjected it, in hope that the creation itself will be set free from its bondage to decay and will obtain the freedom of the glory of the children of God. We know that the whole creation has been groaning in labor pains until now.

Here Paul links the *church* with creation. The hope of the fulfillment of creation is perfected through God's children. Therefore, the church can, in the words of Ola Tjørhom, be described as a "priest for creation."[4]

John makes reference to how Jesus has chosen the Christians *from* the world to be no longer *of* the world. They, like Jesus, will be hated by the world (John 15:18–19). At the same time Christians are called to be *in* the world: "I am not asking you to take them out of the world, but I ask you to protect them from the evil one" (John 17:15). They are in the world with a purpose. They are in fact *sent* to the world: "As you have sent me into the world, so I have sent them into the world" (John 17:18).

Paul draws out the contrast between those who belong to the church and those who do not: "Do not be conformed to this world, but be transformed by the renewing of your minds, so that you may discern what is the will of God—what is good and acceptable and perfect" (Rom 12:2; cf. e.g. Eph 4:17–24). Such a contrast does not assume that Christians who seek to realize the will of God are following something other than God's original will for creation. The problem according to Paul is not that the Gentiles have no opportunity to acknowledge the will of God, but that they did not live by it (Rom 1:18–32). In certain cases, the knowledge of God will even be greater among the Gentiles than among the Christians (1 Cor 5:1).

---

4. Tjørhom, *Visible Church*, 85–71.

The Bible assumes a basic righteousness and morality will also be present among those who are not Christians. Christians are therefore, urged to be good citizens and live up to society's demands (1 Thess 4:11–12). In 1 Peter 2:12, Christians are admonished to live "honorably among the Gentiles, so that . . . they may see your honorable deeds." This presupposes a certain shared understanding of what is right and good (cf. 1 Thess 4:10–12). In the household codes of Ephesians 5–6; Colossians 3–4 and 1 Peter 2–3 it is assumed that certain social structures can be a suitable environment for Christians to live out their calling according to the will of God. In Romans 13:1–7, it is taken for granted that the secular governments are operating on behalf of God. However, according to Revelation 13, earthly rulers can also govern against the will of God.

While Christians are to behave according to the order of society, this order is at the same time made relative through a kingdom of God perspective. For example, Paul believed it is better for those who were unmarried to remain unmarried due to the perceived immediacy of the forthcoming kingdom (1 Cor 7:26–27). Whatever situation one finds oneself in, the point is to see the present life as temporary in the anticipation of God's kingdom to come:

> I mean, brothers and sisters, the appointed time has grown short; from now on, let even those who have wives be as though they had none, and those who mourn as though they were not mourning, and those who rejoice as though they were not rejoicing, and those who buy as though they had no possessions, and those who deal with the world as though they had no dealings with it. For the present form of this world is passing away. (1 Cor 7:29–31)

In the Synoptic Gospels the kingdom of God is given priority over family and marriage relationships: "Whoever comes to me and does not hate father and mother, wife and children, brothers and sisters, yes, and even life itself, cannot be my disciple" (Luke 14:26; cf. Matt 10:37, 19:29). Elsewhere in the Scriptures, such as the Pastoral Letters, marriage and family life is presented in a more positive light.

As the review of these New Testament texts shows the correlation between the church and the world cannot be interpreted in a simple way. On the one hand, an overt emphasis on discontinuity and the corrupt nature of the world may conflict with the insight that the world still is God's creation, and that God as creator is still activity involved in the world. On the other hand, an overt emphasis on continuity and the goodness of the world may conflict with the church's character as witnessing to and giving a foretaste of the coming kingdom of God. The church should simultaneously confirm the createdness of the world and bear witness to a new creation.

GUSTAF WINGREN ON CHURCH AND CREATION

The Swedish theologian Gustaf Wingren is a theologian who emphasizes the relationship between the church and the created order. In his book *Gospel and Church* he argues against, what he calls an ecclesiology without a theology of creation. Such a view Wingren believes should be replaced by "an understanding of the Church as the gathering together of those whose lives have been restored, redeemed, and delivered under their Lord in whom all things have been created from the beginning."[5] According to Wingren, this theological tradition stems from the second century heretic Marcion. This dispute continues influence both low and high church circles today. Such a view tends to see salvation as something *beyond* the created reality, which leads to an understanding of the church as a reality separate from the world.[6]

Wingren's creation theology does not serve to make soteriology superfluous and a theological appendix. The central content of the gospel is the message of Jesus' death and resurrection, and the possibility of forgiveness of sins and salvation for all people. The central salvific event is *baptism* which brings people into communion with Christ. Baptism is not only a one-time event, but has reference to the whole of the life of the Christian up to the final consummation.[7] Through baptism a person becomes part of something that is not yet fully realized. The last judgment may thus be regarded as "the final revelation of the redemption sealed in baptism."[8]

Wingren's central concern is to emphasize the intrinsic connection between what happens in salvation and what is given in, and through

---

5. Wingren, *Gospel and Church*, 5. This book is based upon Wingren's theology of creation from an earlier book, *Creation and Law*. For a broader presentation of Wingren's ecclesiology see Håkansson, *Vardagens kyrka*.

6. Wingren, *Gospel and Church*, 4–5.

7. Ibid., 6–18, 207–23.

8. Ibid., 210.

creation. God's *new* work through Jesus' death and resurrection presupposes God's *original* work that all the people living on earth partake of.[9] Redemption is therefore, nothing but the realization of the creator's original intentions: "Thus the purpose of the Creator to make man in His image is fulfilled in baptism, which in turn is fulfilled in the resurrection of the dead and the life eternal."[10]

As the fulfillment of creation, redemption is seen as being *more* than creation: "Redemption gives more than creation when it restores creation." Redemption does not lead to a special Christian life separated from everyday life; the distinguishing element of a Christian attitude is rather to be willing to *suffer* for the good of our neighbor.[11]

This relation between creation and redemption is also a key to the understanding of the church. Through Word and sacrament the church is the place of fulfillment for the will of the creator. This does not mean that the church is separate from the world. On the contrary, the baptized life means to live life in the created world. The baptized are not freed to live a different life other than life in the world. They are called to live their life in the created world:

> So there comes into being a Church which is the first fruits of a restored humanity. Day by day it turns to the Gospel for its life and to nowhere else. It lives out its life in this world of God's creation, making use each day of the things God has made and having joyful dominion over them. The man whom we see in Christ's Church is the man whom we know in the created world, now freed to make proper use of the good things that God has created.[12]

For Wingren life in God's created world is a calling for the each individual Christian. As a fellowship the church primarily manifests itself in worship. From this worshipping fellowship, the individual is sent out to live their days in the everyday life—with a vocation to work for the sake of their fellow neighbor. Furthermore, the eucharist is realized as an eschatological event, not by separating from the everyday life, but quite the opposite. In addition, argues Wingren, salvation involves a renewal of

---

9. Ibid., 99–100.
10. Ibid., 10.
11. Ibid., 180–81.
12. Ibid., 5–6.

creation, and the realization of the eucharistic gift means to live one's life in the middle of the created life.[13]

For a Christian to live in the world is not just for the world's sake but is also for the sake of the church. The church is in danger to lose its humanity if, for the purpose of preserving its holiness, it distances itself from the world. For Wingren, ecclesiology is Christologically rooted—even as divinity and humanity cannot be separated in Christ, so holiness and humanity belong together in the life of the church.[14]

In my view, Wingren's emphasis upon the importance of a theology of creation gives an important and necessary insight for ecclesiology. A proper understanding of God's work of salvation in, and through the church, needs to be seen through its relation to God's creative work in the world. This means that these two acts of God cannot be separated from each other, nor are they to be identified with each other. Understanding creation theology as a foundation for ecclesiology does not mean that the church is only understood as part of creation. It also does not mean that the church and the world should be simply identified with each other.

Through his eschatological perspective, Wingren safeguards both continuity and discontinuity between God's creative work and God's work of salvation. According to this view, there is a difference between the two acts of God. Not that one is "down here" and one "up there," on the contrary, they are both acts of God's work in, and through the world. The fullness of God's redemption is not "up there," but "ahead" in the future. Although belonging to the future, redemption is also made present in the *now* in an anticipatory and provisional way through the gospel and sacraments of the church.

Wingren's understanding of the life of the baptized as a life in the world also means that the church as fellowship is primarily manifested in the Sunday worship service, and especially in the eucharist. Throughout the rest of the week, however, the church primarily consists of individual Christians going about their daily life. Through the daily life of individual Christians the church lives its life in society: "It is individual men and women in their place of daily work who are the Church."[15] In Wingren's

---

13. Ibid., 17–18, 160–61. Cf. *Luther on Vocation*.

14. "Holiness is then conceived to be a quality which gains in purity in proportion as the Church shuts itself off from ordinary human relationships. Humanity then disappears from the Church." *Gospel and Church*, 53–54.

15. Ibid., 226.

understanding of the relation between church and society there is no room for a distinct Christian sub-culture.

Wingren does not reflect on whether such a way of being church would be possible in every type of society. Moreover, his theology reflects a particular social situation and a presupposed interpretation of this social context of postwar Sweden. This was a society that was previously a homogeneous Christian culture undergoing change where Christianity was beginning to lose its influence upon society. To a large extent, society was becoming more and more *secular* while religion was being confined to its own sphere. Wingren's response to this situation is *neither* to accept the withdrawal of the church into a ghetto mentality, *nor* to advocate a re-Christianizing of society.[16] Instead, he chooses to interpret the new secularization process positively through a creation theology, whereupon the church becomes manifest through the activities of individual Christians in the secular, public sphere.[17] From Wingren's point of view, what characterizes the public life is that it is *secular*, in the sense of a lack of, or absence of religion. The idea that Christians could encounter alternative types of religion in this secular space seems to lie beyond the horizon, at least when it comes to religion as an aspect of daily life. Christianity has faded away and left behind a religious *neutral* vacuum.

The notion that this is a religious neutral space does not mean that it is neutral in terms of morals and values. The battle between good and evil takes place fully in society and everyday life—Christians are called to engage on the side of good. However, concerning the question of *what* is good and evil Christians have no privileged insight (there are no explicit *Christian ethics* according to the Wingren hermeneutic). The specific Christian contribution lies more in the contribution to motivate in doing good, and of the willingness to suffer for the sake of one's neighbor.

A critical question arises of whether this type of moral consensus is possible in every society, or whether it rather reflects a specific historical context as determined by the values of a former Christian culture. It

---

16. In Norway the low-church movements (as typified by the Lutheran voluntary organizations and some of the free churches) have tried to, in a distinctive way, combine these two strategies. On the one hand, through prayer houses and chapels they have tried to build close-knit faith communities. On the other hand, they have attempted to re-Christianize society through, for example, the formation of the Christian Democratic Party.

17. Wingren shares this positive interpretation of the secular society with his contemporaries Dietrich Bonheoffer and Friedrich Gogarten. Zahrnt, *Question of God*, 123–69.

is not difficult to find examples of societies that have been dominated by values very different from a Christian understanding of the creator's will, irrespective of whether these have been based upon secular ideologies, or upon other religious traditions. The sharing of basic moral values in Wingrens' context may rather be an expression of a shared Christian heritage, albeit in a *secularized* version, rather than a proof of the religious neutrality of these values.

In his understanding of society Wingren focuses upon individuals who relate to each other in different situations. The way people in society interact by their participation within different *groups* is not overtly reflected in his argument. Different groups may differ considerably from each other with respect to worldview and basic moral values in societies that are more pluralistic than Wingren's context. In such societies, the church and those belonging to the church will appear as one group among others. Moreover, in a pluralistic society, it is doubtful whether secular alternatives can claim to represent the neutral or general view. In many instances, the Christian worldview would also be closer to those advocated by other religious groups than those represented by more secular alternatives.

My point is not to doubt the possibility of (and necessity for) interaction between people, regardless of faith or belief. Both the church and members of the church are part of, and must deal with, human life in all its breadth. My concern is to stress how problematical it is to interpret the life in the world as being religiously neutral, where the gospel is merely seen as a supplement or confirmation. Life in a given society will always include and presuppose beliefs and practices of a religious or philosophical nature. I would therefore propose that Wingren's understanding of how the church should relate to society is too simplistic, at least in more pluralistic societies in contrast to Wingren's context.

CHURCH AND CULTURE

The issue of the relation between church and society is also an issue about the relationship between church and *culture*.[18] Culture is to be seen as a complex reality, because of its diversity and multi-dimensional aspects

---

18. Concerning the concept of culture see Kraft, *Christianity in Culture*, 45–63. Culture should only be understood as a specific sector of society (arts, music, theater etc.), but is a moreover comprehensive concept.

which co-exist and are intricately interwoven with each other. We can only speak in the plural when considering culture. Culture also includes religion and the religious. We cannot talk about religion as being distinct from the culture, but as being an aspect of the culture. Religion is itself cultural reality.

Although we can find similarities in different cultures, there is not just one overriding human culture. What it means to be human is to be shaped and identified in diverse ways in community with others. This occurs in very various ways, so to talk about a common human culture is therefore meaningless. Every culture is specific and particular. Although cultures and cultural expressions have certain stable traits, they are not constant realities—they are constantly changing and varied in appearance. The ever changing cultural forms, means it is meaningless to speak of one human *common culture*. Such an idea may have some meaning when considering culture at one particular historical time and place, but even then the idea of *common culture* often means the monopolization of a particular hegemonic culture.

When considering the relationship between Christianity and culture it is necessary to clarify that Christian faith has a *trans-cultural character*. Although from its beginnings Christian faith was situated in a particular culture, it was quickly passed on through many different cultures. This means that the Christian faith is both found in different cultures, and has many different cultural expressions. As such, it is impossible to understand Christianity as being just a supplement to a particular culture, or as an isolated element of a culture. Christian faith will necessarily affect other aspects of culture, and will be influenced by culture. Another way of seeing this is to understand Christian faith as being *contextual*.[19]

Interactions with different aspects of culture will, to a greater or lesser extent, lead to *conflict*. Not least, this will happen when the Christian faith is about to establish itself in another cultural context. Such a conflict will mostly occur when faced with the religious elements of culture, especially when the Christian faith seeks to replace other existing beliefs and customs. Even then, we cannot talk about one faith simply replacing the other: in a given culture the Christian faith will often absorb elements from other religious forms that characterize that particular culture.

19. The issue of context and contextualization has been of notable interest in missiology, especially the issue of how best to share the gospel cross-culturally. Hesselgrave and Rommen, *Contextualization*; Bevans, *Models of Contextual Theology*.

Ideas and customs that do not immediately appear to be religious can also come into conflict with Christian faith. Most notably, this can apply to morality, where certain patterns of behavior may be considered contrary to Christian ethics. Such a conflict concerns, not only personal moral behavior, but also social institutions. The church's stand against polygamy is but one example of this. Today other questions related to sexual ethics is a source of conflict between the church and other groups in society, as well within the churches themselves.

Conflicts with culture, in other areas other than the purely religious, may also be related to an unconscious identification of the Christian faith and a particular cultural context. The classic illustration of this was when missionaries brought Western culture with the preaching of the gospel. Another example is, when the cultural codes as created by church sub-cultures are identified as normative expressions of Christian faith. This may result in conflict and separations that are more rooted in cultural conditions than in relation to that of the faith.

A dilemma that arises with regards to the relationship between Christian faith and a given culture is the question of what precisely the core element of faith is and what elements are culturally determined. In other words, how can the trans-cultural element of Christian faith be identified, i.e. the element that should be present in all cultural versions of the faith and makes it possible to talk about one Christian faith and one Christian church. The idea of such a trans-cultural element of Christian faith does not mean that it is possible to isolate and "distillate" this element as culturally independent. The fact that Christian faith is always given in specific cultural forms does not prevent us, however, from recognizing the *same* faith in the culturally different forms of the faith. A question that has no simple answer and continues to be discussed is where are the boundaries between trans-cultural elements and the various contextual and cultural expressions.[20]

In its affiliation to any culture the church should confirm the existence of the dual character of the human reality as being created by God and marked by sin. This means that no culture can simply be rejected as being sinful or demonic, and likewise no culture is free from being marked by sin. Therefore, the church's relationship to any culture cannot

---

20. A contentious and divisive issue in the Western culture today is sexual ethics: For example, the issue of homosexuality and whether the traditional condemnation is a trans-cultural or culturally determined part of Christianity.

support a one-sided conflict model or a one-sided harmony model—it is required to be both affirmative and critical.[21]

When we consider church and culture, it is easy to think these as two *separate* realities and that the church exists *independently* of culture. Such an understanding is untenable, both in sociological and theological terms. Sociologically speaking, the church is both an outworking of human culture and part of the very fabric of human culture. Theologically speaking, the church does not cease to be a part of the created reality. As an anticipation of the redemption of creation the church is still *part of creation*. Since redemption is only *anticipated*, sin still remains present in the church.

Both the world and the church belong to the created reality, and both the world and the church are marked by sin. What makes the church different to the world is that it is the place in the world where God has chosen to bear witness to his presence in a special way and the place of anticipation for his redemptive work with humanity and the world.

A theology of creation outlook is also important for ecclesiology concerning the question of *diversity*. What distinguishes creation in particular is the great diversity between different species and life forms. According to the biblical creation narrative, such diversity is an expression of the will of God. Furthermore, there is a great diversity between people. This applies to the relations between different cultures and groups. This is also true on an individual level, not only are we two different sexes, but people also have different personalities, abilities and talents. Biologically speaking, individual differences are reflected in the vast diversity of genes found in the human species. This diversity is further reinforced by the fact that we go through different stages and experiences of life.

Like all other aspects of the created order, diversity is affected by sin. This means that diversity not only appears as beautiful and as a blessing, but it is also the basis for division and conflict. The solution to this problem is not to abolish diversity. Much of the strife and conflict is a reaction to diversity because we feel threatened by what is different. We try ways to eliminate difference or to put it under our control. Violence and conflict often stem from a fear of diversity and difference.

As an anticipation of the new humanity of the final consummation, the church should celebrate and protect the diversity of human life. This

---

21. A classic description of different models to try and understand the relationship between Christian faith and culture is given in Niebuhr, *Christ and Culture*.

applies not only to the existence of diversity, but gives the *same right* for different groups and individuals to express themselves according to their own characteristics, the exception being when diversity is rooted in violence or injustice. Likewise, we are to reject the notion of diversity that with strains people to a particular identity that limits their freedom.

The church's confirmation of diversity should apply to society in general, but it should also apply to the diversity of the church. The fact that in the church we are all one in Christ, does not mean that we are all the same. Since the original creation of the world was diverse, so there is reason to expect that the new creation will also be diverse. As a foretaste of the new creation, the church should therefore also be a diverse community. To see the church as a diverse community, however, should not be used as an excuse to justify injustice and inequality, and cannot be used to justify divisions and conflicts in the church. As diverse as the church is, it is still called to be one.

A theology of creation means that the church is to be a church for all people and for all cultures. God's work of salvation in Jesus is not only for part of creation, or for one particular people, it is aimed at creation in its entirety and for all people. The fact that salvation has not yet been received by all does not change this truth. The church should not close in on itself and be contempt with its own salvation. Both the church's foundation in creation and God's mission for the church requires a fundamental *openness* towards the world. The church should be no stranger to any person or to any aspect of the human reality. This is not to imply an openness that blurs the difference between the church and the world, but one that is critical of any tendency of the church being self-satisfied in creating walls of division towards the world. The church is for the world's sake and embodies the world's salvation.

THE CHURCH AND THE MISSION OF GOD

In the New Testament the belief that the church is for the sake of the world is encapsulated by the charge that the church is sent into the world. Several texts draw a parallel between the Father's mission of sending his Son into the world to that of the church being sent into the world. In John's Gospel for example, some of the last words of the resurrected Jesus was to send his disciples out: "As the Father has sent me, so I send you" (John 20:21).[22]

According to Matthew's Gospel this commissioning of the disciples after the resurrection was foreshadowed by a former commissioning (Matt 10; cf. Luke 10). In the similar way that Jesus preached the Gospel of the kingdom of God and healed the sick (Matt 4:17), so the disciples too were sent out to do the same (Matt 10:7–8). However, the disciples were not given the promise of success by Jesus in the task set before them. On the contrary, he forewarned them that just as he faced opposition, persecution and resistance so would they (Matt 10:16–25).

While the designated group for the first commissioning of the disciples was the people of Israel, this was expanded to all peoples following the resurrection. According to Acts 1:8, the disciples were called to be Jesus' witnesses "in all Judea and Samaria, and to the ends of the earth." According to the Great Commission at the end of Matthew's Gospel, Jesus sent his disciples out to "all nations" to make them disciples: "Go therefore and make disciples of all nations, baptizing them in the name of the Father and of the Son and of the Holy Spirit" (Matt 28:19–20). Thus, the community of faith was not only a vehicle to preach the message, but also a community to which new people were *added*. The disciples were sent out to make more disciples, and to add them to the fellowship through baptism and teaching. It is interesting to note how the same Jesus who promises to be present when the disciplines *gathered* in his name (Matt 18:20), also promises to be with them as they *go out*: "I am with you always, to the end of the age" (Matt 28:20).

To try and gain some insight in how the Great Commission was understood and practiced in the early church we can turn to the Acts of the Apostles. Here we read that the gospel was first preached in Jerusalem, then elsewhere in Palestine, and eventually throughout the Roman Empire. To begin with it was only Jews that were added to the church, later the church came to realize that even Gentiles could be baptized without being circumcised (Acts 15). The spread of the gospel to new places was, in part, a result of people moving because of persecution or for other reasons (Acts 8:14), and in part, a result of a well thought out mission strategy, or directly through the guidance of the Spirit. For example, after the church in Antioch had gathered for worship they became convinced

---

22. For an overview of mission in The New Testament see Nissen, *New Testament and Mission*.

by will of the Holy Spirit that Paul and Barnabas should be commissioned and sent out together (Acts 13:1–3).

Over time, the term *mission* was introduced to describe this aspect of church life. Through its linguistic root (Latin *missio* means *sending*) the term is related to the idea that God sends the church to complete a specific task. The importance attached to mission has varied throughout the church's history. For many churches mission has been perceived as something belonging to the past and was often associated with the Christianization of each country. In the majority of countries in Europe this meant the task of mission was completed by the Middle Ages. With the seventeenth and eighteenth centuries mission rose to a new importance within Protestant churches, a fact that was partly connected to the idea of the civilization of pagan cultures outside Europe. Besides the commitment to proclaim the gospel in countries beyond the traditional Christian countries, with the developing secularization, mission was also acknowledged as necessary within one's own country. The mission movement grew as a commitment to both overseas and home mission.[23]

In many countries the work of overseas and home missions were organized under the auspices of independent missionary societies. These societies had different kinds of relations with official church structures, and were rarely fully integrated into these structures. In many cases the consequence of this was that mission and church was perceived as being two separate entities. Such a duality can be explained historically, but theologically this is unjustifiable. Mission is precisely the *church's* mission to the world. A church without mission is therefore theologically absurd. Without mission there is no church.[24]

A result of the traditional understanding of mission has resulted in mission being understood as something the church does, as a kind of activity or work alongside others. Thus, mission becomes an *addition* to church life, or even something the church can do without.

In recent missiology and ecclesiology there has here been a development towards understanding mission as being a fundamental ecclesiological category. It belongs on the very nature of the church's identity as

---

23. For an overview of the history of missions see Bevans and Schroeder, *Constants in Context*, 73–280.

24. This is not to exclude the possibility of organizing missionary work under the direction of independent organizations in the service of the church (see chapter 9).

being sent—being "missionary," "missional," or "mission-shaped."[25] The basis for such an understanding is a *theocentric* appreciation of mission as being *God's mission* (*missio Dei*). In essence, mission expresses God's saving work in the world. When the church engages in mission it becomes a tool for God's own redemptive work. As David Bosch puts it: "Mission is, primarily and ultimately, the work of the Triune God, Creator, Redeemer, and Sanctifier, for the sake of the world, a ministry in which the church is privileged to participate."[26]

When mission is sidelined or understood as one activity among many, this often is the result of an inadequate understanding of the relationship between the church and the world. As I have pointed above, this relationship should be understood in light of the church's eschatological position: it is a sign and foretaste of God's new reality, but it also exists in the middle of the old reality. It is an outworking of false theology to act as if God's kingdom is already established on earth, or as if mission is already complete. So long as the church waits for Christ's return, so the church is a pilgrim people, a church *in via*.

A recognition of the church's eschatological position in the world also means that it is unacceptable to limit the mission to specific *parts* of reality. This will happen if we operate from an understanding of the church and the world as being completely separated. A result of such thinking often leads to setting up sharp distinctions between the outside and inside of the church.

Such a view can manifest itself in very different and often mutually incompatible variations. One variant is a type of state church theology based on the idea of being a Christian people. Since most people are baptized and members of the church, the missionary task is virtually complete within the nation's borders. The task of the church is, first and foremost, the notion of maintenance and consolidation. Mission is therefore, not something that should take place within the country, but *outside* among

---

25. While the word *missionary* is traditionally associated with the idea that this is something the church *does* (e.g., overseas missions), the words *missional* and *mission-shaped* (from an American and a British context respectively) have recently been coined to describe mission as something the church *is*. Van Gelder and Zscheile, *Missional Church in Perspective*.

26. Bosch, *Transforming Mission*, 392. In this book Bosch gives a comprehensive overview and assessment of the development of missiological thinking. A similar overview can be found in Bevans and Schroeder, *Constants in Context*, 281–395. For an understanding of seeing mission as *missio dei* see Bosch, *Witness to the World*, 239–48.

people who have not yet heard the gospel. Mission is thus unilaterally delineated as being a "mission to the pagans," in the sense that mission is amongst those who as yet do not belong to a Christian civilization.

In reaction to such limitations of mission, low-church revival movements have claimed that mission must take place even within a Christian country. Even if a majority of the population is baptized and formally members of the church, this does not guarantee that they have personal faith, or that they are part of a vibrant Christian fellowship. Overseas missions must therefore be supplemented with home missions. This type of mission is often perceived as being limited to those on the *outside*. To be on the outside does not mean those people outside the church, or outside Christian civilization, but those who are outside a fairly clearly defined group of believers. Mission is what one group does to evangelize those who do not belong to the group. In many cases, the group's own image of itself can be fairly static. The question remains how to bring people from *outside* to be *inside*. For those who are already in the group the primary concern is maintenance and consolidation.

In their own ways, both state church and the low-church perspectives try to take seriously the fundamental difference between the church and the world. If the church is to take mission seriously, then it must transcend boundaries and go out. However, as the church is not divorced from the world, mission cannot be limited to only those on the *outside*. The gospel of the kingdom of God is a call to repentance and faith for those on outside and for those within—and for those in the uncertain middle ground.[27]

The fact that the church is sent into the world, means it is *for the sake of the world*. Around the 1970's the "church for others" became a major slogan in ecumenical missional thinking. Underlining this concept was the idea that the purpose of God for salvation was not the church, but the world. It was argued that because mission comes from God (*missio Dei*) this meant that God could do his work in the world independent of the church. The church is not to stand in the way of God's work in the world, but rather is to look to the world and participate in the work of God as found there. With the church not being the goal of God's mission, this meant that the church was not, as it was claimed, an end in itself to which

---

27. A similar point is made by Bevans and Schroeder who write that there is "*one mission*" that has "*two directions*—to the church itself *(ad intra)* and to the world *(ad extra). Constants in Context*, 394.

people were called out of the world in order to join the church. Salvation is thus, not something that is bound to the church, but a work God does directly in the world. Since Jesus' death and resurrection, the world is already redeemed and on its way to the fullness of salvation.[28]

Such an understanding of *God's mission* is fundamentally problematical. A basic weakness of this argument is it does not distinguish between creation and redemption. The fact that God works with the world regardless of the church is apparent when it comes to his continuing work of creation. God's work to save the world from the power of sin, however, is related to Jesus' life, death and resurrection, and his continued presence where people are gathered in his name.

It is not as though God's mission is independent of the church. On the contrary, the church is God's instrument in the world. However, it is certainly not the *church*, but *God's kingdom* that is the ultimate goal of God's work of saving. Until the final consummation, the reality of the kingdom of God in the world is directly related to the preaching of the gospel, baptism and the eucharist. More specifically, it is directly related to the church as a fellowship of people gathered in the name of Jesus. In the words of Ola Tjørhom, the church is "the place of salvation."[29]

The church's preaching of the gospel aims at the establishment and growth of the church amongst different groups of people. This applies to places where the church already exists and also in places where the gospel has as yet not taken root. As the church is sent into the *entire* world with the gospel this means mission does not cease even in established contexts, but should continue to break through into different social, cultural and geographical boundaries. According to Acts 1:8, the mission objective is until "the ends of the earth." The fact that the church in mission goes out to the *whole world* is itself a sign that the kingdom of God has come. Conversely, it is a betrayal of the gospel and a false witness of the kingdom of God if the church settles down in familiar contexts and fails to cross new frontiers.

When the gospel is received in new contexts, this happens when new congregations are formed. For example, this is demonstrated by Paul's missionary activity as described in the Acts of the Apostles and the Letters. In the places where Paul went on mission, the goal was to found

---

28. An influential document of its time was *The Church for Others* from the World Council of Churches.

29. Tjørhom, *Visible Church*, 50.

new churches. These newly founded churches were not only instruments for mission, but also the *goal* of mission. To gather in Jesus' name in one place meant that Jesus was present with his saving presence in that place. The church is not just a place where you can hear about God's kingdom, it is also a sign and foretaste of the reality of God's kingdom. The church's mission is not only to point beyond itself but is also *to offer itself*. The invitation of the gospel message to have fellowship with God in the name of Jesus Christ is realized in anticipatory fashion in the church's fellowship.

The view that the church is the goal of mission, however should not be formulated in such a way so that the church is identified with the coming kingdom of God. The *ultimate* goal of the work of salvation for the world is God's kingdom and not the church. While the church is the anticipation and sign of the kingdom of God, it is also part of the fallen world. It is a community that is *on the way*, not a community that has already reached its destination. All ecclesial triumphalism and self-glorification is in contradiction to the gospel and a false witness of the kingdom of God.

THE CHURCH'S HEALING MINISTRY

In the last section I have described two essential aspects of the church's mission: first, to preach the gospel, and second, to add people to the fellowship of faith. We also find these two characteristics in the ministry of Jesus: he preached the gospel of the kingdom of God and called people into fellowship. Jesus' ministry also included a third dimension that should not be overlooked, namely, his *healing* ministry. According to the gospel accounts, preaching the gospel went hand in hand with healing the sick and casting out demons: "Jesus went throughout Galilee, teaching in their synagogues and proclaiming the good news of the kingdom and curing every disease and every sickness among the people" (Matt 4:23). When Jesus sent his disciples out on mission the disciples' ministry was likewise to be characterized by preaching and healing (e.g., Matt 10:7–8).

According to the gospels, Jesus understood both preaching the gospel and works of healing to be demonstrations of the forthcoming kingdom of God. When asked for a sign of whether Jesus was the promised Messiah, he replied: "Go and tell John what you hear and see: the blind receive their sight, the lame walk, the lepers are cleansed, the deaf hear, the dead are raised, and the poor have good news brought to them" (Matt 11:4–5; cf. Luke 7:22–23).

These words bear witness that the salvation of God's kingdom is not restricted only to humanity's spiritual side, but also includes the *whole person*, both soul and body.[30] To encounter Jesus, was not only to receive forgiveness of sin, but also to receive health to the body. In many examples we read that Jesus both pronounced forgiveness of sins and healed diseases. In the story of Jesus' encounter with the paralytic in Mark 2:1–12, the healing was regarded as a sign that Jesus had authority and power to forgive sins.

Although the healing ministry is a *sign* of the kingdom of God, the situation was that not all the sick were healed at the same time, and if they were healed there was no guarantee that they would not get sick at a later date. The narratives about when Jesus raises the dead most clearly illustrate this point (Matt 9; Luke 7; John 11). Even though the power of God's kingdom was manifested in such dramatic way, those who had been raised from the dead would nevertheless die again at a later date. Only at the final consummation will the reality of these signs be made present: a life no longer threatened by death.

Jesus' healing ministry testifies to a second important aspect of God's kingdom as manifesting itself in the world—not only does it speak against human sin, but it also speaks against principalities and powers in the world that would destroy human life. In the gospel narratives these forces are usually personified as evil spirits. In many cases, Jesus' healing ministry takes the form of deliverance. Jesus' encounters against the evil powers demonstrate that the kingdom of God has come: "But if it is by the finger of God that I cast out the demons, then the kingdom of God has come to you" (Luke 11:20).

It remains a topic of discussion how Jesus' healing ministry is to be continued in the ministry of the church today. A key issue being how

---

30. Nielsen, *Heilung und Verkündigung*. According to Nielsen, Jesus sets his healings within "an eschatological perspective, as he understands them to be proleptic manifestations of the forthcoming kingdom of God and the downfall of Satan's reign." The correlation between healing and preaching is one of "interdependence . . . as they are two ways that manifest the same reality, namely God's forthcoming kingdom" (ibid., 288–89, our translation). According to Nielsen, all too quickly in post–New Testament times healing became secondary to proclamation. This was due to a division being made between soul and body (a concept alien to the witness of the Bible), which was to negatively affect the view about the mission of the church.

much weight should be assigned to Jesus' healing ministry as being *miraculous*. There is no doubt according to the Gospel narratives that signs and wonders demonstrate Jesus' extraordinary power (*dynamis*) and authority (*exousia*). However, when Jesus heals, he does not use people as objects to demonstrate power, but he does this out of compassion and love for them. This is exemplified in Matthew 14:14: "When he went ashore, he saw a great crowd; and he had compassion for them and cured their sick." The fact that people are set free from disease and demon possession is not only a sign of God's kingdom but also an anticipation of the kingdom to come. The important thing being is people are set free, and not whether or not they are supernatural and extraordinary occurrences.

Furthermore, acts of compassion towards the needy that have no miraculous element may also be understood as signs of the kingdom of God. According to the parable about judgment day in Matthew 25:31–46, it is those who give food to the hungry, give drink to the thirsty, welcome the stranger, clothe the naked, and visit prisoners, who are exemplified as being the righteousness of the kingdom of God.

The early church saw it as their duty to uphold both the preaching of Jesus and to continue his healing ministry. According to Mark 16:15–18, the preaching of the gospel is to be accompanied by both the expulsion of evil spirits and the healing of the sick. The Acts of the Apostles gives several examples of when the disciples healed the sick (Acts 3:1–10, 5:16, 8:7, 9:34, 14:9–10, 28:8–9). Paul mentions "the gift of healing" as one of the gifts of the church (1 Cor 12:9, 28, 30; cf. Jas 5:16). Alongside this, the early church was in different ways engaged in the relief of human suffering. Not least, they gave to those in need within their own church. For example, the cost for many who joined the church was to the determent of other relationships. To compensate for this loss, other arrangements of support were made within the church (Acts 6) or between the churches (Acts 11:29–30). There is no evidence to suggest that these works were limited only to believers. On the contrary, Paul encourages that "whenever we have an opportunity, let us work for the good of all, and especially for those of the family of faith" (Gal 6:10).

Efforts to take care of the sick, poor and destitute have been an essential ministry throughout the history of the church. Modern health care is partly the result of the church trying to emulate its masters' healing ministry through nursing and medical services. In a similar way, the modern social welfare system is a continuation of the church's care for the poor. Even though the modern welfare state in some parts of the world has taken charge of these responsibilities from the church, this still remains an aspect of the church's mission that cannot be put aside and left only to others to do. To give up this aspect of the church's mission is an abdication of a vital aspect of the church's vocation in the world. To be a witness of the coming kingdom of God is not limited to words alone, but it must also include *the works of the kingdom of God.*

THE DIAKONIA OF THE CHURCH

The activity of doing works of service can be described by the use of the Greek term *diakonia*.[31] The understanding of the church's diakonia has in recent years been the subject of considerable debate. This is a debate that has not only focused upon the practical aspects of diakonia, but has with equal weight of importance, reflected upon a theological understanding of diakonia.[32] A question raised by this debate is whether the church's diakonia should be understood as a continuation of Jesus' healing ministry, or whether it should have another understanding.[33]

Due to the limited scope of this chapter, it is not possible to go into this debate in too much depth. However, it is worth highlighting the issue that has been central to this debate, namely whether this should be understood as an outworking of creation and the law, or of redemption and the gospel. A widely held view in Lutheran circles is to see diakonia as belonging to the sphere of creation and the law. According to this point

---

31. There is no direct equivalent to the Greek term in English. In the following I will therefore use the Greek term in the English text, which has become common in ecumenical documents of the previous years, cf. e.g., Nordstokke, *Diakonia in Context*.

32. Concerning the theological grounds and content of diakonia some recent contributors to this debate include Helge Kjær Nielsen and Kjell Nordstokke. While giving diakonia a broader theological background, both scholars specifically mention Jesus' healing as part of the reason for having diakonia. Nielsen, *Han elskede os først*, 81–82; Nordstokke, *Det dyrebare mennesket*, 45–50.

33. The view I present here, namely that the church's works of mercy are to be understood as an extension of Jesus' healing ministry, is not necessarily universally accepted. For example, see Olav Skjevesland ("Jesu hebredelsesgjerninger og diakonien") who argues against this view in the conclusion of his article about Jesus' healing ministry and diakonia. See also Østnor, *Kirkens tjenester*, 49–55. Conversely, Gustaf Wingren roots diakonia as: "The specific biblical basis of the Church's diaconate or ministry of service is the healing of the sick which from the beginning was a regular part of both Jesus's own messianic activity and the mission of the apostles." *Gospel and Church*, 155. Applying the same basis of understanding for diakonia see Ivarsson, *Kyrkan och diakonin*.

of view, Christian diakonia is nothing more than the work that all people are called to do. This means diakonia falls under another category other than preaching the gospel, which is peculiar to the church. This does not mean that diakonia is not necessary, or that it is something the church can do without. As a necessary result of the faith created by the gospel, it is about the *fruits of faith*. The real reason for the church's diakonia is given in the command of loving your neighbor as yourself, which is a command for everyone.[34]

In my opinion, it is essential to emphasize the relation between diakonia and theology of creation, in the same way as it is when it comes to relating ecclesiology to a theology of creation in general. This does not mean that the church's diakonia can be restricted and understood as deeds only within the context of creation. Such a limitation does not take into account these good deeds are a sign and foretaste of the coming kingdom of God.

Diakonia as a sign of the kingdom does not *exclude* an understanding of diakonia as *also* belonging to the sphere of creation. The possibility for such a twofold interpretation is given by redemption as the restoration and renewal of creation. When people's lives are restored and renewed through the diakonia of the church this confirms God's creative work and is a sign of the renewal of creation with the coming kingdom of God.[35]

As is characteristic of the presence of the kingdom of God in this world, the eschatological dimension of diakonia makes it ambiguous and provisional. Although the diakonia of the church should serve as sign of the redeemed human life, as a sign it will always be both provisional and imperfect.

This raises the underlining question of what substantiates activities of the church as being diakonia. In other words, what is it that happens in the sphere of creation that can *also* be seen as a sign of God's kingdom? The answer to this question surely cannot lie in the *quality* of care

---

34. For example, this view is presented Østnor, *Kirkens tjenester*, and in particular pp. 49–70. Cf. e.g., p. 62: "Diakonia as good deeds commissioned by God that help fellow human beings in need, should be seen as part of *God's creative work* in the constant struggle against sin's corruption of creation and the consequences this has had for humanity. As such, the works of diakonia are not directly linked to God's work of salvation" (our translation).

35. Wingren, *Gospel and Church*, 168: "The distinctive mark of mission and diaconate is that both are vehicles for the restoration of the original creation and to this extent they serve Christ and creation at the same time."

or service that people do in the church. Certainly the church is called to meet people with the same love and care that they too have been met with by Jesus. This is a love that is motivated and willing to give selflessly to one's neighbor (Phil 2:7; 1 Cor 3:5). In practice, however, diakonia will be mixed with selfishness and impure motives. All too common, we put ourselves first where those who are in need are not considered so highly.

What substantiates the church's diakonia is neither its content, nor its special quality, but that it is simply performed in *Jesus' name*. This means that diakonia and the gospel can never be separated from each other. The church's diakonia should always be integrated, explicitly or implicitly, with the message of salvation in Jesus Christ. It does *not* mean that diakonia is nothing more than a tool for preaching the gospel or witness of the gospel, and it also does not mean that the gospel must be taught explicitly in every given situation where diaconal work is in operation. Diaconal works are still diakonia even when the gospel is not explicitly preached. However, the connection to the gospel must always be present, albeit sometimes implicitly and indirectly. When the church works for the benefit of people in the world, it is primarily for the sake for the people it serves rather than for self-promotion and self-preservation. The church does this ministry because Jesus has asked it to do so—the church is *sent* into the world with the mission of Jesus, and in the name of Jesus.

This means that diakonia and church cannot be separated from each other. It is precisely the church that is sent into the world. Due to the church being a community that meets in the name of Jesus, means the works of the church are in a special way, an expression of Jesus' saving presence in the world. The integration of diakonia in the church implies that even when something is done by the individual members of the church, this work is rooted in the fellowship gathered in Jesus' name. Therefore, every work done by a Christian in the name of Jesus is an expression of the diakonia of the church. The idea of diakonia being an individual Christian act of charitable love in everyday life should not be set against diakonia as initiated and carried out by the fellowship itself. The church as fellowship is not just about *being* together, but also about *working* together (see the next chapter).

In the same way as mission has been delegated as a separate aspect of the church's life, so this is true of diakonia. There are, of course, legitimate and necessary reasons for developing expertise and specialization also in this area. However, it is also important that diakonia (as with mission) is not only a concern for part of the church. When rightly understood, diakonia should permeate and affect the whole of church life. It is in the very nature and calling of the church to witness to God's kingdom through its works. A church that is content to *speak* of God's kingdom, but fails to do the *works* of the kingdom, is not being faithful to the gospel of God's kingdom. As it is written in 1 John 3:17: "How does God's love abide in anyone who has the world's goods and sees a brother or sister in need and yet refuses help?"

DIAKONIA AND POLITICS

Traditionally, the church's diakonia has been concerned with the needs of individuals. Although diaconal ministry must never loose focus of the individual, it is an illusion to believe that all problems are due to individual choices or circumstances, and that all problems can be remedied by helping the individual. Human suffering will, in different ways, be conditioned by social structures that help to create, maintain, and justify various forms of injustice and deprivation.

The church and the church's diakonia cannot to be content with just helping the individual as a result of unjust social structures, but must also work to change unjust structural conditions. This means that diakonia should have a *political dimension,* and be ready to highlight injustice in society, for example, in political structures or in certain political decisions made. A diakonia without any political aspects or implications lacks real credibility. The non-political church is either a church that is closed in on itself, or a church that is conformed by the society in which it is a part. In either case, the church fails in its mission to serve the world.

To suggest that the church's ministry in the world will always have political results is not to suggest that the church should understand itself being an ordinary political player. In politics the choice is rarely between good and bad solutions, rather different considerations are weighed against each other. Such a trade-off should not be the task or decision of the church. The church should not act as a political party or align itself to any political party. Instead, it should respect the individual Christian's right to engage in politics holding differences of opinions and evaluations.

The political engagement of the church is, first and foremost, to speak against injustice and fight for human dignity. When people live in poverty and their dignity is undermined, it is the church's mission to speak out, even when this involves the criticism of rulers and political decisions.[36]

In this regard, the church is not to limit itself not only to the human situation. Its service to the world includes the non-human part of the created reality as well. In today's world, we are made aware how the extent of diversity and the balance of creation is being threatened by human activities and consumption. Therefore, it is necessary for the church to speak out for the protection of creation. In doing this, the church not only supports the basis for humanity's continued existence on earth, but places intrinsic value in the non-human world as created and willed by God—as part of the created reality that "will be set free from its bondage to decay and will obtain the freedom of the glory of the children of God" (Rom 8:21).[37]

Above all, a right understanding of the church's relationship to the political world is founded upon the understanding of the church as a witness of God's kingdom. On the one hand, God's kingdom is a restoration of God's created world. The church's witness of God's kingdom will always be the benchmark from which to criticize conditions in society, and a source of inspiration in making conditions better. On the other hand, God's kingdom is a new and different reality, which can not be understood as a result of the gradual evolution of the world as we know it. When God's kingdom comes, it is not at all as a result of human effort, but the sole expression of the work of God.[38]

Even though the church is called to anticipate aspects of the reality of God's kingdom, this cannot be directly applied to society as such. While politics is about governance and decision making, the ideal of God's kingdom is *servanthood*. When Jesus taught his disciples about the attributes of Christian fellowship, he does this in contrast to political authority:

---

36. How much the church should be a political voice, and how far it should make recommendations or criticize specific political debates and outcomes, will always be an important discussion point for the church. This also applies to how far representatives of the church should position themselves in political issues, or whether these issues should be left to the discretion of individual Christians. While these discussions should be based on the self-understanding of the church, any attempt by politicians and the political arena to limit the church's right to express itself politically is to be rejected.

37. The church's ministry for the created world requires the development of an ecological theology. This is a task that has only barely begun.

38. For further explanation concerning this topic see: "The church and the political order in the light of God's lordship" in Pannenberg, *Systematic Theology*, vol III, 49–57.

> So Jesus called them and said to them, "You know that among the Gentiles those whom they recognize as their rulers lord it over them, and their great ones are tyrants over them. But it is not so among you; but whoever wishes to become great among you must be your servant, and whoever wishes to be first among you must be slave of all. For the Son of Man came not to be served but to serve, and to give his life a ransom for many." (Mark 10:42–45)

Here Jesus portrays the Christian fellowship as being a community that is fundamentally *different* to the reality of the general society. This is not a difference that is to be eradicated by applying the ideals of the servant community to society at large. On the contrary, the New Testament recognizes political governments and their right to rule (Matt 22:21; Rom 13:1–7; Titus 3:1; 1 Pet 2:13–17).

This should not be construed to mean that the ideals of community the church is called to represent are completely irrelevant to the world outside the church. Although they cannot simply be applied to society as such, they do give a critical and relativizing perspective upon social power structures. After all, these are only temporary structures that will one day be replaced by the community of righteousness and peace in the kingdom of God. When the church is called to represent an alternative community, it is not primarily for its own sake, but for the sake of the world.

Even though the church represents God's kingdom, the church is also a part of the world and subject to conditions of this world. This means that even the inner workings of church life cannot be completely independent of forms of power and authority. Ecclesial organization must also have procedures for decision making, control, and given the ability to exercise power. The primary focus for all ecclesial activity, however, is that of *service*—for God, for each other, and for the world. Such a position qualifies and relativizes the use of public structures of authority that the church may use at any given time.

From a Lutheran point of view, the relationship between the church and the rest of society is often formulated on the basis of the so-called *two kingdoms doctrine*. According to this doctrine, God governs the world in two ways, partly through the state and the secular sphere, and partly through the church and the spiritual sphere.[39] To truly understand the doctrine of the two kingdoms it is important to see this from an escha-

---

39. Frostin, *Luther's Two Kingdoms Doctrine*; Tjørhom, *Kirken—troens mor*, 234–39.

tological perspective and not as a static and general description of the relationship between society and religion. This describes the relationship between God's creative work and his new work of salvation, where the church is an anticipatory sign of the kingdom of God. Applied as a description of the relative independence of the relationship between religion on the one hand, and politics and culture on the other, its validity is primarily limited to traditional Christian cultures. As Pannenberg points out, this is due to the fact that these cultures are influenced by Christianity's eschatological awareness of the difference between this world and the kingdom of God.[40]

THE CHURCH CATHOLIC

One of the classic statements made about the marks of the church is its *catholicity*. Both in the Nicene and Apostles' Creed *catholic* is one of the basic descriptions of the church. Although this term is used as a name of a specific denomination (the Roman Catholic Church), however as an ecclesiological statement, catholicity refers to every congregation and the church in general.[41] The catholicity of the church is closely associated to its calling to be sent into the world.

Even though *catholic* is not a biblical term, it clearly includes biblical motifs. Linguistically it implies the concept of *the whole*—the universal, that which is common to all. One aspect of the notion of the church's catholicity is associated by the idea of its unity and apostolicity. To be catholic, means to be part of the one and only church that exists wherever people are gathered around the one and only apostolic gospel of Jesus Christ.[42]

The idea of the church being catholic cannot be truly understood if we isolate only to the inner-life of the church. The church's catholicity is not something the church owns, but is something that is given by its relationship to Christ and the coming kingdom of God. The Lord of the

---

40. "The distinction between the spiritual and the secular, and hence also the secularity of the political order and of the cultural shaping of life in the present world, has its basis, then, in the eschatological awareness of Christianity. There could hardly be any sense of it apart from this basis." Pannenberg, *Systematic Theology*, vol. III, 53.

41. See chapter 9 for a more detailed examination of the relationship between the local church, universal church and denominations.

42. Dulles, *Catholicity of the Church;* and Küng, *Church*, 296–313 give a comprehensive account of the history of this term and its various shades of meaning.

church is Christ to whom "all authority in heaven and on earth has been given" (Matt 28:18). The coming kingdom of God means the end of the present world and where "God may be all in all" (1 Cor 15:28). It follows that the relationship to the *world* is therefore foundational to the church's catholicity. Christ is not just the Lord and savior of the church, but of the whole world. Similarly, the coming kingdom of God is not only the church's future, but the world's future.

The church's commitment to the *whole* implies a commitment to the world's *diversity*. The *whole* is not a uniform reality, but a sum of all forms of diversity. Being catholic, the church is called to be a church in different contexts and for different people. Moreover, being catholic, the church is called to welcome diversity and integrate this into its own fellowship—while at the same time maintaining its intrinsic unity.[43]

As with the idea of the church's holiness being interpreted from an eschatological perspective, so this is true of the church's catholicity. It is not something the church owns, but something it has through its relationship to Christ and the coming kingdom of God. Thus, catholicity is something the church participates in, and is also something the church is constantly called to realize.

The church is not called to be introverted and self-seeking, but to be open to the world. Being catholic, the church is sent into the world, indeed to the whole world. Being catholic, the church is not to make its home in only one particular culture, or one particular context, but is continually sent out to all and called to cross new boundaries. The realization of the church as catholic is by its mission "to the ends of the earth" (Acts 1:8) and "to the end of the age" (Matt 28:20).

---

43. These aspects of the church's catholicity are further discussed by Moltmann, *Church in the Power of the Spirit*, 347–52; and Schlink, *Ökumenische Dogmatik*, 587–88.

5

Fellowship with One Another

A BASIC CHARACTERISTIC OF the church is that it is a community. This community has two aspects: First, it is a community with God—whenever people come together in the name of Jesus, Jesus promises to be present and have fellowship with them. Second, it is community with one another. The church is not a place where individuals meet with God on their own, but a place where people meet with God together as a fellowship. Community is thus to have fellowship with other people seeking God in Jesus' name. The church is not an abstract spiritual fellowship, but a real coming together of people from various social backgrounds. As such, it can be described sociologically in line with other human communities. At the same time, it needs to be interpreted theologically in its relation to the triune God and the coming kingdom.

THE CHURCH AS KOINONIA

In recent years, the understanding of the church as a fellowship has been interpreted by the so called *koinonia* or *communio* ecclesiology. This has been spurred on by studies of the New Testament idea of the church being *koinonia* (Greek, translated into Latin as *communio*). As translations like *community* or *fellowship* do not cover all aspects of the concept, it is regularly used in its Greek or Latin version.[1]

---

1. Work regarding the nature of the church as *koinonia* has been of particular concern within ecumenical circles, not least because this concept has proven fruitful as means for understanding the relationship between different churches. This research has also generated material and ideas that are of value to ecclesiology in general. See for example *Communio/Koinonia*; Best and Gassmann, *On the Way to Fuller Koinonia*; Holze, *Church as Communion*; Doyle, *Communion Ecclesiology*.

An important contribution to this research is John Reumann's analysis of *kononia* as expounded in the biblical texts.[2] Reumann makes the point that *koinonia* is never used as a term for the church itself, yet it remains an important *aspect* attributed to the church. How this term is used says something *about* the church and its nature; it is a descriptive concept.[3]

A foundational aspect of the Christian *koinonia* is its *participatory* nature. On the one hand, we are talking about fellowship with Christ. To be a Christian means to be called into community with Jesus (1 Cor 1:9). This community is sacramentally conveyed through the eucharistic bread and wine. On the other hand, the eucharist also means we have fellowship with one another. As we share in the one body of Christ, so we have fellowship with one another: "The cup of blessing that we bless, is it not a sharing in the blood of Christ? The bread that we break, is it not a sharing in the body of Christ?" (1 Cor 10:16–17).

Fellowship with Christ is not some abstract notion, but a real participation in Christ's suffering, death and the hope of glory (Phil 3:10–11; 1 Pet 5:1). Through participating in *Christ's* suffering, believers also share in *each other's* suffering and consolations (2 Cor 1:7, Phil 4:14). Christian fellowship is also a fellowship in *service*, for example, in Philippians Paul speaks about "sharing in the gospel" (Phil 1:5).

Fellowship also suggests that we share each other's resources, including finances. Paul uses the term *koinonia* when writing about the collection for the church in Jerusalem "sharing in this ministry to the saints" (2 Cor 8:4; cf. 9:13; Rom 15:26). In the First Letter of John a profound statement is made about the relationship between fellowship with God and fellowship with one another, as both being rooted in the gospel. According to John, fellowship also shows a willingness to repent and ask for forgiveness for sins committed:

---

2. Reumann, "Koinonia in Scripture." This analysis includes, not only the noun *koinonia*, but also other derivatives from the same root. The term is primarily found in the Pauline Letters and in the First Letter of John, which has its origins in the Greek-Hellenistic world. Although *koinonia* is not found in the Gospels and does not have any derivatives in the Old Testament, Reumann still advocates it articulates aspects of the church that have general validity.

3. Reumann concludes that "*koinonia* is not a name for an interim step called 'the Fellowship' on the way to the Christian church, or the name for the ecclesia itself . . . *Koinonia* is instead an early and important aspect of the church and its unity, in faith, witness and life, including baptism and Lord's supper." Ibid., 62.

Fellowship with One Another

> We declare to you what we have seen and heard so that you also may have fellowship (*koinonia*) with us; and truly our fellowship (*koinonia*) is with the Father and with his Son Jesus Christ... If we say that we have fellowship (*koinonia*) with him while we are walking in darkness, we lie and do not do what is true; but if we walk in the light as he himself is in the light, we have fellowship (*koinonia*) with one another, and the blood of Jesus his Son cleanses us from all sin. (1 John 1:3, 6–7)

In the Acts of the Apostles we are given an example by the church in Jerusalem in how fellowship between Christians can be worked out in real life. Acts 2:42 refers to how *koinonia* is among one of the key components in the life of the church. This fellowship was not an idealized notion, in fact the disciples are reported as having all things in common (*koine*) (Acts 2:44, 4:32).

The New Testament does not seem to make a contrast between a spiritual fellowship and a fellowship that exists in the ordinary interaction of people going about their daily life. In the Letter to the Philippians Paul assumes that *koinonia* in the Spirit impacts the relationship between the Christians:

> If then there is any encouragement in Christ, any consolation from love, any sharing *(koinonia)* in the Spirit, any compassion and sympathy, make my joy complete: be of the same mind, having the same love, being in full accord and of one mind. Do nothing from selfish ambition or conceit, but in humility regard others as better than yourselves. Let each of you look not to your own interests, but to the interests of others. (Phil 2:1–4)

A theme that is often repeated in many passages in the Bible is the notion of mutual love between believers. To *love one another* seems to have been an important ideal for the early Christian church. John's Gospel makes reference to the *new commandment* that Jesus gave his disciples before he left them: "I give you a new commandment, that you love one another. Just as I have loved you, you also should love one another" (John 13:34; cf. 15:12).

The appeal of mutual love in Christian fellowship is also mentioned throughout the Letters, for example the Letters of Paul[4] and John,[5] and in

---

4. Rom 12:10: "Love one another with mutual affection; outdo one another in showing honor." Cf. Rom 13:8; Gal 5:13; Eph 1:16, 4:2; Col 3:14; 1 Tess 3:12, 4:9–10; 2 Thess 1:3; Phlm 5.

5. 1 Pet 1:22: "Love one another deeply from the heart." Cf. 1 Pet 3:8, 4:8.

1 Peter.[6] The love is portrayed as already a part of the Christians' relationship to one another, while at the same time they are encouraged to allow this love to increase to an even greater extent—one that permeates their shared live together. *Perfect* love only belongs to God, but as children of God, Christians are called to mature in love.

Rather than being some sort of idealized notion, love is to be expressed in specific relationships through practical acts of love. The highest call of love is willingness to lay down one's life for the sake of others: "No one has greater love than this, to lay down one's life for one's friends" (John 15:13). Love is also expressed by specific attitudes and actions which have the interest of other's at heart. To love means to serve one another (Gal 5:13) and bear with one another (Eph 4:2; cf. Col 3:13). Christians are to teach and admonish one another (Col 3:16), encourage one another (1 Thess 4:18), seek to do good to one another (1 Thess 5:15), and exhort one another (Heb 3:13; cf. 10:24–25).

In 1 Corinthians 12, Paul depicts the church as being Christ's body. This is not just about the fellowship between Christians and Christ, it is also about the relationship amongst Christians. In the body of Christ the basic underlining principle is one of solidarity and the sharing in each other's joys and sorrows: "If one member suffers, all suffer together with it; if one member is honored, all rejoice together with it" (1 Cor 12:26).

Other terms used to characterize the Christian fellowship with one another also suggest a relationship of mutual respect. For example, Christians are to regard each other as *friends*.[7] As with other aspects of a Christian's relationships, friendship is rooted in Jesus' example of calling his disciples friends (Luke 12:4; John 15:14–15).[8]

A central theme in the New Testament concerns the relationship with God and with each other in terms of family relationships.[9] An essential aspect of this is to call God Father, and to see one another as God's

---

6. 1 John 3:11: "For this is the message you have heard from the beginning, that we should love one another." Cf. 1 John 2:10, 4:7, 11; 2 John 5.

7. This term is explicitly used in, for example: Rom 12:19; Heb 6:9; 3 John 15. For an understanding of friendship in antiquity and the role it played in the New Testament see Sandnes, *New Family*, 49–54, 86–91.

8. Moltmann, *Church in the Power of the Spirit*, 114–21. Moltmann believes the concept of friendship is a central ecclesiological concept.

9. Sandnes, *New Family*, 65–82. Sandnes gives an overview of the role of the extended family in the New Testament. See also Aasgaard, *My Beloved Brothers and Sisters*.

children. The significance of having the same Father is Christians can refer to one another as *brothers and sisters*. In the Acts of the Apostles and the Letters "brothers and sisters" (*adelphoi*) is used as term by which Christians are to relate to another (e.g., Acts 1:15, 11:1; Rom 1:13, 12:1; 1 Cor 6:5).[10] Therefore, the church can be regarded as a *household* (*oikia*), and Christians the "household of God" (Eph 2:19). The reference to the church as family is not primarily referring to a theoretical truth, or to kinship on a purely spiritual level, but rather it is a personal relationship lived out in fellowship with one another and marked by certain qualities (Rom 12:10; 1 Pet 3:8).

As Karl Olav Sandnes has argued in his New Testament study, the church as a family is more than just an idea. In many cases, the early church functioned very much like a family to its members. In some cases, existing families became the backbone of the fellowship. In other cases, when people lost the network of their blood relations as a result of becoming Christians, the church served as a fellowship that became their *new family*.[11]

VISIBLE AND TANGIBLE FELLOWSHIP

As we have reviewed so far, Christian fellowship in the New Testament is understood as a network of tangible and ongoing relationships between people. Fellowship is *rooted* in something that cannot be directly observed in its relation to God and the coming kingdom. At the same time, the fellowship itself is something possible to experience and observe. A New Testament understanding of church as a fellowship implies a tangible and ongoing social interaction between people.

It is not true that *spiritual* fellowship is beyond empirical observation, while tangible fellowship is purely based upon human deeds. As I have noted before, the Spirit works in and through human deeds. Fellowship with one another in the church *is* a spiritual fellowship to the extent that it makes visible the Spirit's work. According to Galatians 5:22–23, love and other such virtues are to characterize Christians in relationship to one another—these are the *fruit of the Spirit*.

---

10. As Sandnes points out (*New Family*, 74), it is appropriate to translate *adelphos* as gender inclusive.

11. Sandnes, *New Family*.

The Real Church

The fact that Christian fellowship *is* a spiritual fellowship does not exclude it from being a sign of something beyond itself. The point being, the visible fellowship is not a sign of some invisible and perfect version beyond itself, but rather a sign of the coming kingdom of God. Even though the kingdom of God is something more than the church, it is still to be anticipated in the life of the church.

Such an understanding of the visible and tangible character of Christian community is not so clearly articulated in most theological works. More often than not, the spiritual and sacramental character of fellowship is set against its visible and tangible nature, or it is suggested that a theological understanding of the Christian community cannot be described in sociological terms.

To give an example of a theological understanding of Christian community beyond that of the fellowship as we experience it, we can once again return to Bonhoeffer's *Sanctorum Communio*. Bonhoeffer does emphasize the interaction between fellowship as we experience it and the real church, but argues this relationship is something that has to be *believed*. He disputes the notion of an *experience of the church* where one would be able to experience other people as members of God's church.[12] Because the visible church consists of both false and true members, what we experience is only the *religious community*. What qualifies the *religious community* as *church*, is according to Bonhoeffer, the administration of Word and sacrament in the empirical church. When the Word and sacrament is administered, it is through the eyes of faith we can be sure that the real church of God is present. Faith does not recognize the church, in what Bonhoeffer polemically describes as the "romantic feelings of solidarity between kindred spirits," but rather in the fact that very different people demonstrate their ecclesial fellowship as they come together around the Lord's table.[13] Bonhoeffer makes reference to the phenomenon that communicants in an urban context may not necessarily have any personal knowledge of each other. While some might regret this situation, Bonhoeffer stresses that when the church celebrates the eucharist in such circumstances, this gives an overwhelming witness that the communion of saints is something more than outward forms of human fellowship. In a situation where the Jew remains a Jew, the Greek a Greek,

---

12. Bonhoeffer, *Sanctorum Communio*, 279.
13. Ibid., 280–81.

the worker remains a worker, and the capitalist a capitalist, any confusion of the Christian *communio* being a community of human sympathy is excluded.[14]

Bonhoeffer certainly has a point when he argues against an identification of the communion of saints with the subjective experience or feeling of being in fellowship with like-minded people. However, this does become problematic when concrete relationships between people seem to be a kind of secondary expression of something that really is beyond experience.

One way of splitting the spiritual community from the concrete fellowship is, what we might call an *actualistic* understanding of the church. This is to see the church as an *event,* rather than an ongoing fellowship. From a certain perspective Matthew 18:20 may be interpreted as supporting this notion: since Jesus made the promise that he would be present with his disciples when they gathered in his name, we might interpret this to mean that his presence is *limited* to this gathering—where the church as a spiritual fellowship between God and one another does not exist independent of the worship service.

An example of a theologian who follows this line of thought is Martin Honecker as articulated in his book on ecclesiology.[15] Honecker's main issue is how we can theologically understand the relationship between church as empirical entity and as something that happens in and through the preaching of the Word. Honecker argues that empirically speaking the church appears to be a human religious institution with social and organizational structures. It is necessary for the church to be an institution otherwise it simply would not exist in history. Honecker distances himself from Protestant tendencies that would understand the church as a purely spiritual society, without external form.[16]

Meanwhile, Honecker still upholds the *difference* between the church as a human religious institution and the church as a spiritual community. What binds these two variables together is the *preaching event.* When the Word is preached, the church as a human religious institution is transformed into the church as eschatological community. In its outer form the church becomes an interaction between the office of preaching and the

---

14. Ibid., 245–46.
15. Honecker, *Kirche als Gestalt und Ereignis.*
16. Ibid., 206.

fellowship of those *listening*. Honecker believes it is solely the preached Word that qualifies the church as a church. The idea that the church is recognized by certain Christian acts or a certain Christian ways of life is therefore to be rejected. While the church's outward forms are ever changing, the preaching of the Word ensures continuity of the church. When Scripture is preached, the church in its visible form is related to Christ and experience of God's judgment and redemptive work.[17]

While Honecker sees the real church as an event, Bonhoeffer sees it more as constant reality. Both seem to agree on one point however, namely that a specific social fellowship cannot be identified with the church as a spiritual and eschatological fellowship. A concrete and visible community can only be the precondition for, or the consequence of, the real spiritual community and not the community itself. In my opinion, such an understanding is difficult to reconcile with a New Testament picture of church as a specific and continuous *koinonia* between Christians.

The fact that Honecker puts so much emphasis upon *preaching* can probably be attributed to the influence of neo-orthodox *Word of God* theology. It would be possible to develop Honecker's line of thought towards a more sacramental theology where eucharist is understood as the primary carrier of God's presence—making the church a spiritual community. Regardless of how such a position formulated in detail, the question still remains whether the church can be understood as a spiritual community when it is not gathered around the Word and sacraments.

The legitimate point proposed by an actualistic ecclesiology is undoubtedly in how the church worship transforms a human community into the church. It is theologically impossible to imagine a church that is not gathered in the name of Jesus through Word and sacrament. One can also argue that the church is most unambiguously present when gathered together. However, when the people are not gathered together, this does not mean they cease to be a church. The church as gathered in the name of Jesus does not cease to exist when this gathering is over. Church worship is the center of the church's life and the source from which the daily life flows. The belief that the church as fellowship is rooted in the eucharist does not imply that the ecclesial community is limited to the celebration of eucharist itself. On the contrary, the celebration of the eucharist points

---

17. Ibid., 205, 210–11.

Fellowship with One Another

outwards towards the life in the world of the church—a life that is in accordance to what is received in the sacrament.

The correlation between eucharist as a sacramental fellowship and the actual living fellowship between Christians is particularly emphasized by Martin Luther in a treatise on the eucharist from 1519.[18] Here Luther presents an understanding of the eucharist as a sacrament of fellowship, whereupon he distinguishes between the eucharist as *sign* and its *significance*: the sign is the bread and wine and its "significance or effect . . . is fellowship of all the saints" (50).

Those who receive the bread and wine, receive "a sure sign of this fellowship and incorporation with Christ and all saints" (51). This fellowship is characterized, above all, by the fact that they share everything, both the good and the bad. This applies to the relationship between Christ and believers, but also the believers themselves. The eucharist is therefore, a sacrament of *love*, where those that receive love should "in turn . . . render love and support to Christ in his needy ones" (54). When a Christian suffers, he or she must therefore "go joyfully to the sacrament of the altar and lay down his woe in the midst of the community and seek help from the entire company of the spiritual body" (53). Such help and support are not only symbolic in character, see for example of Luther's (somewhat idealized) description of the condition of the church in former times: "Christians cared for one another, supported one another, sympathized with one another, bore one another's burdens and affliction" (57).

An interesting point is the comparison Luther makes between the believing fellowship and the fellowship in an urban community:

> It is like a city where every citizen shares with all the others the city's name, honor, freedom, trade, customs, usages, help, support, protection, and the like, while at the same time he shares all the dangers of fire and flood, enemies and death, losses, taxes, and the like. For he who would share in the profits must also share in the costs, and ever recompense love with love. (51–52)

The analogy to the city still has its limitations, partly because the communion of saints is not just about fellowship amongst people, but also about fellowship with Christ. Furthermore, fellowship not only applies

---

18. "The blessed sacrament of the holy and true body of Christ, and the brotherhoods" (WA 2:742–58). *Luther's Works*, vol. 35, 49–73. The parentheses in the following text refer to pages in this edition.

to this life, but also to life after death. The eucharist is also a sign of the communion between the invisible and eternal realities (65–66).[19]

THE CHURCH AS MORAL COMMUNITY

In recent years, the idea of Christian communities having ethical qualities has come to the attention of both individual theologians and in ecumenical discussions. For example, the World Council of Churches (WCC) has attempted to apply *koinonia* ecclesiology to the discussion about social ethics.

In the report of a WCC conference of 1993, the emphasis was on the church as a *moral community*.[20] The report states that the church's moral practice is not a secondary outcome of the church, but rather it is an expression of the very nature of the church. Moreover: "The church not only has, but is, a social ethic, a *koinonia* ethic" (6). This does not mean that all members of the church must agree on all moral issues. Nevertheless, there will be limits to the ethical diversity, because there will always be cases where "certain decisions and actions are in contradiction to the nature and purpose of the church and the central teaching of the gospel" (7.4). Church unity that does not take into account moral issues is a *cheap unity*, meaning forgiveness without repentance, and baptism without discipleship. In contrast to this is a *costly unity*: "Costly unity is discovering the churches' unity as a gift of pursuing justice and peace" (7.6). The report points to cases where Christian unity has been broken because the churches have followed a moral practice that has been in conflict with the Gospel, for example the South African churches' support of apartheid (7.4).[21]

---

19. Luther seems to want to relativize the importance of the community's visible character in the shadow of death: "Therefore it is also profitable and necessary that the love and fellowship of Christ and all the saints be hidden, invisible, and spiritual, and that only a bodily, visible, and outward sign of it be given to us" (65). Instead of speaking about exterior/interior, visible/invisible, it is possible to maintain the same theological point by talking about the visible communion as an anticipation of something that has not yet been realized. Such a notion seems to be behind Luther's point when he assumes that we will at the end "attain to the eternal things also with sight and senses" (66).

20. Best and Granberg-Michaelson, *Costly Unity*. The parentheses in the following text refers to paragraph numbers in the final report, pp. 84–104.

21. In the New Testament we also see how moral issues may lead to a breakdown of fellowship with other Christians. See for example: Matt 18:15–17; 1 Cor 5:1–13; 2 Thess 3:6. The use of *church discipline* has a long ecclesial tradition.

Fellowship with One Another

This does not mean that the Christian moral efforts constitute the church. On the contrary, the church is constituted by God's grace as communicated through the sacraments. However, as the report points out, the church still needs to discover the moral meaning of the sacraments, and to see its sacramental life as a carrier of unity and solidarity with each other, and with the world (8).

The idea of the Christian community as a distinct moral community has consequences not only for ecclesiology, but also for the understanding of Christian ethics. Instead of seeing this as a contribution to a common social ethics, many theologians believe that the Christian community is the primary context for Christian ethics. The most influential representative of such a view is probably Stanley Hauerwas.[22]

For Hauerwas, the church is a community with a very distinct structure and culture. It is a *colony*, a cultural island in the middle of an alien culture. The reason why theologians are beginning to embrace this idea is because the homogenous Constantinian culture is but history today in the Western world. In today's world Christian faith has become the foreigner, and any attempt to legitimate Christian faith within society is not only misguided, but also contrary to the gospel. Hauerwas emphasizes the importance of the *practice* of Christian faith, as "new living rather than new understanding."[23]

Hauerwas distances himself from the type of political theology that perceives the primarily Christian task to change the world. The church's *political* task lies in being itself, being church: "The main political task of the church is the formation of people who see clearly the cost of discipleship and are willing to pay the price."[24] "The church," Hauerwas continues, "doesn't have a social strategy, the church *is* a social strategy."[25]

In a certain sense, the community aspect of being a church is secondary to the church's deeds. Hauerwas can thus describe the community as a "by-product" or as something that "happens," when people seek to be faithful to the will of Jesus.[26] How the Christian community should be,

22. For an introduction to Hauerwas' theology, see Rasmusson, *Church as Polis*.
23. Hauerwas and Willimon, *Resident Aliens*, 24.
24. Ibid., 48.
25. Ibid., 43.
26. "Christian community, life in the colony, is not primarily about togetherness. It is about the way of Jesus Christ with those whom he calls to himself . . . In living out the story together, togetherness happens, but only as a by-product of the main project of

is first and foremost, a response to Jesus' call to discipleship.[27] The possibility of living out the Christian moral life, without being a part of the Christian community, is something Hauerwas strongly denies.[28]

The church is in Hauerwas' view, a distinct society, a "colony" or a new "*polis.*" The underlining principle for his ethical thinking is how people can live for Jesus in the context of fellowship. The question is not, therefore, how the church can change the world, but how it can be faithful to its calling.

I would like to challenge two aspects of Hauerwas' position. First, is the question of whether by starting with ethics this may lead to a work-oriented church. The community character of the church is not only a prerequisite and a consequence of Christian life, but is itself an aspect of the salvation that God gives. Second, Hauerwas can be criticized for interpreting the Christian faith and the church's relationship to the world in far too negative terms. Based upon a theology of creation, the church's relationship to the world can be described as both continuity and discontinuity. The church is not of the world, but still it is in the world and sent to the world. Its mission is to be faithful to the gospel, not for its own sake only, but for the sake of the world (see the previous chapter).

As a community the church is both a distinct community, and in a complex way, interwoven into the social structures of society. To ignore the fact that such correlations exist, is both sociologically naive and theologically unsustainable. The tensions inherent in this relationship are not easily eliminated, neither theoretically, nor practically. The church can never be divorced from the reality of this tension, at least until God's kingdom has come. The tensions between the church's distinct character and it being interwoven with the very fabric of society will continue even if one stresses (as Hauerwas does) the church as a distinct community.

However, the opposite position of identifying the church as community with the social relations of the general society is no better. This can occur, for example, within a state church theology that sees the church

---

trying to be faithful to Jesus." Ibid., 78.

27. "What sort of community would be required to support an ethic of nonviolence, marital fidelity, forgiveness, and hope such as the one sketched by Jesus in the Sermon of the Mount." Ibid., 80.

28. Ibid., 80–81. An understanding of Christian ethics that primarily concerns the Christian life is taken up within the Lutheran debate by, among others, Reinhard Hütter, see *Evangelische Ethik*.

as the religious dimension of society.²⁹ Likewise, a Lutheran theology of vocation may stress the individual Christians' vocation in society in such a way that gives little room for the shared efforts of the church as a community.³⁰ As a corrective to these one-sided views it is important to stress that the church has a calling in the world, which cannot be achieved by individual Christians alone, but requires a shared action. At the same time the church as a community finds itself woven into the social fabric of society.

FOLK CHURCH AS CHRISTIAN FELLOWSHIP

Throughout history the church has related to the surrounding society in various ways and has taken various social forms. While the early church was a relatively distinct fellowship, later it became the state religion of the Roman Empire and became increasingly integrated into society at large. Right up until modern times, what has characterized the situation in Europe has been the synthesis between the church and society. Since the Enlightenment this synthesis has gradually been dissolved, resulting in the emergence of more distinct and independent ecclesial organizations. The remnants of this Constantinian synthesis, however, still lives on.

The current situation is characterized by great diversity, both between various countries and within countries where churches have different social structures and different relations to the given society. Not least, such differences depend upon whether the church represents a majority of the population, or whether it is a minority church. A church representing the majority of the population will be, to a greater extent, embedded in society and more difficult to distinguish from society. A minority church, on the other hand, will be more distinct as a community. Of course, such differences can also be related to ecclesiology and the theological ideals of the given church. For example, many free churches have made a deliberate choice not to be part of a church that is, in their opinion, too embedded within society.

---

29. Such a position has e.g. been advocated by the Norwegian folk church theologian Sevat Lappegard, e.g., in "Folkekyrkjeteologi."

30. The church after the church worship as being a principally *individual* affair in everyday life of a Christian is the direction Gustaf Wingren's ecclesiology seems to point to. See chapter 4.

THE REAL CHURCH

From a historical and sociological perspective, the differences between denominations make for interesting analysis.[31] Keeping to the subject of this book I would prefer to focus on questions relating to *theological interpretation* of the current situation. The task of theological interpretation is particularly challenging in the cases where there is a high degree of integration between church and society. How should the church as community be identified in such cases? What is the church and what is not the church?

The Nordic Lutheran churches are a good example of churches with a high degree of integration between church and society. These churches have a close connection to the state, and have a majority of the population as its members.[32] These and similar churches are often referred to as *folk churches* as a way to describe their close relation to the general population.[33]

In the case of the Church of Norway, almost 80% of the population are baptized members. Adherence to the church is shown by high attendance figures during the holiday seasons such as Christmas, as well as for special occasions such as baptisms, confirmations, weddings, and funerals. Both at a national level and at a local level, the church may play an important role in gathering people for festivities and tragic events. This is not to say that being a church member necessarily guarantees they share basic beliefs of the church. In fact, the vast majority of church members rarely go to the weekly services.[34]

Alongside this rather broad definition of church membership, the Church of Norway is also host to a variety of groups and fellowships within the church. These groups may be formally organized, or they may function as informal *core congregations*, comprising of the active participants in the weekly services and in various activities throughout the

---

31. The analysis of the various social forms, of which Christian groups are one example, is a subject of the sociology of religion. Furseth and Repstad, *Introduction to the Sociology of Religion*, 133–50.

32. An introduction of the situation of the Nordic Lutheran churches is given in Eriksson et al., *Exploring a Heritage*.

33. The English translation *folk church* does not truly capture the richness of the meaning and context of the Norwegian word *folkekirke* (or the German word *Volkskirche*).

34. In a survey carried out in 2000 among members of the Church of Norway, 59% said, with differing degrees of uncertainty, that they believed in God, while 56% were content to call themselves Christians. In the same survey 8% said that they go to church at least once a month. Høeg et al., *Folkekirke 2000*.

church. The workforce needed for both voluntary and paid ministries are often recruited from these groups, including the members of the elected parish councils. To some degree these groups have been the product of the revivalist movements of the nineteenth century up to the present day. In contrast to Sweden, these groups have mainly stayed within the folk church rather than form their own independent churches.

This historical background has led to, what could be called, a *twofold social* formation of the church. On the one hand, it is a folk church for the majority of the population, and on the other hand, active congregational life and Sunday worship attendance remains relatively low. As these two social groupings of the church interact with each other in the church's rhythm of life we can see how the Church of Norway is simultaneously both a majority and a minority phenomenon.[35]

The existence of the two different social formations within the Church of Norway raises a number of issues, both in terms of sociological interpretation, theological assessment, and church strategy. From a sociological perspective there is the issue of what distinguishes these two social formations of the church and what is the relationship between them. I believe this should be understood on the basis of their differences, as well as how they mutually co-exist and influence each other.

The key *theological* issue that arises is in how this can be interpreted in light of the church as *communio,* or fellowship, as outlined earlier in this chapter. If the church is to be understood as a fellowship of people gathered in Jesus' name, will this not exclude those church members who rarely or never set his foot in a church? Can the folk church be perceived as a Christian fellowship if it is, as I have argued, an experienced reality?

The relevance of this issue is not limited to the Church of Norway, or to other churches with a similar configuration. Most churches have a proportion of passive or nominal members within their fold. These members may have a formal connection to the church, for example, they may show up from time to time, or they may simply understand the church as *their* church. This situation even applies to smaller free churches. Not always have this group of people got the theological attention it deserves.

The understanding of the *communio* of the church as a visible and tangible fellowship has often led to identifying the church by its active

---

35. I have analyzed this phenomenon in Hegstad, *Folkekirke og trosfellesskap*; and "Minority within the Majority." Cf. the notion of the "vicarious religion" of the minority on behalf of the majority, in Davie, *Religion in Modern Europe*.

core members. Such an understanding presumes that the nominal members do not belong to the *communio* in the truest sense of the word. In fact these passive members are a *mission field*. Attempts to understand the folk church as such as *communio* has often meant a downplaying of the church as concrete and visible fellowship, either by stressing the invisible aspects of the *communio*, or by withdrawing into the formal organization of the church as represented by the clergy. As I have argued in this book, such an approach is highly problematical.

An understanding of the church as visible and concrete fellowship, however, does not imply an exclusive identification of the church as *communio* with the core group of active members. This group should definitely be understood as an expression of the *communio*, but not in an exclusivist manner. Such an approach is both theologically and sociologically inadequate, as it does not take into account the complex character of human fellowships. Such fellowships seldom have so clearly defined boundaries and they are often interwoven with other fellowships. This is especially true in a folk church setting, where the church is highly integrated into the social fabric of society. In this setting it is impossible to a make sharp distinction between Christian fellowship and human fellowship in its more general sense. In many instances Christian fellowship may be an aspect of family life, friendships, and neighborhood networks. When families meet together at baptism or funerals for example, this is obviously an expression of relationships at a local level and between family members, but can also be seen as an expression of Christian fellowship. The same is true for families when the practice of faith may be part of the relationship between spouses, parents, and children. Even when the religious make-up and world views within society is pluralistic and an understanding Christian fellowship as being an integrated part of society is increasingly untenable, both at the local community level and within families, this point is still relevant.[36] When talking about the real church as concrete and visible fellowship, this is not to suggest this can be naively identified as being only the core group of active participants in the church. As in other social realities, the ecclesial fellowship may be fluid and ambiguous when it comes to demarcation. It is precisely because the

---

36. In the folk church there has to be a balance between two areas of strategic concern: On the one hand, the church should strengthen and make use of its influence in society—not isolating itself. On the other hand, it needs to build fellowship groups that may serve as a place for more explicit Christian fellowship and for the nurturing and strengthening of faith.

Fellowship with One Another

church is a complex social reality that it constitutes a concrete fellowship. From this point of view, the folk church is as much the *real church* as the core group.

Even if social realities may be fluid and ambiguous they usually have some identifying center. With respect to the church, this center is the coming together in the name of Jesus. This, of course, means that an actual group of people who come together on a regular basis are of crucial importance for the church being church. At the same time the church is more than a group of people that are gathered at a certain time and place. Actually, the community exists before and after the church service. This means that the fellowship is not limited to those who are present at the church service at any given time. This seems to be the outcome of an actualistic ecclesiology: if the church exists only in and during the church service, it consists of only those who are present in the act of worship. An understanding of the church as an ongoing fellowship that is constituted by communal worship and exists even when there is no church service, means one belongs to the gathered community without necessarily having to be present every time when the community gathers together. The early church practice of taking the consecrated eucharistic elements to the church's sick can be seen as an indication that the sick too were considered part of the eucharistic community, even if they were unable to physically participate in the actual church gathering.[37]

Not even in a closely-knit free church are all the members present all the time for church worship. No one would imagine that those who were unable to attend a worship service are no longer part of the church. In my opinion, a similar line of argument may be used concerning members of the folk church who rarely participate in a church worship. Nevertheless, theologically speaking their connection to the church is related to the church as a worshipping community. They belong to the fellowship even if they rarely attend church worship. In the context of a church worship they became part of the church through baptism. This relationship is further strengthened and reiterated in their lives, and in the lives of people close to them, by going to baptisms, confirmations, weddings, funerals and other occasions that take place in the context of church worship.

If the fellowship includes more than just those present at worship, then those who are present in fact have a kind of representative role for

---

37. See for example Justin Martyr in his First Apology, chapter 67. *First and Second Apologies*, 71.

those not there. They worship, not only for their own benefit, but for the benefit for the whole community.[38] This requires a radical *openness* by those who are at worship towards those who are not present at worship.[39]

The idea of those who are worshipping at the church service representing the baptized members who are not there, must not be perceived as some kind of ecclesial norm or ideal state. The fact that so many members of the church are not present at worship is a great challenge for the church. While wanting to affirm that church members belong to the fellowship, the church, nevertheless, must find ways to facilitate and challenge all members to find their place in the worship of the fellowship to which they belong through baptism. The church that allows for, and includes, its more passive members must not conversely lead to any undervaluing the regular churchgoers. On the contrary, a healthy folk church is dependent upon those who are willing to take responsibility for maintaining the worship of the church.

To see the church as a fellowship is not to give any clear-cut theological demarcation between members, especially not in a folk church situation. What is characteristic of a majority of members in the folk church is precisely their ambiguity with regards to Christian faith and practice. Any attempt to set clear delineations can falsely exclude those who actually belong to the church, or falsely include those who have no wish whatsoever to be included. In this situation, the church's attitude should be characterized by a "naiveté of love," which takes all types of commitment to the church seriously, while not having any false illusions about the quality of this adherence. A broad and nuanced empirical research about the meaning of church membership for church members can guard against extreme folk church romanticism as well as skepticism.

---

38. Such a thought is the theme of the eucharistic hymn by Svein Ellingsen (Norsk salmebok 657): "We carry many with us / When we go to receive / What Jesus gave and gives us / Is theirs we do believe / For all you've set the table, / The baptized are at home, / We carry many with us, / And pray that they will come" (translation by Gracia Grindal).

39. Huber, *Kirche*, 108: "The church is never completely present at worship, as regrettably there is often only a small fraction of the church present at a given time. Nevertheless, those who are present at worship are addressed as the congregation. Those who come together at worship represent the church in its entirety. Therefore, we are only speaking about the worship of the congregation when it is noticeably and explicitly marked by an openness for those who cannot, or will not come, and those who have turned away, or are indifferent" (our translation).

Fellowship with One Another

Empirically speaking, the Christian fellowship in the folk church is a rather amoebic reality. Any theological interpretation should not seek to eliminate this ambiguity, but seek to interpret the phenomenon in all its indistinctness and complexity. The fact that the ecclesial community cannot be unequivocally demarcated supports the theological eschatological perspective of the church as a pilgrim people characterized by faith and unbelief, holiness and sin.

It is advantageous to see this complex situation of the social shape of the ecclesial fellowship from its center rather than from its margins. Social anthropologist Paul G. Hiebert, who has been particularly influential within evangelical missionary thinking, has formulated two alternative approaches when describing group membership.[40] One approach, which is mostly prevalent in Western cultures, is the *bounded set*. A *bounded set* is a category marked by clear boundaries where the various objects belonging to this category share certain basic characteristics. Another approach is the *centered set* approach which is mostly prevalent in Eastern cultures. A *centered set* is created by defining a center where different objects are related to this centre. The distance to the center is not so significant, as the objects moving *in the direction of* the center. It is not necessary therefore, to either define clear boundaries for the group, or to focus on any similarities between the objects. While a *bounded set* is a static concept, a *centered set* is dynamic, where the roles of the objects within the group constantly change.

Hiebert also suggests how these two different ways of understanding groups can be applied to the church. To understand the church as a *bounded set* thus implies an emphasis on the church's *boundaries*, where the main concern of ecclesial strategy is in how to get more people within the boundary of the church. The tendency here is to perceive those who are *in* the church in a fairly undifferentiated way.

Rather than seeing the church from its boundaries, the *centered set* defines the church by its center, and by the type of relationship people have to the center. This is to recognize that people may have a very different relationship to the center, and that there are different levels of participation and involvement in the church. The central concern of an ecclesial strategy is thus to strengthen the center and to work to ensure that people are moving in the direction of the center.

---

40. Hiebert, "Sets and Structures" and *Anthropological Reflections on Missiological Issues*, 107–36.

In my opinion, to understand the church as a *centered set* facilitates a positive interpretation for the folk church. This prevents a one-sided focus on the church's boundaries that has so often characterized the debate about the folk church. This will also enable a discussion about church membership in more differentiated categories, ranging from those most involved to those less involved. To interpret the ecclesial community in this way means we can still have clear *structures* even if the *boundaries* of the ecclesial fellowship remain unclear. This is not a structure determined by its outer boundaries, but is one that is theologically understood and determined by the center of the fellowship.

Understanding fellowship from its center does not mean that the fellowship has no boundaries at all. There are people who obviously *do not* have any positive relationship to the church's center, and it would be pointless to count them as part of the church. There will always be people and groups who claim to have a relationship with the church's center, but in reality represent something entirely different from the biblical gospel. In the face of the overt heresy, what might be claimed as the church has to be understood as non-church.

THE CHURCH AS PUBLIC

Although the church is a fellowship with its own special character, the New Testament does use analogies from other social settings when describing the distinctive character of the church. I have already made reference to the New Testament understanding of the church through the social reality of the *family* in antiquity. However, it is clear that the family is not the only analogy used to describe the church.

Reinhard Hütter points to the fact that the understanding of the church as a family or household (*oikos*) in the New Testament is complemented by an understanding of the church as a political and public community (*polis*). The most obvious example of this is found in Ephesians 2:19, where the Gentile Christians are told they are "citizens with the saints (*sympolitai*) and also members of the household (*oikeioi*) of God." Hütter believes that the fact that these concepts are combined in this way is remarkable. In antiquity *polis* and *oikos* were regarded as two quite distinct spheres where women, for example, were limited to *oikos*. In the church the dichotomy between these two spheres is eradicated by the creation of a unique social reality, where the old divisions between the sexes and classes no longer had any justification (cf. Gal 3:27-29).[41]

Hütter is most concerned about the church as *polis*, or what he calls the *public*. The question concerning the church as public is not, according to Hütter, primarily a question of how the church is to appear *in* or is *part of* the public sphere, but rather the church is to be understood *as* public.[42] He distances himself from, what he describes as monolithic political liberalism of the public, which presupposes the idea of one common public to which everyone is answerable. Hütter does not exclude the possibility of dialogue and overlap between various publics, but argues nonetheless that it is necessary for the church to emerge as a *polis sui generis*, as a public of its own. Besides political liberalism, Hütter also objects to a Protestant theology that primarily understands religion as a private and personal matter. It is necessary, argues Hütter, for the church not to be reduced to the private sphere, or to be subjected to the secularized public arena.

Hütter bases his understanding of church as public upon the ancient city-state (*polis*) and its uniqueness as a human space for interaction as typified by a common goal (*telos*) with certain visible common norms. Within this framework, the city-state was distinguished by a basic freedom for all citizens. The city-state was further characterized by the fact that it had a particular *locality*. It was not a vast geographical area like that of an empire, rather it was tied to the interaction and dialogue of a specific population.[43]

In a similar way the Torah constituted the Israel of the Old Testament as a public by providing a framework for common practice. In a similar manner the Spirit at Pentecost initiated the eschatological public of the *ekklesia*—an eschatological *polis* constituted by the *kerygma* and of certain core practices (especially baptism and the eucharist). As the public of

---

41. Hütter, *Suffering Divine Things*, 158-71; *Bound to Be Free*, 30-37. According to Sandnes, "Ekklesia at Corinth," this picture is too harmonic: the understanding of church as public contributed in limiting the role of women in the church.

42. Hütter distances himself from Wolfgang Huber's position concerning the church as public. Huber (*Kirche und Öffentlichkeit*) understands the church as *part of* the general public, not as a public of its own. See also Wannenwetsch, *Political Worship*, who perceives church worship as a distinctive public gathering which has ethical and political implications.

43. Hütter develops his theory based upon Hannah Arendt's analysis. *Suffering Divine Things*, 160-63.

the Holy Spirit the church has salvation as its *telos*. As such it is defined by its core practices rather than by its boundaries.[44]

As public the church has a unique *discursive practice*. Through its discourse the church reflects on its *telos*. In a similar way that the secular public has it discursive practice of political dialogue and debate, so theology is the discursive practice of the church as public. In this discourse the church publicly gives account of its core practices and doctrine. Based upon this concept, Hütter continues to develop his understanding of theology as church practice.[45]

Whether it is appropriate to speak of the church as public will primarily depend on how we define this term. If we understand this to mean what is common to all citizens in a society, we cannot talk about the church as public. However, an alternative interpretation of the term will make it possible to think of different groups in society as separate "publics" based upon their own premises. This could be applied to groups that are bound together by certain ideals and practice that are not shared by the rest of society. Applied to the church, this understanding of the term public would give emphasis to the church as a distinctive community, undergirded by its own distinct self-understanding.

In my opinion, it is necessary to place greater emphasize than Hütter concerning the interface between the church as public and other publics, including the general public arena. On the one hand, the church is not unaffected by whatever else is happening in society. On the other hand, church members will be part of various publics besides the church, and will therefore be in discourse with different groups and their objectives. In contexts such as the Nordic countries where the ecclesial and the general public sphere interconnects so profoundly, it will often be unclear which discourse a certain issue primarily belong to. Moreover, the actions and interpersonal relationships can be interpreted within the framework of various publics. Charitable works could be seen as an example of this, where they could be understood as human philanthropic actions, as well as part of the *diakonia* of the church. In the context of the folk church

---

44. "As the public of the Holy Spirit, the church is constituted not through 'boundaries' but through a 'center' that in the core practices creates 'space' and 'time' and is expressed authoritatively in *doctrina*. This center is of an utterly christological nature, and as such also does indeed demarcate the one 'boundary' the church never transcends." Ibid., 165.

45. Ibid., 166. The subtitle of Hütter's book is "Theology as Church Practice."

most church members will be, more or less, unaware of belonging to any specific ecclesial public.

The understanding of the church as public, not only serves to underline the church as a distinct community in relation to other communities, but it also serves to say something about the nature of the church as community. On the one hand, being a public the church's fellowship is open to the outside world, both in the sense that nothing in the church is secret or hidden from the world, and that all are welcome into the church fellowship.

On the other hand, the understanding of the church as public says something about the internal structure and operation within the church community. Not least, this can complement the idea of the church as family. As I have referred to in Hütter's work, the idea of church as *polis* and *oikos* mutually reflects one another. A one-sided emphasis of the church as a family has, in many cases, led to a church ideal rooted in intimacy—as the church is a family, church members should ideally be in a close personal relationship with each other. While the church certainly should be a place for personal and intimate relationships, this should not exclude other more *impersonal* relationships. In any case, it is necessary for the church to be not only a *family* but also a public.[46]

This is the key point in Patrick Keifert's book *Welcoming the Stranger*. Keifert refers to the North American context that imagines the church as an *extended family*. Such a notion implies the idea that worship should offer warmth and intimacy. In a world filled with pseudo-communities and empty, public spaces, the church can provide intimate and loving relationships.

Keifert sees several problems with such a perception. If the church remains an extension of the private sphere, one outcome is the church loses its character as public space. The church becomes a reflection of an intimate society that has relegated religion to the private sphere. Keifert believes the idea of a public space where people can encounter each other as real *others* without requiring intimacy is threatened both in society and in the church. In the intimate society, worship becomes an attempt to transform the private into a public arena where faith easily becomes a therapeutic exercise. A new form of clericalism is created where the

---

46. According to Sandnes, "Ekklesia at Corinth," Paul's emphasis of the church's public character served to counterbalance the tendency of "familism" of the local congregation.

clergy are understood as mothers or fathers who provide care for the needs of the congregants.

Keifert contends that the most serious result of this ideal means the church no longer welcomes *the stranger*. From a biblical point of view, hospitality for the stranger is an important attribute for being God's people in the world. Only by engaging in public interaction can the church be able to include the stranger. In contrast to the ideology of intimacy that tends to abolish diversity, the church as public space enables the church to embrace plurality and become a source of meaning and value when showing true hospitality towards the stranger.

According to Keifert to understand the church as "a company of strangers" results in, firstly, a reduction of the importance of the church's boundaries, and instead gives focus upon the church's center.[47] Secondly, it gives weight to the importance of ritual in public Christian worship. Through public, impersonal interaction the stranger is allowed to be a part of worship.[48] One of the main points in Keifert's book is the relationship between evangelism and liturgy, which are so often not associated with each other.

The strength of Keifert's thesis is the emphasis he places upon the church's public character. His criticism of the church as being solely understood as a family may be applied to other contexts other than just North American. His argument, however, can lead to over-emphasis of the public sphere at the cost of the church as family. Church as a community of strangers is *also* a community of friends and brothers and sisters.[49]

---

47. "In this sense, the church as a company of stranger engaged in an evangelical conversation is defined more by its center than by some criteria of who is in and who is out; who is a part of the family and who is not. Engagement with this center, which authorizes the church's conversation and life, is the sufficient ground for membership in the conversation. This center of the company, which authorizes the church's conversation and life, continuously opens the church to the world." Keifert, *Welcoming the Stranger*, 91.

48. "Ritual builds the social barriers necessary for effective interaction. It provides the sense of cover that allows most people to feel safe enough to participate in expressions of religious value . . . We need tangible barriers within which enjoyable and purposeful social interaction can take place. Ritual is, among many things, precisely these tangible barriers that make possible such social interaction." Ibid., 110–11.

49. A difficulty with Keifert's presentation is that he does not distinguish between the stranger as an ontological category, which he describes as "the irreducible difference between two persons that exists in any encounter" (in the sense that *the other* will always be a stranger, ibid., 9), and as a sociological category that refers to someone I do not know (as yet).

Fellowship with One Another

It will probably serve us well to distinguish between different types of relationships among church members. Clearly the idea of church as a family is not to say that everyone should have a close, personal relationship with everyone in a church. In the very least, such an ideal would have limits in how many people a congregation could reasonably include. At the same time, it is obvious that the church should include such relationships, and that every Christian should have at least *some* close and personal relationships to other Christians. Even if the community of the church is not identical with the private and familiar, it should also make room for this aspect of life. The church should encourage close and personal relationships between its members, without assuming that everyone will have the same type of relationships with everyone. However, we should not distinguish too clearly between those whom we have close relationships to, and those we do not. As members of God's family every Christian is to see other Christians as their brothers or sisters and act accordingly. We should distinguish between the *possibility* of close personal relationships with any fellow Christian, and how close these relationships *actually* are.

In the life of the church we are to differentiate between diverse forms of interaction and the various arenas for such interaction. There will, for example, be a difference between small groups of committed members and that of public worship. While the former, to a greater or lesser degree, is typified by personal intimacy, the latter is a place to welcome the stranger as a valued participant.

There should be no absolute separation between these two forms and arenas of interaction however. On the one hand, intimate interactions in smaller settings takes place on the basis of, and with a view of, what takes place in the bigger settings. On the other hand, the church as God's family should convey openness for all to enter into close relationships with brothers and sisters in the church. To deny such a possibility, in theory and in practice, is to deny the character of the church as God's family.

The relationship between these different forms and arenas of interaction will certainly vary. One variable is how the relationship between private and public spheres is understood in a given cultural context, and what belongs to these two spheres. Another variable will be the actual size of the church. In situations where a church is made up of a small number of people, it could exist as a fellowship where most people have a close personal relationship with each other. In larger churches (including the parishes in the folk church) a too close identification of the fellowship of the church with certain close-knit groups, may result in alienation and a feeling of exclusion among church members who do not belong to such groups. Furthermore, the dynamics in which a particular group becomes hegemonic within a church may come in conflict with the idea of church as family where all members of the church are God's children with the same right to be included and belong.

THE FELLOWSHIP AND THE INDIVIDUAL

Throughout this chapter I have stressed the nature of the church as community and fellowship. This is a topic that would not be adequately covered if we did not also consider the question of the relationship between the community and the individual, and the relationship between the communal and the personal aspect of Christian faith. On the one hand, it is necessary to avoid a Christian individualism, which understands faith as a purely individual matter. Various forms of individualism can be found, for example, in individualistic piety found in Pietism, or in a privatized folk church religion. Equally, it is easy to go too far in the opposite direction where religious collectivism can virtually absorb the individual into the communal. Collectivism can take many forms, for example in a collective worship piety that makes little sense of individual devotion and individually formulated prayers. It can also take the form of a folk church rationale that emphasizes the religious collective at the expense of the individual, personal relationship with God. Or it can take the form of subordination of the individual's rights to support the needs of the community.

Much of what has been written in this chapter, and elsewhere in this book, serves as an argument against Christian individualism. At the same time, an ecclesiology that emphasizes the collective and social aspects of Christianity can accentuate this view in such a way so as to conceal the importance of the individual and the individual's relationship to God. While faith and the relationship to God should not be reduced to individualism, it still remains clear that there is a real, personal dimension to faith. The idea of God being made present in the Christian church in a special way, does not rule out the fact that he is also made present to the individual. For example, according to the otherwise very much church-oriented Letter to the Ephesians, Christ dwells in the heart of a believer by faith (Eph 3:17). Jesus' presence in the church, and within each person, are not mutually exclusive, but are moreover closely connected. In New Testament passages to judgment day, it is first and foremost the individual who is answerable to God (Matt 25; Rev 20:11–15). In Romans 9–11 Paul sees salvation corporately via God's chosen people (Gentile Christians being engrafted into Israel's tree, see 11:17–24), as well as personally by an individual's confession of faith (10:9–10).

When it comes to spiritual practices, the collective and the individual presuppose and complement each other. In the New Testament prayer is both collective (Acts 4:24–30) and individual (Matt 6:5–6). When God speaks to people, this is to both the church as a fellowship (Acts 13:2) and to individuals (Acts 9:4–6, 10–16).

The relationship between the individual and collective can also be seen from a human rights perspective. According to international declarations of human rights the individual has inalienable rights that not even the interests of the larger society can dispense from. It is essential that the church must endorse the same fundamental human rights, both for its members and nonmembers.

The right to freedom of religion is one the human rights that is especially relevant to our discussion.[50] At times, religious freedom has been used as an argument against the church's right to hold on to a particular doctrinal foundation. In the name of religious freedom it has been argued that alternative forms of belief or disbelief should have their legitimate place in the church. This way of thinking, however, does not take seriously into consideration the church's character as a faith community, of what it means to be a community of people with the same faith. There may of course be good theological reasons for the church allowing a certain flexibility in the formulation of this shared belief. This does not hinder the church, however, from setting limits to what is acceptable for the church in belief and practice, for example, especially for those who have responsibility to act on behalf of the church. In this case, religious freedom is safeguarded through the right to leave the church, or to choose not to serve as a representative of the church. If you no longer identify

---

50. The Universal Declaration of Human Rights, article 18: "Everyone has the right to freedom of thought, conscience and religion; this right includes freedom to change his religion or belief, and freedom, either alone or in community with others and in public or private, to manifest his religion or belief in teaching, practice, worship and observance."

with what a certain church stands for, there is the freedom to join another denomination or religion, or even freedom to start a religious group of your own.

Even if every member has the freedom to leave the church, the church should not take the question of individual members' rights within the church too lightly. The attention to individual members' right should not be understood as something imposed upon the church from the *outside*, but is rather grounded in the church's very own self-understanding. The church cannot be content by just applying general formulations of human rights, but should formulate its own understanding of indispensable rights within the church for all members.

Wolfgang Huber has attempted to formulate such a set of *basic internal church rights* and the impact these could make to the practice of the church. Huber proposes five rights:[51]

1. Everyone has the right of access to the faith and to know Jesus Christ. When the church withholds the gospel within a closed inner circle, or is content to provide religious *services* only for its members, it violates this right. The church must be missional in its structure to safeguard this right.

2. Everyone has the right of conscience and freedom of opinion. This means that the church cannot promote its own teachings or beliefs by force. It is only possible to fight for the truth by spiritual means. This does not exclude the necessity for the church, in certain instances, to draw limits for what is said, and done in the church. Such cases should be treated fairly and with broad and open dialogue in the church where theologians and pastors have no monopoly of opinion.

3. Everyone has the right to personal integrity. This means that the church must respect basic legal rights and formalize rights for its employees. Important decisions should not be reached through closed and informal forums, but through open processes governed by legal regulations.

4. Everyone has the right to equality. This means that every Christian has the right to share the gospel in accordance with their gifts. This excludes a hierarchical structure of the church with sharp distinctions between clergy and lay. When someone represents the church, this is to be on behalf of the whole church. The right to equality is also incompatible with all forms of discrimination based on gender, race, nationality or social position.

---

51. Huber, *Kirche*, 133–37.

Fellowship with One Another

5. Everyone has the right to participate in church decisions. The church cannot be governed by clergy alone, but requires participation from all church members. This is realized through a democratic structure in which the members elect their representatives to synodical bodies.

Clearly, several of Huber's rights raise questions beyond the scope of this chapter. However, his summary of rights makes a crucial point, namely that the idea of church as community has not, under any circumstances, the right to infringe the rights and personal integrity of individuals. This applies in relation to both those who belong to the church, and to those who do not belong to the church.

6

The Church as an Organization and Institution

IN THE PREVIOUS CHAPTER I represented the church as a community and stressed the character of this community as a fellowship of interacting relationships. This basic social character is not a secondary attribute of the church—church *is* essentially a fellowship made up of people. As such, the church is open to sociological analysis like that of any other social group. In the same way as other communities can be understood as organizations, so too can the church. To understand the church as an organization includes the issue of its institutional character and how it is legally regulated. In an ecclesiological context, this should be linked to seeing the church as a fellowship in relation to the triune God.

THE CHURCH AS AN ORGANIZATION FROM A SOCIOLOGICAL PERSPECTIVE

The human interaction within a community includes various forms of routinization of this interaction. This means that different routines or patterns of social interaction are established when different people are given different roles they are expected to enact. Such practices can be very informal, or they can be formalized through agreements or rules. These rules may have been established by the members of the group, or they may be based upon an inherited set of rules the group is expected to adhere to. This applies to both within the group, and in relation to other groups. Many of these rules (although not all) may be legally binding in one form or another, and can be analyzed from a legal point of view accordingly. Different social groups will have different degrees of formalization, depending upon the type of social group in question, and how long it has been in existence. It is a known fact that the need for formalization tends to increase according to the age of a given group.

Formalized social interaction can be described as an *organization*. Organizations may be described as social systems that are deliberately constructed to achieve specific goals.[1] The study of these types of social systems is a theme taken up by organizational sociology and other forms of organizational research. As a social system it is also normal to understand the church as an organization. Internationally there is an increase of scholarly research that is describing and understanding the church and other religious communities from such a viewpoint.

In an article by Harald Askeland on the understanding of the church as an organization, he emphasizes that the term organization is to be seen as a conceptual abstraction of a given set of social relationships.[2] Therefore, organizations are not in themselves directly observable realities: what are observable are specific forms of social interaction that may be subsumed under the concept *organization*. Askeland points out that the concept of organization is not so different from the concept of church: both concepts are based upon realities that are not directly observable, but represent certain interpretations of a complex set of relationships between people.

However, the concept of organization is not a suitable way to describe all forms of social interaction. Askeland points to the fact that organizations, unlike less formal forms of social interaction, are about a *condensation* of relationships as a type of formalization and structuring. In the form of organizations, social interaction involves a greater orientation towards goals and usually involves standardization of the repertoire of organizational roles and role behavior.[3]

On the basis of such understanding, it is clear that the church can be interpreted as an organization. It does not mean the concept is equally suited to all aspects of the church, however. For example, more informal relationships between people in the church will fall outside of this concept, because they do not have the formal and structural qualities that an organization requires. A description of the church as an organization is only a partial description. Seen from an organizational perspective, some

---

1. Scott, *Organizations*, 26.
2. Askeland, "Hva betyr det om kirken forstås som organisasjon," 23–26. Cf. *Ledere og lederroller*, 132–53.
3. Askeland, "Hva betyr det om kirken forstås som organisasjon," 25.

aspects of the church's existence are more apparent than other aspects, and some aspects may even go beyond such descriptions. Furthermore, to understand the church as an organization does not exclude complementary perspectives, including those from theology and other areas of the social sciences. For example, from a general sociological perspective, the more informal social relationships and systems are of equal interest as the formal (this is also true of the church). For general sociology organizational sociology only represents a partial perspective on social reality.

According to Askeland, there are two basic lines of division within organizational theory.[4] One dividing line is to see organizations as rational systems as opposed to natural systems. While rational approaches are most interested in seeing organizations as instruments designed in order to achieve clearly defined goals, natural systems approaches may be more concerned with the informal processes of the organization. These are often linked to activities that ensure the group's survival rather than that of achieving the organization's official goals.

The second dividing line is between seeing organizations as closed systems protected from the surroundings, and between seeing organizations as open systems that interact with, and are dependent upon, the surroundings. It is clear that organizations actually work in junction with their surroundings, therefore this distinction applies primarily to the *emphasis* given to certain aspects of specific case studies.

From Askeland's point of view, the natural and open system approaches provide the best alternatives for analyzing the church. This viewpoint allows for the investigation of the distinctive culture and identity developed within any group, and it also sharpens the awareness of the interplay between the ecclesial organization and its general organizational context.

The organizational sociological viewpoint not only enables seeing the church in comparison to other organizations, but also it raises questions about what makes the church unique as a *religious* organization. Askeland believes the following are some distinguishing features that make religious organizations different from other organizations:

---

4. Ibid., 29–32. Askeland bases his review of trends within organizational sociology upon the work of Richard W. Scott.

The Church as an Organization and Institution

- Religious organizations are often not so concerned about achieving specific goals. Existing organizational structures and activities are often ends in themselves.

- An imbedded universalism results in a drive toward expanding the membership, making it necessary to be able to socialize new people into the fold.

- This universalism also means religious organizations will try to reach all segments of the population and all age groups. They tend to have a wider range of services and programs than most secular organizations. This broad range approach makes great demands on employees and volunteers.

- Religious organizations usually show a high degree of loyalty and commitment among their active members. They would like to perceive religious norms as overriding other norms.

- In religious organizations underlying *values* often have greater impact in decision making than in secular organizations.

- Due to its voluntary nature, religious organizations tend to be more decentralized than the commercial and governmental organizations.[5]

Such a list like this clearly is more applicable to some churches and congregations than others. For example, a state-funded folk church can be quite centralized and will not necessarily have the same drive to incorporate new members. The most important thing about this type of investigation is it not only enables us to see churches in light of other types of organizations (e.g., commercial or public), but it also enables us to reflect upon the distinct organizational characteristics of churches compared to other organizations.

It would be interesting to go beyond the question of what characterizes the church as a religious organization in a general sense, and consider what might be the organizational outcome based upon identity as the *church*. In other words, are there any distinct organizational structures and modes of operation that can be derived from the church's self-understanding as a community gathered around Word and sacrament? To begin such an investigation we would probably have to ask what role *worship service* has in the ecclesial organization. To my knowledge this

---

5. Ibid., 33–34.

issue has not been a central issue in organizational sociological studies concerning the church.

Especially in the more popular theological works, a common distinction is made between the church as an *organization* and *organism*. In such theories the term organization is often used to describe the church's exterior, empirical side, while the term organism to describe the church's inner and spiritual side. I would like to make two points concerning the use of the term organism. Firstly, the term organism is a biological concept that when applied to the church can only be seen as a metaphor.[6] To say that the church is an organism, in a literal sense, is simply meaningless. The use of the term organism usually reveals a desire to point to certain aspects of the church as being *analogous* to a biological organism. When using this type of analogy it is important to specify *in what respect* the church is analogous to a biological organism. This is not self evident, even if those using this analogy believe it to be so.

Secondly, it is necessary to point out that the term organism is also used in organizational sociology to describe organizations in general.[7] The metaphor of the organism is not just used about the church, but is generally used to denote various forms of social communities. It is suitable to use this term to describe organizations in the way that living organisms are extremely coordinated bodies that perform tasks as a result of the close interaction between many and various small units. To use organism as a concept does not make the church into something less than an organization, but portrays it as a particular type of organization with emphasis upon unity and coherence.[8]

THE CHURCH AS AN INSTITUTION

One developmental aspect of social structures is they eventually appear as objective realities abstracted from the people who belong to them. In sociology the term institution is used to describe this type of reality.[9]

---

6. Concerning the church as the body of Christ see chapter 2.

7. Morgan, *Images of Organization*, 33–69. To a large extent, this term corresponds to the concept of *natural systems* (as made reference to above).

8. One aspect of seeing a social organization as an organism within organizational sociology is the interaction with the organization's social *environment*, i.e., with the *social ecology* of which it is a part. Accordingly, this aspect of the organism metaphor could be more readily applied to the church.

9. The correlation between the concepts organization and institution is not immediately clear. Organizational sociologist Amitai Etzioni believes that the term institution

The Church as an Organization and Institution

According to W. Richard Scott, institutions are "multifaceted, durable social structures, made up of social elements, social activities, and material resources."[10] Even though institutions change with time, they are usually more stable than other social realities. Among other things, stability is ensured through norms and regulations associated with the institution. These norms have two aspects to them, the more formal and legal alongside the more moral. Institutions are also maintained by specific cultural patterns and common notions.[11] In addition, institutions operate by the fact that they possess material resources. For example, real estate, objects and economy are material aspects of institutions that help to maintain the institution.[12] Institutions are often represented by certain people who are authorized to act on behalf of the institution, they be the owners, spokespersons or employees.

In many situations the church will appear as an institution. In European history the church is *the* institution that has displayed the greatest degree of stability and continuity over a two thousand year span. A significant degree of institutional continuity is found in the Roman Catholic Church, but other churches have also had stable institutions (normally within national boundaries).

One aspect of the church as institution is the possibility to understand it as an objective reality that is, more or less, independent of the people who are part of the institution. As an institution the church is something you relate to, rather than something we see ourselves as being part of. As an institution the church is represented by its buildings, clergy, employees, and elected bodies.

In European history such an understanding of the church as institution has been further emphasized due to the difficulty of being able to distinguish the church as community from the society at large. To be a citizen and church member in Christendom was, to a large extent, sim-

---

can have different meanings and should be dropped in favor of the concept organization. *Modern Organizations*, 3. There seems to be a tendency to use the concept organization when speaking about the modern phenomenon of organization, while the term institution is used regardless of the historical era.

10. Scott, *Institutions and Organizations*, 49.

11. Scott suggests "the three pillars of institutions" as being: "the regular pillar," "the normative pillar," and "the cultural-cognitive pillar." Ibid., 51–61.

12. Mutual funds and charitable foundations are examples of institutions where material resources are the primary, and social interaction within the institution are secondary.

ply two sides of same coin. The church was understood as an institution that primarily encompassed certain (religious) functions within society. Therefore, the institution was largely identified with the *places* where these functions took place (church buildings) and with the *people* that oversaw these functions (the clergy and other church officials).

Although Christendom's homogeneity is largely part of a previous world, many churches, including the Nordic folk churches, still continue in the legacy of Christendom. To a greater extent the folk church functions as an institution one *goes* to rather than as community that one *belongs* to. Since to go to church is to seek out religious rituals, the priest/pastor has come to function as the main representative of the church as institution, based upon of his/her role as administrator of rituals.

With the increase in numbers of church employees and the introduction of new types of positions, it is easy to interpret the church as being primarily a professional organization, whose members are perceived as *clients* or *customers*. As such, the church can be seen as one service provider among many alongside the private sector and state sector.[13]

The shaping of the church as an institution is not only a result of sociological factors, but is also tied to, and undergirded by, theology. In Roman Catholic ecclesiology, emphasis upon hierarchy as constitutive for the church has contributed to an understanding of the church as an institution lay Christians relate to through its ordained and authorized representatives. According to Avery Dulles, the First Vatican Council was an expression of the culmination of Roman Catholic institutionalism, where the hierarchy was seen as those who upheld the church's primary functions and where the laity became recipients and objects of these functions. To a large extent, the church was identified by its structures and functions. The Second Vatican Council, on the other hand, represented a theological reorientation away from such institutionalism and allowed for a greater emphasis of the church as a community of God's people.[14]

---

13. An interesting empirical study from a theory of service perspective of people's relationship to the church is found in Per Pettersson's study of the Church of Sweden. Pettersson's results show that, although many church members rarely make use of the services of the church, to maintain a life-long relationship to the services of the church is still highly regarded and valued and transcends the value for each individual service provided. See "Church of Sweden in a Service Theoretical Perspective" and *Kvalitet i livslånga tjänsterelationer*.

14. Dulles, *Models of the Church*, 34–46.

The Church as an Organization and Institution

In Lutheranism, overemphasis upon the administration of Word and sacrament as being constitutive of the church has contributed to a similar institutionalism. When the preaching and administration of the sacraments is performed by the minority (the clergy) for the service of the majority (the laity), the character of the church as an institution is accentuated in such a way that the notion of the church as fellowship is downplayed.[15]

In comparison to Roman Catholic institutionalism, Lutheran institutionalism comes across as relatively modest. While the Roman Catholic institutionalism identifies the church as a complex organization with a number of different clerical ministries and ecclesial levels, Lutheran institutionalism has been focused on the pastor and the pastor's administration of Word and sacrament. This focus has lead to an understanding of the office of the pastor as being the main institutional element of the church. Other aspects of the organization of the church have often been perceived as secondary, non-constituting elements. Within the framework of the state church system, organizational and legal conditions have even been managed by agencies outside of the church.

An attempt to base ecclesiology on an understanding of the church as institution is found in the Neo-Lutheranism of the nineteenth century, for example in the writings of Friedrich Julius Stahl.[16] For Stahl, the understanding of the church as *institution* is the key when describing the church's empirical side. Stahl is particularly concerned to argue against any understanding of the church as a voluntary coming together between individuals. Instead, he stresses the church's objective character: that its origin is in God and is his instrument for human salvation. As a divinely founded institution the church is recognized by the preaching of the gospel, the administration of the sacraments, the ordained ministry, and the ecclesiastical governance.

For Stahl, the concept of the church as a divinely founded institution was given as an argument against the idea of a religious democracy. The

---

15. The Augsburg Confession VII balances the institutional with the personal and communal: The church is a fellowship where ministerial practices take place. Therefore, we cannot conceive of one without the other. Much of the ecclesiological divergence in Lutheranism can be described as a difference of emphasis placed upon the relationship between the institutional and the personal element as described in AC VII.

16. The following points about Stahl's ecclesiology are based upon Fagerberg, *Bekenntnis, Kirche und Amt*, 197–225. Cf. Sundberg, "Ministry," 83–84.

church is not the outcome of people coming together, but is an objective reality that is *above* the people and equipped with the divine powers as exercised by the ordained ministry.

According to Stahl, however, the institutional character of the church does not invalidate the church as a fellowship. Following the Augsburg Confession art VII (Word and sacrament are administered to people gathered), Stahl argues that the twofold, defining characteristics of the church is simultaneously institution and fellowship or congregation. While the church as an institution of salvation is the fruit of God's work, the church as fellowship is an outcome of human response to the salvation of God through prayer and a holy life.

Although Stahl tries to keep the church as institution and congregation together, he makes an untenable distinction between the church as institution and fellowship. Another difficulty with Stahl's distinction between the church as institution and fellowship is his attempt to associate this as a differentiation between the church as a visible and invisible reality. Such a correlation implies that the visible church is the institution and the invisible the fellowship. As a congregation the church is an invisible fellowship in faith, and in the Spirit. As institution the church is visible, principally through the administration of Word and sacrament and through the ordained ministry. The visible church is thus the institutional church. The fact that this institution implies a fellowship of believers is reduced to a theological idea by Stahl, and to something that is not empirically accessible.

To understand the church as institution is evident from a sociological perspective, and is relatively unproblematic theologically. However, theological difficulties arise when the institutional perspective becomes dominant in such a way that ignores or invalidates the church's fundamental character as a fellowship, or if fellowship becomes secondary in comparison to the institutional. A difficulty also arises when the church is understood solely as an agent of ministry without acknowledging that service flows from the ministering fellowship. Likewise, difficulties arise when the clergy serve on behalf of the church without being truly anchored in the fellowship. Finally, and of equal relevance, there are difficulties when the church is understood as a venue for religious services detached from the foundation and framework of the church as fellowship.

The Church as an Organization and Institution

IS THE INSTITUTIONALIZATION OF THE CHURCH THEOLOGICALLY UNTENABLE?

Not all would agree that the institutionalization of the church is theologically necessary or legitimate. Emil Brunner, for example, is a theologian who consistently reacted against the tendency to accentuate the church's organizational and institutional aspects at the expense of its character as fellowship. In his book *The Misunderstanding of the Church*, he makes a fundamental distinction between the church as found in New Testament (in his opinion the term *ekklesia* is more suited to describe this church) and the latter institutionalized church. According to Brunner, the New Testament *ekklesia* is quintessentially a fellowship of persons. Brunner believes there is a sharp contradiction between the church as understood as fellowship and institution: "The New Testament *Ecclesia*, the fellowship of Jesus Christ, is a pure communion of persons and has nothing of the character of an institution about it."[17]

Brunner argues that the fact that the New Testament *ekklesia* was something other than an organization or institution is not to say it was without order. As the fellowship in the Spirit, the church was orderly, even if it was not legally organized. The legal system of the church, as we know it, *replaces* the Spirit's order: "The organization of the church and in particular its legal administration is a compensatory measure which it becomes necessary to adopt in times and places where the plenitude of the Spirit is lacking. Canon law is a substitute for the Spirit."[18]

So long as the early church was a messianic community that was waiting for the return of the Lord, there was no need for legal regulation or institutional frameworks. The emergence of these frameworks is to be interpreted as part of the decline of the church:

> The emergence of ecclesiastical rule and jurisdiction is coincident with the loss or weakening of the community's messianic consciousness ... The community which waits in hope for the return of the Lord and which lives by faith and love in the possession of His Spirit, cannot be an institution, a church.[19]

The basis for Brunner's argument is both theological-ecclesiological and historical. Theologically, he argues that the church by nature is not really a

17. Brunner, *Misunderstanding of the Church*, 17.
18. Ibid., 51.
19. Ibid., 59.

legal institution, but rather a fellowship of people. Historically, he argues that the church as fellowship was an adequate description of the New Testament church, but as the church gradually became institutionalized this moved the church from its origin. According to Brunner, a notable aspect of institutionalization was the emergence of a clerical hierarchy and a sacramentalism (where the sacraments were understood institutionally, rather than as an act of the fellowship). In this way the church developed "from a spiritual communion with its utterly personal character into a sacramental collective with its essentially impersonal centre and therefore impersonal structure."[20]

Although existing churches have moved away from their origins, they still have elements of early church *ekklesia*—the husk hides the precious core. Brunner believes the vocation of today's churches is to facilitate the growth of the true *ekklesia*, the true fellowship of Christ in the world.[21]

Brunner's concerns about ecclesial institutionalization clearly raise many significant points. If the church as an institution replaces the church as a fellowship this is highly problematical. As I have pointed earlier, a danger is the institutionalized church can function in such a way that it excludes or marginalizes the ecclesial fellowship. Brunner argues that this will *always* be the case. It is not just *certain* institutional and legal regulations that are problematical in relation to the church as a fellowship, but *any* institutional and legal forms. Brunner assumes that there is a fundamental contradiction between the church as fellowship and any institutional form of church.

From a sociological and historical perspective this position is untenable. As I have pointed out previously, any human fellowship will over time develop communal patterns of behavioral interaction. The degree of formalization of these patterns and behaviors will vary however. It is a well-known sociological fact that the degree of formalization usually increases with time. While the first Christian church seemed to have a fairly informal organization, this gradually changed as the church under-

---

20. Ibid., 77. Brunner's historical hypothesis is indebted to the work of Rudolph Sohm. Working from a Norwegian context, the lay movement leader Ludvig Hope presents a similar dichotomy between the church as an institution and the church as spiritual society. Like Brunner, Hope is indebted to the work of Rudolph Sohm. Hope, *Kyrkja og Guds folk*.

21. Brunner, *Misunderstanding of the Church*, 101, 106–15.

went formalization and institutionalization through the successive generations. Central to this process was the development of defined offices and the codification of church law. Similar trends can also be seen in the churches and ecclesial movements of recent times. In my estimation, such a development is both natural and necessary.

Theologically speaking, there is no basis for claiming that the Holy Spirit works more directly in the less formal frameworks, or that a community is less spiritual the more formalized it becomes. In reality, the Spirit always works through human structures even if these forms can vary considerably.

As the Spirit always works through specific forms, so the Christian fellowship will always have a certain form. Even though the degree of formalization and the forms can vary greatly, there is no reason to distinguish between fellowship *in itself* and the forms of the fellowship: a fellowship will always be a community with a particular outward shape. This also means we do not need to make the distinction between the church and its organization as if they are two completely different things. It is not as if the church *has* an organization separate from the real church. On the contrary, the church *is* an organization. To regard the church as an organization is to see the church from one particular viewpoint. It is untenable to make the organization of the church into something other than the church itself, as it is untenable to *reduce* the church to its organizational dimension. In the same way that other social realities are more complex than simply describing them as organizations, so this is true of the church which is more than just an organization.

This is not to say that any form of ecclesial organization is equally good or expedient. The church's organizational structure should always be open to critique. Craig Van Gelder makes the point that ecclesial organization should always be made accountable to the church's nature and how it best can serve the church's mission: the church does what it is, and it organizes what it does:

> The nature of the church provides the basis for understanding the ministry of the church—the church is. The ministry of the church provides the framework for understanding the organization of the church—the church does what it is. The organization of the church provides the structures for the church to carry out its ministry—the church organizes what it does.[22]

22. Van Gelder, *Essence of the Church*, 155–56.

Van Gelder does not agree with ecclesial institutionalism when this makes certain forms of religious organization as an end unto itself. There is nothing wrong in the church having institutional structures, but all such structures should be appraised according to whether they serve the church's mission.[23]

Difficulties arise in Van Gelder's argument when he attempts to determine the relationship between the nature of the church with its mission and organization as being grounded in what the church *does,* and only *indirectly* by what the church *is.* The church's organization is not only to serve what the church *does,* but must also ensure that the church *is* what it is called to be. The organization of the church is to facilitate the church's mission. This must not lead, however, to an activist church, a church that can only define itself by what it *does*—but by what it is, a church that bears witness to God and his kingdom to come. It is important that the church is organized in such a way as to not go against its primary witness. For example, this can occur when the church becomes a hierarchy of those who rule and those who are subordinate, rather than a fellowship of equals. In addition, the question of *power* remains a constant challenge for any church organization. Even if the church can never avoid adapting organizational forms from contemporary society (including forms of governance), Jesus' example will always be the source by which we can critique such adaptations (Matt 20:25–28).

CHURCH AS A LEGALLY ORDERED

An important aspect of social organization is the formulation and application of rules and regulations, both within organizations and in society at large. To begin to understand and describe the communities and social groups we, therefore, need to consider the judicial and legal aspects. In the same way other perspectives can be applied to the church, we should avoid making the legal perspective absolute. Although laws and regulations are important factors in the shaping of a society, this is not exclusively so. While laws and rules regulate social relationships, they are also features of social relationships.

As the legal aspect of church life has had such a major role to play in the church, it is important to examine this. Throughout its history the church has been legally regulated in different ways, both through internal

---

23. Ibid., 157–62.

The Church as an Organization and Institution

church law and by general law. The legal side has also been theologically significant in ecclesiology to a great extent that it has primarily referred to its legal regulations rather than to its social formulations. Not least, this has been true of Roman Catholic ecclesiology which has tended to identify the church as delineated and defined by Roman Catholic canon law.

It is not my intention to disparage the importance of church law, or argue against the necessity of having a legally regulated church system. Nevertheless, I think the close association between theological and legal perspectives has often been too dominant in ecclesiology and necessitates a sociologically grounded corrective.[24] However important the legal standpoint may be, it is still only a partial truth about the reality of society. Legislation is the codification of a social reality, but it also has other aspects to it than the codification itself. Although legislation is of crucial importance for society, society is far more than legislation, and for that matter, far more than what is legally regulated. If legislation was to collapse, society would still exist (even if new legislation would subsequently have to be developed).

A similar argument can also be applied to other social groups, including the church. Although internal legislation in most cases is crucial for congregations and denominations, these congregations and denominations are not to be identified just by their legislative ordering.[25] An empirically oriented ecclesiology should not tie itself down solely to describing legal structures, but should also investigate the social reality that is being legally regulated. In order to understand the church as empirical reality, a formal and legal ordering has to be based upon a comprehensive understanding of the church as social reality, both by its internal life, and as a social phenomenon within society.

An example of how different viewpoints arrive at different conclusions can be seen by the issue of continuity and discontinuity during the times of great legal and organizational upheaval in the church. An interesting case at hand, is to reflect upon what happened in Norway (then under Danish rule) during the Reformation. After the Danish king decided to break away from Rome, canon law suddenly become invalid and a new

---

24. Peter Berger discusses the relationship between a sociological and legal perspective in *Invitation to Sociology*, 40–41.

25. Regarding *legislation*, I do not primarily refer to public law, but more so to church constitutions and church law. In a state church system, church legal regulations often have the status of public law as well.

church constitution was ratified. If we deem canon law as constitutive of the church, this means the Reformation was the introduction of a *new* church in Norway in 1537. According to such an interpretation the old church was expelled and not to return to Norwegian soil until 1843 with the re-establishment of the Roman Catholic Church in Norway. An alternative understanding is to highlight the continuity between the pre-and post-Reformation church. Although the church's legal system was of great importance, the church lived on through the people and in the congregations that constituted the church. Thus a new church was not formed, but the old church was reformed.[26]

The fact that the church as a social community is foundational to the legal regulations of this community has implications for the understanding of church law. Hans-Richard Reuter points that church law should primarily be rooted in ecclesiology.[27] Accordingly, he distances himself from the tradition of German Protestant theology that sees church law through the theological interpretation of the concept of justice.[28]

On the one hand, Reuter rejects those who have claimed a fundamental incongruity between the church and church law (such as Rudolph Sohm). As a continuous historical reality the church cannot do without the legal means to regulate its conditions of existence. On the other hand, the legal regulation of the church does not *constitute* the church, but it is more accurately *consecutive* and *regulative*.[29] Church law does not create the church, but church law has to be created because the church already exists. At the same time, church law is more than simply a codification of a state of affairs that already exists. On the contrary, as in any other institution the church's legislation is an effective tool to modify and regulate existing forms of human interaction.

The anchoring of church law in ecclesiology means that it has to be grounded in a theological understanding of what it is to be church. This

---

26. This idea of continuity is also true of the self understanding of the Church of Norway. In a statement endorsed by the General Synod in 2004 it states: "The Church of Norway is a continuation of the church that was established in Norway at the end of the first millennium." *Den norske Kirkes identitet og oppdrag*, para. 2 (our translation).

27. Reuter, "Kirchenbegriff." Reuter's position concerning this issue is shared by Per-Otto Gullaksen, *Stat og kirke i Norge*, 42–56.

28. Reuter thus distances himself from scholars of church law such as Johannes Heckel, Erik Wolf and Hans Dombois.

29. Reuter, "Kirchenbegriff," 30–31.

is not to say that church law can be deduced directly from the theological principles. Church law should always serve the church as it exists in a certain situation as shaped by a particular history and context. The development of church should always respond to specific issues found in concrete situations, while being conscious that it functions in a manner that is consistent with the church's character and mission.

The issue of church law is only one (although very important) aspect of the broader question of how the church should organize its life and work. This is partly, but not exclusively, a legal question. The legal regulation of an organization does not provide a complete picture of the actual patterns of interaction. The actual life of an organization can be more informal, and in certain cases function differently to what the law presupposes. The question of how the church should be regulated legally is but one issue among many in how the life of the church is to be organized.

7

A Fellowship of Ministries

As A CONCRETE COMMUNITY the church is characterized by specific structures. Such structures also mean that members of the fellowship do not have identical functions. In other words, there is a differentiation of roles and tasks. Such a differentiation does not override the fundamental equality between all the members of the Christian fellowship, even if differentiation often has been practiced in a way that obscures this equality. An ongoing challenge for the church is the centuries old tradition of the two graded distinction between clergy and laity. In this chapter, I will argue that such a dichotomy should be replaced by a theology of ministry that emphasizes the fellowship of the church as a plurality of different ministries.

A TRADITIONAL DISTINCTION BETWEEN CLERGY AND LAY

The distribution of functions within social groups can be understood in many different ways. Some are strongly hierarchical, while others are more egalitarian. In some cases the members' roles are very static, while in other contexts they are more flexible. While some groups are characterized by differentiated patterns of interaction, other groups are characterized by a polarity. Some examples of this can be seen in schools (teacher—pupil), in health care (physician—patient), and in retail (seller—customer). In these examples, differentiation of roles usually only exists on the "professional" side of the polarization. In the health care, for example, we find other types of professionals besides doctors, but in practice they tend to work in a subordinate role under doctors. To be a patient is a relatively passive and relatively undifferentiated role.

A Fellowship of Ministries

A comparable polarity can be found in the church where divisions are made between *clergy* and *lay*. In a similar way to that of the health care system, a further differentiation of roles has primarily been applied to the clergy in the form of differentiated clerical offices. The majority of *lay* church members have often been attributed to a more passive and receptive role.

Historically, such a dichotomy became prevalent when the church became the majority of a given society, for example, when Christianity was the state religion of the Roman Empire. The large influx of new members led to a professionalization of the clergy and gave rise to more clearly defined distinctions between clergy and lay.[1] Such a dichotomy still exists in many churches today. In part, this is an outcome of historical and sociological factors—this is especially true of churches that understand themselves as folk churches. However, this is also an outcome of an ecclesiology that serves to justify such a dichotomy.

Throughout church history, such a dichotomy has been challenged and criticized by various movements which have sought to achieve a greater degree of equality between church members. This has been particularly the case in free church movements. On the one hand, these movements have developed a theology that has been able to substantiate a greater sense of shared ministry. On the other hand, these movements are based upon sociological conditions that have further realized this in practice, as they often have consisted of fewer and more dedicated members.

Even within the larger folk churches there has been a tendency to question such a dichotomy. Central to the Lutheran Reformation was the protest against a theology that operated with a principled distinction between clergy and lay. In its place, the reformers renewed the New Testament idea of Christians being a "holy priesthood" (1 Pet 2:5) as being the quantifier of Christian equality in the church. Despite the ideal of the *priesthood of all believers,* in practice the Reformation churches continued to maintain the relatively distinct differentiation between the clergy and laity.

In theological thinking and church practice during the twentieth century, there was a renewed emphasis that all Christians are called to minister, not just pastors and other office holders. This applied, not only to Protestant churches, but also to the Roman Catholic Church. The

---

1. Skarsaune, "The Constantinian Turn," 304–5. A critical account of this development is given by Haag, *Upstairs, Downstairs.*

Roman Catholic Church, while defending theologically the principle of distinguishing between the clergy and laity, also stressed the importance of all believers participating in the life and ministry of the church. For example, this was articulated in the Second Vatican Council document about the church, *Lumen gentium*. This document reiterates the position and ministry of the laity and states that the church is primarily to be understood as the people of God where all the baptized share in the holy priesthood.[2] While giving an ecclesiological rationale for the role of the laity in church life, this document still upholds a distinctive theology for the ordained ministry. The underlying principle in Roman Catholic theology of the ordained officeholder is based upon the apostolate. Bishops as the apostles' successors are confirmed in their position and calling to fulfill the mandate that Jesus gave to the original twelve. Since the apostles were the ones who founded and led the early church, the ordained ministries still have a certain priority vis-à-vis the rest of the church.[3]

In Lutheran theology the theology of ordained ministry has also had a semi-independent status from ecclesiology in general, due to it being linked to the doctrine of grace. Since Word and sacrament are the means by which God gives us his grace, the ministry of teaching the Word and administering the sacraments is a prerequisite for the church. On this basis, it can be argued that the ordained ministry has a certain priority vis-à-vis the church in general. This emphasize was especially adhered by representatives of Neo-Lutheranism of the nineteenth century. According to Wilhelm Löhe the congregation originates from the pastoral office, not the office from the congregation. The ordained ministry is thus the source of the congregation. The fact that the gospel logically precedes faith in the gospel, therefore gives support to the notion of giving precedence to those who preach the faith in relation to the gathered faithful.[4]

In many cases such theological reasoning has created a two parallel ecclesiological discourse with their own starting points and conceptual frameworks. On the one hand, there is a developed ecclesiology of seeing the church as a fellowship—an ecclesiology that is primarily used to justify the position and responsibility of the laity. On the other hand, there is a developed theology of ordained ministry that is used to jus-

---

2. *Teachings of the Second Vatican Council*, Constitution on the Church, para. 10 and 30–38, pp. 85, 119–30.

3. Ibid., Constitution on the Church, para. 18–29, pp. 96–119.

4. Sundberg, "Ministry," 85.

tify and qualify the ministry of the pastor and other ordained ministries. What remains an issue is these two discourses often function relatively independently. In many cases it seems that theology of ordained ministry receives priority when it clashes with a more general ecclesiology.

Such a situation is unsatisfactory, not only because it is shows little cohesive ecclesiological thinking, but also because of the unfortunate consequences it has in ecclesial practice. By basing the roles of lay and ordained ministries upon two separate theological rationales, contributes to conservation of the inherited distinction between clergy and lay, both in ecclesial theory and practice.

A DIVERSITY OF MINISTRIES

In my opinion, the only way to overcome this difficulty is by developing a general ecclesiology that is able to incorporate the concerns represented by theologies of ordained ministry. This can be done by promoting a more all-inclusive *theology of ministry* within the framework of a more comprehensive understanding of the church's identity and mission. The basis for such a theology can be found in the New Testament, most notably through Paul's teaching about the *different ministries and spiritual gifts* in the church (see, for example: 1 Cor 12; Eph 4; and Rom12).

Paul does not think within a polarized pattern of thought where he restricts himself to one specific ministry in relation to the rest of the church. Rather, what Paul presents is *plurality* of *different* ministries and spiritual gifts that all serve the *one* church. The *raison d'être* of Paul's theology presupposes *equality,* and is based upon the underlining principle of unity between the Christians. Paul's position does not assume unity and equality exclude diversity. On the contrary, unity and diversity sustain one another. For Paul, the *unity* of the church is based upon the gift of salvation that all Christians share in common:

> ... making every effort to maintain the unity of the Spirit in the bond of peace. There is one body and one Spirit, just as you were called to the one hope of your calling, one Lord, one faith, one baptism, one God and Father of all, who is above all and through all and in all. (Eph 4:3–5)

Diversity is rooted in the reality that God gives different gifts and different ministries to different Christians. In Ephesians 4, after attesting the fundamental unity of Christians, Paul describes how God equips people in different ways: "The gifts he gave were that some would be apostles, some prophets, some evangelists, some pastors and teachers, to equip the saints for the work of ministry, for building up the body of Christ" (Eph 4:11–12). The one and only God accordingly gives different ministries to different people in order to build up the church.

In 1 Corinthians 12 Paul gives his most extensive discourse about the correlation between unity and diversity. Paul demonstrates how God works through a variety of spiritual gifts and ministries:

> Now there are varieties of gifts, but the same Spirit; and there are varieties of services, but the same Lord; and there are varieties of activities, but it is the same God who activates all of them in everyone. To each is given the manifestation of the Spirit for the common good. (1 Cor 12:4–7)

Paul adopts the image of the church as being one body: The body is one, but still consists of many different members. For the body to function, it is necessary that the members have different ministries and tasks. Even the ashamed, weakest parts are necessary for the body to function (vv. 12–26).

Applied to the church, this shows how individual Christians are like the members of one body, the church: "Now you are the body of Christ and individually members of it" (v. 27). The various members are analogous to the various ministries in the church: "And God has appointed in the church first apostles, second prophets, third teachers; then deeds of power, then gifts of healing, forms of assistance, forms of leadership, various kinds of tongues" (v. 28).

The main Greek term that Paul uses to describe the various gifts and ministries of the Holy Spirit is *charisma* (which is translated by the NRSV as spiritual gifts). A common way to interpret this term is to see it as a kind of supernatural, personal gift or quality. In Paul's use of the concept he combines the personal equipping for ministry and the ministry itself: when God gives someone a ministry, God also equips them for the job. The reverse is also true: when God equips, this is not for personal gain, but for serving the church fellowship. In the words of Olav Skjevesland: "A spiritual gift is a ministry based upon God's grace, made effective in the Spirit's power with the aim of edifying the church."[5]

---

5. Skjevesland, *Levende kirke*, 61 (our translation).

A Fellowship of Ministries

The broad meaning of the term *charisma* is also reflected in the specification of the ministries the Spirit gives the church. Here we find the office of apostles, prophets and teachers, and also the more impersonal gifts such as miracles, healing and speaking in tongues (v. 28, cf vv. 9–10; Rom 12:6–9).[6]

There is good reason to assert that the interpretation of spiritual gifts that Paul outlines in texts like 1 Corinthians 12, should be the central starting point for any theology about the church and its ministries. This is claimed, among others, by Edmund Schlink in his analysis of the theology of ministry. He suggests that "even if there is no reflection on this plurality in most other New Testament texts," Paul's statement is "so universal and rudimentary that it cannot be historically relativized, but has to be included in a doctrine of church and ministry."[7]

The same view is supported by Hans Küng in his ecclesiological work, *The Church*. Küng represents the church as "continuing charismatic structure."[8] To do this he begins with Paul's teaching about the spiritual gifts and claims that this teaching has important ecclesiological and ecumenical implications: "The rediscovery of the charisms is a rediscovery of specifically Pauline ecclesiology, the importance of which for the problems of Catholicism and ecumenism cannot be overestimated."[9]

Based upon a comprehensive exposition of the concept of *charisma*/spiritual gifts, Küng goes on to discuss the more *permanent ministries*, which he understands as "public functions within the community ordained by God and which must be exercised regularly and constantly."[10] These ministries/offices should not be understood as anything *other* than spiritual gifts/charisms, but more as special *forms* of these. *Charisma*, therefore, is the broader term, office the narrower term.[11]

---

6. Sandnes, *I tidens fylde*, 235–39, provides a comparative overview of the various spiritual gifts in Pauline theology. He argues that these spiritual gifts are not an exhaustive list, but *examples* of spiritual gifts available in the church. Cf. Banks, *Paul's Idea of Community*, 91–112.

7. Schlink, *Ökumenische Dogmatik*, 597–98 (our translation).

8. Küng, *Church*, 179–91.

9. Ibid., 180–81.

10. Ibid., 394.

11. "The charism cannot be subsumed under the heading of ecclesiastical office, but all Church offices can be subsumed under the charism." Ibid., 187.

Miroslav Volf also refers to passages such as 1 Corinthians 12 in his description of the ministries and officeholders in the church. Volf believes the church is "a communion of interdependent subjects," and should consequently be understood not as "a monocentric-bipolar community but fundamentally a *polycentric-participative community*."[12] The church should see the fellowship in the Holy Spirit that works through the spiritual gifts of every believer as its center, rather than those of certain officeholders. Since all Christians have spiritual gifts, Christ is made present through all the church members and not just through the clergy.[13]

In the same way as Schlink and Küng, Volf recognizes the importance of certain offices and officeholders in the church. With them, he believes that these offices should be understood on the basis of the concept of *charisma*: "Ecclesiastical 'offices' are a particular type of charismata."[14] This insight relativizes any distinction that may be made between officeholders and others: "On the basis of a common baptism, all Christians have become priests and realise their priesthood in their own way on the basis of their respective charismata. Hence all members of the church, both officeholders and 'laypersons', are fundamentally equal."[15]

This means that ministry is not the reserve of one particular group of church members, but is something all Christians share in the church. At the same time, there is of course, a *difference* between ministries, both in terms of content, scope, authority and commitment.

In an important ecumenical document, *Baptism, Eucharist and Ministry*, the so-called Lima document, a proposal is made to understand ecclesial offices in the context of Paul's teaching of the spiritual gifts. The chapter titled "Ministry" begins with a general ecclesiological section headed "The Calling of the Whole People of God." Here it is noted that the Holy Spirit gives gifts to all members of the church.[16] These gifts are

---

12. Volf, "Community Formation," 231.

13. "And since all Christians have charismata, Christ is also acting through all the members of the church, and not merely through its officeholders." Ibid., 232.

14. Ibid., 235.

15. Ibid.

16. "The Holy Spirit bestows on the community diverse and complementary gifts. These are for the common good of the whole people and are manifested in acts of service within the community and to the world. They may be gifts of communicating the Gospel in word and deed, gifts of healing, gifts of praying, gifts of teaching and learning, gifts of serving, gifts of guiding and following, gifts of inspiration and vision. All members are called to discover, with the help of the community, the gifts they have received and to

seen in conjunction with the biblical concept of spiritual gift/charism: "The word *charism* denotes the gifts bestowed by the Holy Spirit on any member of the body of Christ for the building up of the community and the fulfillment of its calling."[17]

Ordained ministry is to be understood in this context. It is a special kind of spiritual gift that does not replace the others, but rather encourages other Christians in their own ministries:

> The ordained ministry, which is itself a charism, must not become a hindrance for the variety of these charisms. On the contrary, it will help the community to discover the gifts bestowed on it by the Holy Spirit and will equip members of the body to serve in a variety of ways.[18]

THE LUTHERAN CASE: THE ONE MINISTRY OF THE CHURCH

Whilst most denominational traditions have had some notion of plurality in their view of ministries in the church, Lutheran churches have traditionally focused their attention on the ministry of the pastor as the foundational ministry in the church. The understanding of this ministry and its basic function for the church is based upon article V of the Augsburg Confession: "So that we may obtain this faith, the ministry of teaching the gospel and administering the Sacraments was instituted."[19] Even if this article does not exclude the possibility of other ministries in the church (which is obviously beyond the scope of this article), the traditional Lutheran theological view has seen this as the only ministry of the church. This limitation has been further re-enforced by the Latin title customarily assigned to the article: "*De ministerio ecclesiatico*," "of the ecclesiastical ministry." Although this title was not part of the original text,[20] it has served as a key to interpreting this article and has

---

use them for the building up of the Church and for the service of the world to which the Church is sent." *Baptism, Eucharist and Ministry,* Ministry, para. 5, p. 20.

17. Ibid. Ministry, para. 7a, p. 21.

18. Ibid. Ministry, para. 32, p. 27.

19. Kolb and Wengert, *Book of Concord,* 41.

20. According to Kjell Olav Sannes this title was introduced in editions as late as 1669. Sannes, "Leadership and Ministry," 321. Kolb and Wengert, *Book of Concord,* 41, translates this as "Concerning Ministry in the Church."

subsequently contributed to the understanding of the ministry within the Lutheran church as being one ministry.

In Lutheranism there have traditionally been two schools of thought in how to interpret this "ecclesiastical ministry." Some suggest it refers to the *personal* ministry of the office of ordained pastors. Others suggest it refers to a *functional* ministry that is not tied to a certain office, even if the pastor normally will have the main responsibility for carrying out this ministry.[21] In other words, it points to the *function* of preaching the gospel and administering the sacraments. A *common* denominator that holds the *personal* and *functional* views together is the belief that there is only *one* ministry. As a result, the question of other offices and ministries has generally been outside the scope of Lutheran debate.

In the Lutheran tradition this single ministry (*the* ecclesial ministry) has generally been identified with the ministry of the pastor. Even if the pastor has taken care of other functions in the church as well, the core of pastoral ministry has been understood as a *ministry of Word and sacrament*. In the light of this, the office of the bishop (in those Lutheran churches that have this office) has not been understood as a separate ministry, but as a particular form of the pastoral ministry. Other ministries in the church, such as church wardens, organists, etc., have often been perceived as ministries in a subordinate role in the service of the pastor.

A consequence of this view of the pastorate being the main ministry of the church has been the perception that the members of the congregation are passive recipients of the pastor's ministry. This understanding and practice was profoundly challenged by the Pietist renewal movements of the eighteenth and nineteenth centuries. Referring to the New Testament idea of spiritual gifts being available to all Christians who share in the life of the church, this movement upheld the idea of the priesthood of all believers. This led to the active involvement of lay church members within the life of the church, and in many cases this was through independent mission organizations.[22] The rediscovery of the priesthood of all believers and the spiritual gifts however, had its most profound impact upon lay ministry and not that of the theological interpretation of the pastor's min-

---

21. An example of such a discussion can be found during the nineteenth century. Fagerberg, *Bekenntnis, Kirche und Amt*; Sundberg, "Ministry;" Sannes, "Leadership and Ministry," 318.

22. This is primarily within the Norwegian context, but similar developments can be seen elsewhere in Europe.

istry. The theology of ordained ministry and the theology of lay ministry and spiritual gifts continued to be largely distinct and grounded upon two different theological rationales. The relative independence of the lay movement vis-à-vis the official church structure also provided different organizational frameworks for these two forms of theological rationale. This meant there was no real integration of these views.

A similar pattern can be discerned in the Charismatic movement, which since the 1970's has also had an influence in the Lutheran church. In a similar fashion to the lay church movements, spiritual gifts were central, but with a greater emphasis placed upon their supernatural and extraordinary character. Again, the understanding of the spiritual gifts had no direct effect for the understanding of the pastor's ministry. Of course pastors could also be equipped with special spiritual gifts, but if this was the case, these were seen as being in addition to pastoral ministry.

The strength of this kind of theology of spiritual gifts, both with its Pietist and Charismatic forms, was it underpinned that all Christians have a ministry in the church. Its weakness was that it functioned *alongside* the traditional theology of ordained ministry, without any real integration between the two. In the light of what has been said above concerning the Pauline concept of the charisms, there is reason to assert that such a dichotomy between the theology of ordained ministry and the theology of spiritual gifts is a division that should not be there. In other words, these two theologies of ministry belong together. From a New Testament point of view, all ministries in the church—both ordained and lay—are charisms of the Holy Spirit. In my opinion, these two variables that have largely been divided should be integrated by a renewed New Testament understanding of the meaning of the charisms.

In last few decades the traditional monopoly of the pastor has been challenged within the official church structures, for example in the Church of Norway. This has been the result of the introduction of new categories of independent ministries, such as catechists, deacons and cantors. This has led to a debate about the theological interpretation of these ministries as related to the traditional Lutheran theology of ministry. The proposal of seeing these ministries as lay ministries has been felt unsatisfactory. An alternative option has been to interpret these new ministries as forms of the one ecclesial ministry as mentioned in the Augsburg Confession—as a form of *differentiation* of this one ministry. An obvious weakness in this argument is it interprets these ministries as having different tasks of the one ecclesial ministry, which leads ministry to be understood in rather abstract terms. This is in contrast to the passage in article V of the Augsburg Confession, which describes the ministry in a rather concrete manner: "teaching the gospel and administering the sacraments."[23]

In my opinion the solution of this dilemma is not to be found in expanding the one ministry to include various forms of ministry, but rather in leaving behind the idea of the singular ecclesial ministry. In a Lutheran context, the Pauline concept of a diversity of charisms would allow for a flexible interpretation of new ministries alongside that presented by the traditional Lutheran position. Rather than present these ministries under the same abstract category of the ecclesial ministry, we could understand ministries such as the pastor, catechist, deacon, and cantor as various ministries, each with their own task and distinctive character. Instead of finding out what these ministries have *in common*, we could strive to develop ministries according to their own characteristics, based on what each one can contribute to the church's identity and mission.

For historical reasons, I believe it is more reasonable to see the statement in the Augsburg Confession article V as a statement about the ministry of the pastor. The fact that only this ministry is mentioned in the Augsburg Confession, however, does not mean that there are not other ministries in the Lutheran church that may also have theological authenticity.

UNIFIED STRUCTURE OR DIFFERENT MINISTRY PATTERNS

From a historical and empirical perspective the great diversity in forms and patterns of ministry is a striking feature. This applies to both differences between churches (even within the same denomination) and to the development that has occurred over time within churches. Even the traditional and widely held ministries such as the ministries of the bishop, priest/pastor, and deacon may include quite a variety of definitions and functions. A difficulty with having a theological discourse on ministry as it exits within churches and within ecumenical dialogues and documents, is the lack of interest or understanding concerning its diversity. Having the motive of wanting to give precise dogmatic definitions of the ecclesial ministries and their structures, can quite quickly end up in giving a styl-

---

23. Regarding this development and debate, see Hegstad, "Én kropp—mange lemmer."

ized and idealized image of something that is in reality very complex. This tendency is further reinforced by ecumenical processes concerning questions related to ordained ministry. In a situation where the goal is perceived as the mutual recognition of ministries, we look for maximum convergence in describing patterns of ministry in the various churches.

In recent times, the so called threefold ministry has conspicuously been brought into the debate as a possible model that all churches might agree upon. According to the Lima document, the threefold pattern of bishop, presbyter and deacon that exists in churches like those of the Roman Catholic Church and Anglican Communion, is proposed for consideration for those churches that have not previously held such a view of ordained ministry. It is hoped that this will lead to a mutual recognition of each other's ordained ministries and thus provide greater church unity.[24]

Important objections can be raised to the idea of having a threefold ministry as the norm of the ecumenical community. First of all, this pattern is not revealed in the New Testament, but developed during the second and third centuries. Secondly, the meaning of such a pattern of ministry consisting of various offices has changed throughout history.[25] One obvious difference is what was initially perceived as three different ministries, gradually began to be understood as different degrees of the one and same office.[26] Furthermore, the content of ministries has changed over time, even if titles have remained the same.

It is regrettable if, based upon the desire for a unified pattern of ministry, that historical arguments are used which in reality, are ahistorical, or not supported by empirical evidence of what ministers actually do. Worse still, is when congregations and churches neglect the needs of the current situation when developing their ministerial patterns in order to align their practice to a theological correctness in these matters, as either derived from their own confessional tradition, or from the ecumenical discourse.

---

24. *Baptism, Eucharist and Ministry,* Ministry, para. 19–25, pp. 24–25.

25. Some of these objections are also mentioned in the document (ibid.), yet the overriding hope remains that if a generally accepted pattern of ministry is adopted this will lead to a greater unity amongst churches.

26. Skarsaune argues that there is nothing in the earliest sources that suggest that these three ministries come under one heading *the ordained ministry* in the singular and definite form. In the early church there is no single ordained ministry differentiated into the ministries of deacon, priest, and bishop. Rather, the three ministries were understood as separate and independent ministries. Skarsaune, "Det tredelte embete og det éne," 27.

Another negative side effect of a standardized pattern of ministry is it does not adequately value *diversity* as an ecclesiological quality. When Paul describes the various services and gifts the Spirit gives the church, this is marked by the picture of diversity and variation. There is nothing in the New Testament to suggest that the unity of the church depends on whether you have the same ministries and patterns of ministry everywhere, and at all times. Unity lies in the mission that the various ministries help to realize.

When it comes to ministry patterns, this is not an argument for an ecclesial anarchy. Undoubtedly, congregations and churches need fixed and predictable patterns and ordering for essential ministries. This is necessary, both for the church's sake and for those who will serve in these ministries. There is good reason to ascribe considerable weight to historical patterns of ministry, whether these come from one's own tradition or are based upon experiences of other traditions. The difficulty arises when such patterns are made absolute and unchangeable, thus preventing diversity and flexibility when it comes to the church carrying out its mission in the given context. In new situations, historically inherited patterns of ministry have to be given new content. New ministries may arise while other ministries may become obsolete.

An important undertaking for any theology of ministry as based upon the historical and empirical would be to consider how church ministry patterns have evolved within different traditions and throughout different historical epochs. It is necessary to understand these patterns so as to aid the church with its present challenges. An interesting contribution to this research is Martin Percy's study of developments in the priesthood in the Church of England. Percy explicitly distances himself from ahistorical and idealized theories of ordained ministry, and instead tries to show how patterns of church ministry have developed as a result of specific historical processes and social contexts.[27]

---

27. "The patterning of the ecclesiologies with which I take issue often seem to be based upon some (claimed) divine blueprint, which is itself, obviously, contestable. Moreover, such narrations tend to take little account of the contextual features that have actually had a distinctive role in determining the shape of ecclesial and ministerial identity . . . The pattern proposed in place of this is a theological reconstruction of ministry that takes the role of the environment and the functioning of the contextual—in relation to shaping theological and ecclesial development—much more seriously." Percy, *Clergy*, 1.

A Fellowship of Ministries

INSTITUTED BY GOD?

A major theme that comes up in discussions about church ministry is the concept of divine institution of a specific ordained ministry and patterns of ministry. Based upon the formulation of the Augsburg Confession article V, such a theme is also an important within the Lutheran context: "That we may obtain this faith, the ministry of teaching the gospel and administering the Sacraments was instituted." In the German text the subject of this institution is plainly stated as: "To obtain such faith God instituted the office of preaching, giving the gospel and the sacraments."[28] Other traditions ascribe to a divine institution of other offices, whether it is the threefold, the Petrine office (papal office), or patterns of ordained offices according to the Reformed tradition.

The idea of certain ministries as instituted by God is often substantiated with reference to how the early church recruited its leaders. Jesus' calling of the apostles has been interpreted as the beginning of a successive line of church leaders. In Orthodox, Catholic and Anglican traditions this has been seen as starting point for the succession of bishops.[29] Paul's appointment of elders in local churches (Acts 14:23), or the references to local church leaders in the Letters have also been used to legitimize certain types or patterns of ministry. In the Calvinist tradition the list of ministries in the New Testament has been the basis for a pattern of four ministries in the church: pastor, teacher, elder, and deacon.[30]

Clearly these New Testament passages that describe the ministry and leadership in the early church are acutely relevant in our understanding of ministry today. At the same time, we should be careful not to use these descriptions as a blueprint for ministry in the church for all times and occasions. Descriptions of ministry patterns in the early church as recorded in the New Testament passages are rather sketchy, and there was probably no uniform pattern of ministry in all local congregations.

Regarding the understanding of certain ministries being a continuation of the ministry of the apostles, it should be noted that the apostles had a very specific task, namely to be eye witnesses of the life, death, and

---

28. Kolb and Wengert, *Book of Concord*, 40. The Augsburg Confession was written both in German and Latin. Even if the Latin text is usually used as the basis of translation for other languages, the German text has the same formal authoritative status.

29. This understanding of apostolic succession is e.g., outlined in Lumen Gentium. *Teachings of the Second Vatican Council,* Constitution on the Church, para.18, pp. 96–97.

30. Regarding Calvin's understanding, see Niesel, *Theology of Calvin*, 199–206.

resurrection of Jesus. Unlike the bishops after them, they were not local church leaders, but rather missionaries and founders of churches.

Such observations do not preclude us, however, from understanding ministries in today's church in continuity with ministries of the early church, be it the ministry of the apostles or other types of ministries. The church of today surely should see itself, and its ministries, in succession with the church of the apostles, even if this does not mean its pattern of ministry can be simply copied or prolonged.

An interesting point made by those who argue for a threefold ministry, is they admit such a pattern cannot be found in the New Testament. Historically, this pattern developed in the second and third centuries and its development is understood as a result of the Spirit's guidance of the church.[31]

In my opinion, the idea of the continuing guidance of the Spirit with regards to patterns of ministry is a valid point. The Sprit was not only active in the New Testament church, but has continued to guide the church ever since. Two objections can be raised, however, when this view is presented to substantiate the threefold ministry as a normative, ecumenical pattern. First, we may ask why the guidance of the Spirit is limited to patterns of ministry as formulated during the first three centuries. Is the Spirit not active in other centuries and in other traditions? Second, we may ask why the guidance of the Spirit is understood as the process of standardization and uniformity, rather than guidance through changing patterns of ministry. It is a paradox that some want to find ecumenical unity in a pattern of ministry that is more standardized than the patterns found in the New Testament. The fact that the New Testament patterns of ecclesial ministries seems to be so varied, should give us caution within the current context when proposing standardizing ministerial patterns as being the ideal. When it comes to church ministry, diversity should not be seen as a predicament, but more as a resource.

---

31. For example, such a rationale is outlined in the Lima document: "The New Testament does not describe a single pattern of ministry which might serve as a blueprint or continuing norm for all future ministry in the Church. In the New Testament there appears rather a variety of forms which existed at different places and times. As the Holy Spirit continued to lead the Church in life, worship and mission, certain elements from this early variety were further developed and became settled into a more universal pattern of ministry. During the second and third centuries, a threefold pattern of bishop, presbyter and deacon became established as the pattern of ordained ministry throughout the Church." *Baptism, Eucharist and Ministry,* Ministry, para. 19, p. 24.

A Fellowship of Ministries

Rather than looking for one specific action and statement made by Jesus, or to one formative phase in church history, divine institution could be seen as the Spirit's leading throughout church history. In this respect, various patterns of ministry would not be a deviation from the guidance of the Spirit. When Paul refers to God who has called some to be, apostles, prophets, teachers, etc. (1 Cor 12:28), this could just as easily be construed as something God continually wills, rather than the institution of a particular set of ministries once for all. This means that in order for churches to fulfill their calling, patterns of ministry could be developed as led by the Spirit and according to the needs of their given context. This also means that all ministries of the church could be seen as an outpouring of the Spirit's work, and not only those mentioned in the Bible, or those upheld within tradition. All ministries in the church are spiritual gifts, and should be interpreted and assessed according to their contribution to the mission of the church in the world. This means there is no distinction between spiritual ministries and the purely practical tasks in the church.

The Spirit's work is not limited to just the early church (and for that matter, limited to the Reformation), but the Spirit is at work in the church today. This means that when the church devises its ministries it cannot only be content with referring to tradition, or to alleged biblical patterns. The church today, through the leading of the Spirit, is bound to ask how it can be true to its vocation in the now. This does not mean that the church should reinvent itself and its pattern of ministry in every new situation and context. The church should rather look for the guidance of the Spirit in the tension between tradition and renewal, knowing that sometimes renewal comes through learning from tradition.

Through history the ministries of the church have taken shape and color from models of leadership found in contemporary society, and this is also the case today. The understanding of church leadership is, for instance, influenced by contemporary understanding of leadership and management in secular organizations. At the same time of course, the church has its own identity and mission which has to be reflected in its leadership and ministry patterns. Since being a church is basically to gather in the name of Jesus, the church needs ministers that can celebrate and lead the fellowship in worship. Since the church is committed to the world in evangelism and diakonia, the church needs ministers that can lead and shape this aspect of church life. Since no congregation is the church alone, so the church needs ministers that can bring churches and ecclesial traditions together. Some of these ministries will have a permanent and public character, and these posts will be assigned to people with a special sense of vocation and commitment, in many cases even given permanent employment and a salary. Other ministries have a more informal and free reigning character. What ministries belong to these categories will vary according to each situation and context. At the same time churches should be open to learn from each other and treasure the accredited riches of tradition.

PASTORAL MINISTRY

In the middle of all these changing patterns of ministry there seems to be a relatively stable trait that runs throughout church history, namely the existence of church leadership having the responsibility of leading the congregation in public gatherings—as worship leaders, celebrants of baptism and communion, and as preachers. As is true of most ecclesial traditions, such a ministry is given various names, such as pastor, priest or minister. The theological and practical interpretations of this ministry will vary greatly. What is seen as the primary task in some traditions (for Protestants this is preaching, and for the Roman Catholic and Orthodox this is celebrating the eucharist), has not always been equally important in other traditions. The relationship to other ministries within the church can also vary greatly. In some traditions the pastor or priest has a monopoly of certain aspects of ministry (above all, the sacramental ministry). Different traditions also assign special areas of responsibility which in other traditions could be done by others. A common denominator for these various traditions is the notion of ministerial leadership for the whole congregation, often expressed by the metaphor of the shepherd (Latin: pastor) tending for the flock (cf. Acts 20:28; 1 Pet 5:2). This pastoral duty is not primarily carried out in a managerial way, but through the role of presiding at the worship of the congregation. In article V of the Augsburg Confession the necessity of having this role of providing the congregation with Word and sacrament is the rationale behind the notion that this ministry is instituted by God.

Even if this ministry has a special role in the church it is important to stress that it is but one ministry amongst a fellowship of ministries. As previously mentioned, it is regrettable to describe the pastor or priest as having *the* ecclesial ministry—as if there were no other ministries and offices in the church. The idea of a diversity of ministries is to place pastoral ministry among other ministries, as well as allowing for diversity in the understanding and shaping of pastoral ministry itself. Pastoral ministry is not an unchanging ministry for all times and for all places. Such a notion does not take into account the various forms of pastoral ministry as it exists in reality. Like all other aspects of theology, a theology of pastoral ministry must be contextual. This validates the possibility of differentiated forms of pastoral ministry within the church.

A view that is upheld in many church traditions is to ascribe pastoral ministry special priestly qualities as attributed to in the Old Testament. This view makes it difficult to understand pastoral ministry as part of the fellowship of ministries in the church. In the Old Testament the priests were a special group of people who were the only ones allowed to enter the holy place of the temple and make sacrificial offerings on behalf of the people (see for example, Exod 28). In contrast, the point is made in the Letter to the Hebrews that Jesus Christ was the final mediator and great high priest who offered himself once for all, so that all believers can have direct access to God (Heb 10:11–14, 19–22.). Any geographically located temple is therefore no longer necessary. According to Paul, a Christian's body is now the temple of God (1 Cor 3:16–17, 6:19; cf. 1 Pet 2:5).

Any priesthood continuing in the Old Testament pattern as a ministry for the Christian church is an alien concept in the New Testament. In the New Testament the priesthood is a "holy priesthood" consisting of the *whole church,* one that gives its life and ministry as "spiritual sacrifices acceptable to God through Jesus Christ" (1 Pet 2:5; cf. v. 9; Rev 1:6, 5:10, 20:6). For the reformers the idea of the priesthood of all believers was an important part of their ecclesiology and theology of ministry. As all Christians share in the priestly ministry there is no special priestly class in the church. Even though all Christians are responsible for the life of the church, this does not rule out the possibility and necessity of certain offices in the church.[32]

In the original New Testament Greek the term *hierevs* is used to denote the Old Testament priests. However, this term is never used to denote ministries in the church. A term used in the New Testament is *presbyteros* (elder or presbyter; cf. Acts 14:23, 20:17; 1 Tim 5:17,19),

---

32. On the subject priesthood of all believers, see Eastwood, *Priesthood of All Believers*; Muthiah, *Priesthood of All Believers*; Wengert, *Priesthood, Pastors, Bishops.*

which has transliterated into "priest" in English (and similarly in other languages). However, in most Bible translations "priest" is not used to denote the New Testament presbyters, but only the Jewish temple priests (as the continuation of the Old Testament *hierevs* (e.g. Matt 21:15; Luk 1:8; Acts 4:1) and their heathen counterparts (Acts 14:13). At the same time "priest" in ecclesial terminology has been used to denote the presbyters of the New Testament. This confusing terminological situation has not contributed to clarity in this matter.[33]

However, the confusion is not only due to terminology, but also to the fact that pastoral ministry in post-New Testament times was accredited qualities and traits of the Old Testament priest. In line with this development, the eucharist became to be understood as a sacrifice with the priest acting at the altar as a sacrificial priest.[34]

Rooted in the biblical idea of the priesthood of all believers the reformers criticized the understanding of the priest as a sacrificial priest. In many Protestant churches the word priest ceased to be used and was replaced with such terms as pastor or minister. Other churches reinterpreted their understanding of the priest, but continued to use the term.[35]

While Reformation churches principally do not recognize the priesthood as being analogous to the Old Testament priesthood, this is not so clearly defined in the Roman Catholic Church. Even though the Second Vatican Council's constitution on the church clearly backups the biblical notion of the priesthood of all believers, it also supports the existence of "the ministerial or hierarchical priesthood" (*sacerdotium*).[36]

---

33. See Skarsaune, "Det kirkelige embete" for a more detailed explanation of terminologies.

34. Ibid., 223–26; Molland, "Das kirchliche Amt," 218–21; Schillebeeckx, *Church with a Human Face*, 144–47.

35. Within the Anglican Communion the term priest is still kept, as well (in its linguistic parallels) in the Lutheran churches in the Nordic countries. In Germany the confessional division is expressed in the terminological difference between the use of *Priester* in the Roman Catholic Church, whereas the Evangelical Church uses the term *Pfarrer*.

36. *Teachings of the Second Vatican Council*, Constitution on the Church, para. 10, p. 85. The Latin *sacerdos/sacerdotium* is the translation of the Greek terms *hierevs/hieratevma* (priest/priesthood). The Lima Document describes the ordained ministry with reference to features from the Old Testament priestly ministry, but it roots this concept in the priesthood of all believers: "Ordained ministers . . . may appropriately be called priests because they fulfil a particular priestly service by strengthening and building up the royal and prophetic priesthood of the faithful through word and sacraments, through

A Fellowship of Ministries

The use of such sacerdotal concepts in the understanding of a certain ministry in the church is difficult to defend from the New Testament. This critique applies both to its Roman Catholic version as well as to the *de facto* situation in other churches that continues to practice a certain priestly separateness. In my opinion, this is a serious obstacle for developing a more comprehensive theology of ministry. It is also a hindrance for developing the understanding of the pastor's ministry as part of the fellowship of ministries within the church.

ORDINATION TO MINISTRY

From the early church onwards, the church has *dedicated* people to a ministry by prayer and the laying on of hands. In latter ecclesial terminology this practice has been described as *ordination*. Ordination is often understood as being a significant sign and acknowledgement for particular ministries as distinct from other ministers. When referring to the ministries of priests, bishops and possibly deacons, these ministries are frequently referred to as *the ordained ministry*, or *ordained ministries*.

Ordination as ecclesial practice clearly has its roots in New Testament passages such as 1 Timothy 4:14 and 2 Timothy 1:6. In addition, other New Testament passages can also be read as allusions to some sort of dedication to a particular ministry.[37] As I have previously pointed out in this chapter, the spiritual gifts (charisms) have a central role for understanding the various ministries in the church (cf. 1 Cor 12). With this as a backdrop, it is interesting to note that two main references to the practice of ordination explicitly links this practice to the concept of *charisma*: "Do not neglect the gift (*charisma*) that is in you, which was given to you through prophecy with the laying on of hands by the council of elders" (1 Tim 4:14), and: "For this reason I remind you to rekindle the gift (*charisma*) of God that is within you through the laying on of my hands" (2 Tim 1:6).

This implies that ordination is not only a formal transferring of authority, and the charisma is not only a personal supplementary tool to the ministry itself. On the contrary, the ministry itself is understood as a charisma, and to enter into ministry is to share in the charisma. The

---

their prayers of intercession, and through their pastoral guidance of the community." *Baptism, Eucharist and Ministry*, Ministry, para. 17.

37. Skjevesland, "Ordinasjonen i Det nye Testamente."

real agent in ordination is not the one who is doing the ordaining, but the Spirit "who allots to each one individually just as the Spirit chooses" (1 Cor 12:11). The Spirit, however, does not act unmediated, but through people's participation. In the context of ordination, this involves human participation, both for those being set-apart for ministry, and by those who call and install someone into ministry, by praying the Spirit to be upon the person with the Spirit's gifts. The fact that the church trusts that it will be heard when asking for such gifts, is founded on the promise that the Spirit *desires* to give the church gifts. At the same time, ordination is no magic event—the Spirit is *free,* so accordingly we must *pray* for the gifts of the Spirit. Also the gift that was once given is not something we own, once and for all, regardless of the Spirit's regenerating work. In view of this Timothy is exhorted to rekindle the *charisma* he once received (2 Tim 1:6).[38]

Such a charismatic view of ordination is frequently sustained by the different liturgies for ordination. In the Church of Norway, for example, the liturgy for the ordination of a priest the following prayers are said: "Come, Holy Spirit, Lord God, pour out your spiritual gifts upon the soul and heart of those being sent and kindle your fire of love upon them!"[39]

Ordination is set within the framework of the church's public worship where people are gathered in the name of Jesus. This illustrates how ordination is a public declaration of setting apart certain person(s) for ministry with the blessing and authority of the church. As a public event, this act is led by the church's principal leaders—for those churches with bishops this is an episcopal task.

Those that are ordained can serve in the congregation or can be given a commission for ministry elsewhere. The latter was the case with Paul and Barnabas who, after the church had fasted, prayed and laid hands on them (Acts 13:1–3), were sent out in mission. In this example the dedication by the laying on of hands is not connected to a well defined ministry. This is the case with Timothy also, where we are given no detailed description of the ministry he was consecrated for, other than that he had some kind of function as a church leader. In Acts 6:6 we read that the apostles consecrated seven men to take care of the charity work in the church (the first deacons). This is obviously a very different kind of min-

---

38. Regarding the understanding of ordination, see *Baptism, Eucharist and Ministry,* Ministry, para. 39–50, pp. 30–32.

39. *Gudstjenestebok for Den norske kirke,* vol. 2, 165–66 (our translation).

istry to that which Timothy was ordained for. This means that ordination is not linked just to one single ministry. In the diversity of the gifts which the Spirit gives the church, dedication through the laying on of hands and prayer may be applied to different charisms.

This obviously does not mean *every* spiritual gift of the church needs a similar ordination rite—not every ministry is an *ordained ministry*. In the New Testament the rite of ordination seems to be linked to regulated leadership positions. While some churches practice a threefold pattern of ordained ministry, some churches have only one ordained ministry, while other churches have other patterns of ordination for various ministries. This also means that some churches ordain to ministries where other churches do not. These differences have been theme for ecumenical conversation between churches, and as a result of such conversations this has led some churches to reconsider their practices (e.g. regarding the ordination of deacons). Not that this should led to an idealized form of complete uniformity, as conversely the Spirit works through diversity. The somewhat blurred line between ordained and non-ordained ministries is also a reminder that ordination does not mean a division of God's people into two separate groups. Even if vocation and responsibility may differ, the whole church shares in the same divine calling.

ALL CHRISTIANS HAVE A MINISTRY

Even if church is a fellowship of ministries, some ministries are more elementary than others. There are certain ministries that the church cannot do without. This is probably what is in mind when article V of the Augsburg Confession mentions the ministry of Word and sacrament as God's tool for creating faith. The rudimentary character of some ministries does not mean that other ministries are unnecessary. New Testament passages like 1 Corinthians 12 suggest a fullness and richness of diverse ministries.

Of course the church can operate with less during difficult seasons and still be a church. In some instances, the ministry of the pastor or priest is almost the only functioning ministry in the congregation. Occasionally, a congregation may even be without an ordained minister. As long as the sacraments are celebrated and the gospel is preached, the church is still a church. The only thing the church cannot manage without is the gospel and someone to preach it (Rom 10:14–15). What is *possible* under such certain circumstances is far from *ideal*. The church needs its ordained ministry, as well as it needs the diverse spiritual gifts of all its members.

The necessity of a certain ministry for the church to be church is challenged by Miroslav Volf in his critique of the episcocentric structure found in Roman Catholic and Orthodox theology. The argument proposed by this type of ecclesiology is that bishops are necessary for the church to be church. The bishop represents Christ to the church and the church towards Christ. Between the church and the bishop there is a basic bipolar asymmetry: the bishop acts, while the church receives.[40] As I have already pointed out, in Lutheran theology we can also find a comparable way of thinking about the relationship between ordained ministry and the church—the congregation as coming from the ministry, and not vice versa.

Volf argues that the church is not a single subject, but a fellowship of subjects where salvation is permeated through all the members of the fellowship and through their shared confession of faith. According to Volf, a clergy centered ecclesiology is neither theologically nor sociologically valid. Theologically Volf bases his argument on an understanding of the church as a fellowship of equal subjects. Volf supplements his theological argument with an additional sociological observation. He observes that such an ecclesiology overestimates the role of the officeholder in the actual life of the church, while the role of the ordinary church member is underestimated. When people come to faith and keep the faith, it is often because other church members have created the necessary plausibility structures. During the worship service, it is not only the clergy that are active, but also the rest of the congregation through song, prayer, and reading—yes through their presence.[41] A theology that emphasizes the church's character of a fellowship of ministries is more likely to reinterpret what is actually going on in the congregation. Such reinterpretation is an important starting point for changing and renewing church practice. Volf believes the most noteworthy theological factor in keeping church members passive, is a lack of theological emphasis about the constitut-

---

40. Volf, *After Our Likeness*, 223–24.

41. "The model according to which the Spirit constitutes the church through officeholders (ordained in the apostolic succession) obscures the ecclesiologically highly significant fact that in all churches, faith is mediated and kept alive above all by the so-called laity, that is, in families, in one's neighborhood, or in the workplace; without this lay activity of faith mediation, there would be no living church." Ibid., 227.

ing role the laity have in the church.⁴² I believe this argument proposed by Volf can offer an important corrective to certain lines of thought and practice.

As I have said in the introduction of this chapter, the church's development towards becoming a church of the majority has been a sociological condition for the division of the clergy and lay people, which has been an important trait of many churches throughout history. To some degree, these sociological premises are still present and in new forms in churches that still maintain a folk church profile, for example the Nordic folk churches. In these churches many church members understand their relationship to the church as that of a customer or client. For these members it would be a strange concept to think that they have a ministry or spiritual gift in the church. Instead, this responsibility is left to the priests and other church employees.

This leaves us with the paradox of confirming such an attitude in the name of being an inclusive church. In order to avoid treating this group as some kind of second-class member, there is a risk to treat all church members as though they are not part of the fellowship of ministries. The result of this may be that lay members who want to be active and serve in ministry, can find little room to do this. This in turn, can lead to passivity, or to people leaving the folk church in order to serve in other churches.

In a folk church setting it is also important to adhere to the fact that spiritual gifts belong to each and every church member. This is not to say that every church member might be aware of this, or are willing to see themselves from this standpoint. The church must of course respect this opinion, and even appreciate its passive members as part of the fellowship. The idea of what constitutes a ministry should not be so restrictive and identified solely upon being active in church work. When parents present their children for baptism and raise them up in the Christian faith, this is also ecclesial ministry. At the same time, the church must challenge its members to see themselves as part of its fellowship of ministry, and to develop specific ministries of service. Such a challenge is not necessary only because the church needs these ministries, but because discovering and utilizing one's gift is part of the richness of being a Christian. A church that gladly accepts their members' passivity and reduces them to being clients to be served, robs them of something significant.

---

42. Ibid., 223–28.

Ironically, the idea of the priesthood of all believers is sometimes used to justify the lack of responsibility and engagement in the life of the church of ordinary church members. This may occur when the priesthood of all believers is presented as just having a personal relationship with God—the right to draw near to God without an intermediary. However, this is only one side of the issue, in 1 Peter 2 Christians are seen as priests ready to *serve*: They bear "spiritual sacrifices" (v. 5) and "proclaim the mighty acts" of God (v. 9). The priesthood of all believers means *those who serve*. As Volf points out, to discover one's special charisma and unique call to minister in the church is a crucial aspect of being part of discovering oneself as belonging to the priesthood of all believers.[43]

THE LEADERSHIP AND GOVERNANCE OF THE CHURCH

The theme of church ministry also raises the question of *leadership* and *governance*. This is an extensive field that can only be discussed very briefly in this context. In traditions that have emphasized the bishops' role as successors of the apostles, bishops (and the priests who represent them) are often regarded as being the true leaders in the church, irrespective of whether areas of responsibility are delegated to others.[44] In Protestant churches, the question of leadership and governance is more complex. One of the outcomes of the Reformation was the transference of power away from ecclesiastical hierarchy to representatives of the laity (in the main, power was given to kings and the aristocracy). Some churches took this further and developed a more democratic church administration. In line with the overall democratic development of society, more and more churches moved towards democratic synodical structures. Such systems of governance give responsibility and influence to elected members of synods and church councils, as well as to administrative leaders employed by these councils. The growth of this type of leadership has, in many instances, created tensions with traditional forms of leadership as exercised by the clergy.

The growth of other types of leadership not only creates tension with traditional forms of leadership, it may also question the basis for such

---

43. Ibid., 225–26.

44. In the Roman Catholic Church the leadership of the church is first and foremost episcopal: "As vicars and ambassadors of Christ, bishops govern the particular Churches entrusted to them." *Teachings of the Second Vatican Council,* Constitution on the Church, para. 27, p. 113.

leadership. This has for instance, been the case in the Church of Norway, where the introduction of administrative leaders has led to a discussion of the meaning of pastoral leadership in its relationship to other forms of leadership in the church.

The pastor's role as a leader has not traditionally been accentuated in Lutheranism. For example, in the ordination liturgy of the Church of Norway the leadership role of the pastor is not explicitly mentioned. Representatives of the Neo-Lutheranism of the nineteenth century even argued for a distinct ministry of governance separate from the pastor's ministry. As the minister of grace they suggested it was, in principle, impossible for the pastor to exercise power, this in turn should be left to a separate office of governance.[45]

Nevertheless, there are still good reasons for maintaining that pastoral ministry today should include dimensions of leadership. This leadership role is primarily rooted in the pastor's role as presiding over the church's worship. As worship is the central event in the life of the church, the ministry of leading worship necessarily exercises leadership in the church. At the same time, there are also good reasons to have other leadership positions in the church. A variety of leadership positions seems also to have been the case in the New Testament church. In the list of different charisms in 1 Corinthians 12, "teachers" and "forms of leadership" are seen as two distinct ministries (v. 28). By seeing all ministries in the church as charisms, as gifts of the Spirit, we no longer need to distinguish between the more *spiritual* and more *practical* or *administrative* acts of service. To reserve the term *spiritual leadership* for the ministry of the pastor only is problematic, as all activities in the church should be seen as the Spirit's work through the various gifts and ministries.

Alongside the question of *who* should be a leader, is the question of where leadership is *anchored*. Where does the leader get her mandate and mission from? To whom is the leader accountable? And who can overrule or even remove the leader? Such questions are important in any context, and not less, in the church.

The immediate answer of where leadership comes from and is anchored is of course God himself. According to Paul, it is the Spirit who gives the spiritual gifts. This means that each person's ministry in the church, including the leader's, have their mandate from God. This is not

---

45. Fagerberg, *Bekenntnis, Kirche und Amt*, 295.

to say that this mandate only comes as a direct and unmediated, personal inner calling. On the contrary, the Spirit works through the fellowship. Although some may have a special ministry given of God, others too in the fellowship share of the same Spirit. Any ministry must be rooted in, and given authority by the fellowship.

This does not mean that everything in the church, at any time, should be subject to collective decision making. Having a ministry involves being given an assigned task by the church. This in turn, allows for a certain autonomy and authority. This is articulated by the liturgy of ordination, for example. A pastor cannot be reduced to the church's *trustee*, but is empowered to address the church on God's behalf. At the same time, everything that transpires in the church is subject to the review of the fellowship. The fact that someone is designated a special task is not to suggest they can go above the fellowship's right to judge what is being said and done.

Luther makes the point that preaching and leadership in the church is to be grounded in the fellowship of the church community in his treatise: "That a Christian assembly or congregation has the right and power to judge all teaching and to call, appoint, and dismiss teachers, established and proven by the Scripture."[46] According to Luther, in a situation where the leadership of the church goes against the gospel, the local congregation has the right to decide who should preach the gospel to them: "We should have no doubt that the congregation which has the gospel may and should elect and call from among its members someone to teach the word in its place."[47] Luther believes, however, that under normal conditions bishops are given the right to choose ministers, so long as this does not contradict the will of the church.

How the church expresses its view will vary according to different historical and cultural circumstances. In our present context, it is difficult to imagine anything other than that church's sovereignty over its own affairs is expressed through democratic structures and processes. In many churches such awareness has led to the development of democratic structures in congregations and denominations. It is important that such structures are perceived and practiced as coming from the priesthood of all believers and not that of universal civil rights. As all ministries are

---

46. *Luther's Works*, vol. 39, 305–14 (WA 11:408–16).
47. Ibid., 311.

A Fellowship of Ministries

to be perceived as services given by God for the church, being elected to synods or church councils and exercising power is on behalf of God for the church.

This view will also affect how we understand the basis of how decisions are to be reached by synods and church councils. In democratic bodies, the task of those who are chosen is to represent the interests and views of the electorate, basing decisions upon good judgment and accurate information. Of course, this way of doing things is not irrelevant for ecclesial councils, but in addition another important process must take place, namely the obligation to seek God's will when leading the church. Decision making of ecclesial councils should be understood as a process of seeking God in each given situation. Since the Spirit is the active presence in church life, discerning God's will is not purely based upon general principles by which we can deduce certain guidelines for decision making, but is about seeking God's will for each specific situation.

In many forms of Christian spirituality there has been a concern to discern the leading of the Spirit for each person. This insight can also be applied to the church fellowship as a whole. To say that decision making is about coming together to seek God through the leading of the Spirit does not mean that other features of a typical decision making process are made redundant, such as the ability to reason, discuss, vote, and exercise leadership. The Spirit's work is actually made present through people filled by the Spirit, and through the Spirit-filled fellowship. To see the decision making process as a shared seeking the will of God, enables this process to be seen in a distinctive light. It is natural therefore, and necessary to include other factors that are not usually included in secular decision making processes, such as Bible reading and prayer. As an outworking of a collective process, it is important that procedures are not dominated by individuals, but each member of the fellowship is given space to voice their opinion.[48]

The idea of decision making in the church as a form of spiritual leadership is confirmed in the Acts of the Apostles. On four occasions we read that the church gathered to seek God's will concerning matters where decisions had to be made (Acts 1:15–26, 6:1–7, 11:1–18, 15:1–35). The decision making procedure described in Acts 15 stands out as a clear example of how a decision was reached after thorough discussion by the

---

48. Spiritual discernment as an important part of the life of the church is considered in Morris and Olsen, *Discerning God's Will Together,* and Keifert, *Testing the Spirits.*

"apostles and the elders, with the consent of the whole church" (v. 22). The confidence of reaching the decision as being led by the Spirit was later outlined in the letter sent to Antioch: "For it has seemed good to the Holy Spirit and to us . . ." (v. 28).

To invoke the will of God to support decisions made can clearly be a risky business. Any decision made must be under the disclaimer that we can never have full knowledge of God. It is possible to make mistakes, even for a Christian fellowship that has asked for the Spirit's leading. Therefore, no decision is beyond reproach, and there must be space to reconsider decisions. The church cannot claim infallibility. The fact that the Spirit works through people does not mean that we can ever fully identify our actions with that of God's. An important component that should accompany any ecclesial decision making process, is *spiritual discernment*: to be able to distinguish between true and false, between what is of God and what is not. The gift of "the discernment of spirits" (1 Cor 12:10; cf. Rom 12:2; 1 John 4:1) is one of the most important gifts God gives to the church.

8

Worship: As Gathered in the Name of Jesus

IN THIS BOOK I have argued to see the church as a fellowship of people who are gathered in the name of Jesus, and I have discussed implications of such an understanding on various aspects of church life. In this chapter the focus will be upon the gathering itself. How should we understand worship in the light of the church being a fellowship gathered in Jesus name?

WHAT DOES IT MEAN TO BE GATHERED IN THE NAME OF JESUS?

A natural place to start in addressing this question is by defining and contextualizing what it means to be "gathered in the name of Jesus." Different denominations use different concepts to denote this central event in the life of the church. Orthodox churches talk about the *divine liturgy*, the Roman Catholics the *mass*, and Protestant churches use terms like *church service* or *worship service* (or just *worship* or *service*). Some free churches and low church movements prefer to talk about *meetings* or *gatherings*. Differences in terminology may reflect different styles of worship, and even the same term can include a range of different worship styles. While some traditions model their worship after predetermined patterns such as liturgical texts, in other traditions worship is more informal.

In the following I will for practical reasons, speak of the *worship service* despite the inconsistent use of this terminology. I will use the term in an *inclusive* sense, including everything that could reasonably be described as being gathered in the name of Jesus. Thus the concept also includes gatherings that lack formal traits immediately associated with a worship service, but still may be a gathering in the name of Jesus in *theological* sense.

To call the Sunday morning gathering, that includes a sermon and the celebration of the eucharist, a worship service is obvious, but what are we to say about an evening worship service which does not have the eucharist? Or what about a youth meeting, a bible group, or a homily given at a nursing home? What about the liturgy of the hours in the Roman Catholic tradition (such as lauds, vespers, etc) that does not include celebration of the eucharist? Furthermore, what about ceremonies such as funerals and weddings? Even though many of these occasions do not include the Sunday service's traditional elements, is not to deny they are gatherings in the name of Jesus in the sense of Matt 18:20. When discussing the worship service from a theological perspective, we should be careful not to exclude other forms of worship that also may belong to the phenomenon proposed. It is necessary, however, to make the distinction between the worship service, in its more *complete* form, compared to gatherings that include *aspects* of this form. Besides certain elements such as Word and sacrament this *completeness* includes the gathering of the whole congregation (and not just limited to a few). In its complete form the worship service will normally be public service open and accessible to all.

Even though a congregation may have many types and forms of services, there will usually be one particular service (or a smaller number of services) in the course of a week that will be regarded as the main service. In most churches the main service takes place on Sunday morning.[1]

Any attempt to determine what belongs to the main service in its more complete form should not exclude other types of Christian worship services that differ substantially from the services in one's own tradition. To say that a Sunday service at a Pentecostal church or in the Salvation Army is something less a worship service is obviously too restrictive. Even though nobody would probably want to disagree about this, in practice much of what is written on the subject of worship often refers to one particular form of worship. The majority of what scholars have written

---

1. An interesting question to reflect upon is how we are to understand the situation when a congregation actually has more than one main worship service (gathering different groups of people). One possible solution is to consider these various worship groups as sharing a common organizational structure, but in reality are really different congregations that gather under the same roof. Martin Modéus argues for the necessity for a congregation to have only one main service, as this is a way to truly show unity of the church in all its diversity. *Mänsklig gudstjänst*, 122–23. For further reflection about this issue see chapter 9.

Worship: As Gathered in the Name of Jesus

about the theology and history of worship refers, in the main, to a particular liturgical tradition, usually limited to churches with more formal liturgies. Very little has been written with reference to churches that have more informal worship, or it is written in such a way as to be polemical in nature.[2] When the terms *liturgy* and *liturgical* are used to denote the worship service (as is common within the academic discipline *liturgical studies*) this usually refers to more formal forms of worship.

As exemplified by the writings of the liturgical scholar Gordon W. Lathrop, terms like *liturgy* and *liturgical* can also be used in a more broad and inclusive sense. Another classic concept used by Lathrop and others to denote the gathering of the church is *assembly*. The term infers that worship consists of people who actually come together in order to do certain things.[3]

THE DISTINCTIVENESS OF CHRISTIAN WORSHIP

There is no unifying concept for Christian worship in the New Testament. The terms used simply refer to the act of coming together (*synagesthai/synerchesthai*, see Matt 18:20; Acts 4:31, 20:7; 1 Cor 5:4, 11:18, 20, 14:23). In James 2:2 the noun *synagogē* is used to describe the Christian worship (see also Heb 10:25). This indicates that the first century Jewish synagogue worship was seen as a model for early Christian worship. This worship included prayer, scripture reading and exposition, and no animal or other sacrifices.[4]

When looking at the concepts used about worship in the New Testament, it is important to note how the terms are *not* used. It is inter-

---

2. For example, Frank C. Senn who writes more than 700 pages about the history of the church worship from its beginnings up until the present day, barely mentions the twentieth century Pentecostal movement (Senn, *Christian Liturgy*). In another book when he does mention the Pentecostal movement and other renewal movements with alternative worship patterns that differ from more traditional liturgical patterns, this has a certain polemical undertone (Senn, *People's Work*). In his comprehensive introduction to the liturgy Karl-Heinrich Bieritz gives a broad presentation of the service patterns found in Orthodox, Roman Catholic, Lutheran, Reformed, and Anglican traditions, but barely mentions the Pentecostal and Charismatic worship traditions that includes hundreds of millions of Christians (Bieritz, *Liturgik*).

3. "Assembly, a gathering together of participating persons, constitutes the most basic symbol of Christian worship." Lathrop, *Holy People*, 21.

4. Concerning the relationship between worship in the synagogue and Christian worship see Senn, *Christian Liturgy*, 67–73; Skarsaune, *In the Shadow of the Temple*, 377–422.

esting to see that there are *no* terms borrowed from the Old Testament temple cult, or from other forms of (non-Jewish and non-Christian) cult worship. The New Testament does use terms relating to the Old Testament sacrificial system, but never uses these directly when referring to the Christian church service.[5] This is hardly a coincidence, but seems rather to have been related to an understanding of Christians gathering in the name of Jesus as being something unique compared to other forms of religious cult, including the temple cult.

This does not mean a rejection of the temple cult. On the contrary, the first Christians of Jewish origin continued to make use of the temple in Jerusalem (Acts 3:1, 21:26, 24:17-18). At the same time, however, they thought that the temple service, and in particular the sacrificial system, was no longer necessary in light of Jesus' death. According to the Letter to the Hebrews, the *new covenant* has replaced the *old covenant* (Heb 8:13) with Jesus' death being the sacrifice that has replaced, and has made obsolete all other forms of sacrifice (Heb 9:12). This is not to say that the temple and sacrificial terminology disappeared completely from the Christian language. To a large extent, it has been transferred over to the Christian life and ministry as a whole. Therefore, Christians and the Christian church can be described as God's temple (1 Cor 3:16; Eph 2:21; 1 Pet 2:5). This also applies to concepts such as *latreuein/latreia* used to describe the Old Testament cult (Rom 9:4; Heb 8:5, 9:1, 9). These are used figuratively about other aspects of the Christian life and ministry (e.g. Rom 1:9, 12:1; Heb 9:14, 12:28), but never directly about church worship gatherings.

While the New Testament does not seem to interpret the church gathering as continuing with or analogous to the sacrificial system of the temple, the idea of such continuity or analogy gradually became a relatively important element in the understanding of the church's worship. Not least, the understanding of the eucharist being a sacrificial offering led to an understanding of the worship service as analogous to the Old Testament sacrificial cult. This led to the adoption of symbols and concepts from the sacrificial cult into Christian worship, such as the eucharistic table being the "altar," and the use of special priestly garments.

---

5. For the following, see Brunner, "Zur Lehre vom Gottesdienst," 99–115. "What happens in Christian worship is something quite new. In essence this event is not only completely different from the pagan cult, but also from Israel's worship" (ibid., 104–5, our translation).

Worship: As Gathered in the Name of Jesus

There are good reasons to be critical towards this development, especially when objects or persons are assigned a specific form of holiness and godly presence at the expense of the New Testament perspective that sees all Christians as holy to whom Jesus has promised to be present whenever they call upon his name. This is not to say that the traditional concept of the altar cannot make sense as a eucharistic table, or that there are no good reasons for liturgical garments. There are, however, plenty of examples were the use of such objects and metaphors have had unfortunate outcomes, for example, the separation of clergy and lay during worship.[6]

An example of how the Christian worship increasingly came to be seen as analogous with other form of worship can be found by the use of the term *liturgy* (and the associated description of the one presiding as *liturgist*). The Greek word *leiturgia* was basically a political term that meant "service for the people."[7] It was used to describe the tasks (often political in nature) performed by significant people who had the best interest of the community at heart. However, the term was also used in religious context for those who performed religious ceremonies. It is in this sense the term is also used in the Septuagint (and in Luke 1:23) for the priests and Levites serving in the temple. In the New Testament *leiturgia/leiturgos* is never seen in terms of what happens in worship, but used figuratively to denote Christian service (Rom 15:16, 2 Cor 9:12; Phil 2:17, 30).[8]

Naturally words change meaning over time, and it is possible to legitimately use the term liturgy when referring to Christian worship. Nevertheless, such terms tend to carry with them historical overtones, for example, when the pastor/priest is referred to as "liturgist" who "officiates at the service" on behalf of the church.

To try and get a New Testament understanding about the worship service is made difficult by the fact that we do not find any clear or detailed picture of the early church worship service. What we can say with certainty is Christians gathered together and they attributed high value

---

6. Most notably during the fourth century when Christianity became the state religion of the Roman Empire these distinctions were further increased. In order to protect the sense of the sacred, different spaces in the church and special rituals were created to distinguish the clergy from the laity. Bradshaw, "Effects of the Coming of Christendom on Early Christian Worship."

7. When this term is sometimes explained as *the people's work*, this is not in accordance with the term's original historical usage.

8. Brunner, "Zur Lehre vom Gottesdienst," 101–4, 109–10. Acts 13:2 is a possible exception to this, see ibid., 103 n. 9.

to these gatherings. The details of these gatherings, however, remain unclear. We do not know whether they had a fixed structure, progression, and to what extent the content varied. There is reason to believe that these gatherings had a more informal and improvised feel than orders of worship of later church history, even if they probably included some constant elements as well.

It is in the Acts of the Apostles and Paul's letters, and possibly some of hymns in Revelation, that we are able to gain some insight about the early Christian gatherings. While the Acts of the Apostles relates some scenes from the Christian gatherings (e.g., in Acts 4:23, 13:2–3), it is Paul who gives us a glimpse into early Christian worship practice (e.g., 1 Cor 10–14; Eph 5:19; Col 3:16–17). Despite the fact that we do not get a comprehensive, detailed picture, it is still possible to identify some recurring elements. A kind of summary is found in Acts 2:42, where it is said that the church "devoted themselves to the apostles' teaching and fellowship, to the breaking of bread and the prayers." Some of the key elements were the preaching of the gospel (apostles' teaching), the eucharist (breaking of the bread), and the common prayer. "Fellowship" (*kononia*) probably should not be seen as a fourth attribute, but regarded an inclusive item that incorporates all the elements together. Worship is therefore, more than just specific actions performed by individuals, but more something you do in fellowship.

HISTORICAL AND CONTEMPORARY SOURCES

While our understanding of early Christian worship is relatively limited, we have a far better grasp of the later developments of church worship up until the present time. We are inundated with a rich variety of sources, such as texts that describe, or prescribe, what shall be done and said during a church service. These sources are probably an important reason why a lot of theologians' work about worship has a more historical bent. In many cases, historical sources about the church service has not only been used to *describe* development, but has been used to promote a *normative* perspective. Patterns and elements from early liturgical sources, more often than not, become established as the normative basis for the understanding of Christian worship today.

Such a normative use of early sources may be used for both upholding a tradition and for critiquing a tradition. Historical sources are used to *preserve* tradition when later developments are understood as continuing the patterns and elements inherited from the early church. Historical sources are also used to *critique* tradition when contemporary forms of worship are seen as restoring elements from early church forms of worship. For example, this was a major concern in the nineteenth century liturgical restoration movement, which led to liturgical reforms in many churches.[9] Often the preserving of tradition and the critique of tradition go hand in hand. In fact we can be engaged in extensive discussions of liturgical details without ever actually questioning the underlining patterns and frameworks of tradition.

There are several reasons why it is useful and necessary to use historical sources (from different time periods) when considering Christian worship today. In order to understand the present situation, it is necessary to know something about how this came to be. To understand one's history helps to understand one's present situation. To work with historical sources is not only necessary when trying to understand one's own history, but contributes to a richer understanding of how a Christian worship service may be shaped. This may contribute to both the enrichment and criticism of one's own tradition. Such a comparative perspective, however, is not limited to historical sources, but must also include the worshipping life of the various Christian churches today.

To look at the ways other Christians worship and have worshipped, is not only important because we can always learn from others, but it is ecclesiologically rooted in the catholicity of the church. While each congregation is fully church in its own time and place, it is called to be church together with other churches, past and present. Each congregation is called to seek fellowship with other churches not only within its own confessional domain. Its practice of worship should also be based upon the fact that there is only one Christian church in the world. What happens in the worship service is basically the same everywhere and at all times—that is to say Jesus is in the midst of people who are gathered in his name. Even though there are various forms, these are in essence, forms of the same basic event. Therefore, the experience of the universal church is relevant when a congregation wants to give shape to its own worship. As a rule, the interchange between different Christian traditions and experiences enrich and challenge each other.

9. For a description of this movement and its ideology, see Senn, *People's Work*, 284–304.

When studying different worship services, both past and present, this should not be limited solely to the study of liturgical *texts*. Research has often concentrated on such texts because these documents are readily available. It is important not to confuse texts with the actual service itself. Liturgical texts are primarily a tool used to describe and regulate aspects of what is enacted, especially by those that lead in worship services. To study these texts is not the same as studying what *actually* happens in a church service via the interaction between all those present. Texts can be an important source of understanding this interaction, but they are far from being the only source.

When it comes to comprehending the Christian church service today, we can simply observe what is going on and converse with the worshippers. Such qualitative, empirical methods have extensively been used in the exploration of Christian churches in recent years. Surprisingly, these investigations have mainly been limited to what goes on outside the church service. Sociologists of religion and other empirical religious scholars have been eager to determine how many people go to church and why they attend and leave the church, with little concern about what actually happens during the worship service. Empirical studies about the service should be an equally important source as liturgical texts in the field of liturgical theology.[10]

The disadvantage of one-sided focus upon texts is the tendency of favoring particular churches and traditions that have their own written records. Historically, it is far from certain that what is written in recorded liturgies truly represents the breadth of Christian worship throughout the ages. An emphasis upon written sources will also favor the more formalized forms of worship, rather than more informal styles. In our own time, we can easily overlook traditions that do not produce liturgical texts and handbooks, e.g., the Pentecostal and Charismatic movements.

A theological understanding of Christian worship should relate to the biblical material that describes the early Christian gatherings, as well as to how Christians have worshipped throughout the ages. A

---

10. Martin D. Stringer's study of the worship life of four churches in Manchester (*On the Perception of Worship*) is thus a pioneering research. Some studies have also been made of the worship of Charismatic and Pentecostal churches, see Albrecht, *Rites in the Spirit,* and Steven, *Worship in the Spirit*. In another study Stringer has considered the social meaning of worship from a historical perspective. Stringer, *Sociological History of Christian Worship*.

theological understanding cannot be based purely upon a reconstruction of historical originals, or upon a distillate of what can be found in all Christian worship traditions. Instead, we should look for the very essential features that make a gathering of people a Christian worship service, and what role worship plays in the church. This does not mean that the worship service should be constructed simply from a set of principles, regardless of how Christians have celebrated and actually worship today. Any work with both theory and practice of worship must relate to the actual worship. This also relates to the social and cultural context in which worship takes place.

WORSHIP AS SIGN

An understanding of the church as a sign and an anticipation of the fellowship between humanity and God in the realized kingdom of God (see chapter 3), must also have consequences for understanding the worship service. If the church is to be understood as a sign and foretaste, this applies as much to the worship service as it does the very essence of the life of the church. A key question is to understand the relationship between the character of worship as *sign* and its character of *foretaste*. To what extent does the worship service point to the future, and to what extent does it actually realize that what it is pointing to?

The understanding of the worship service and its various components as pointing beyond itself is a central theme in liturgical theology of Gordon W. Lathrop. He uses both the terms *sign* and *symbol*. Based upon an Augustinian-Lutheran understanding of the sacrament, Lathrop looks at the relationship between the sign and what the sign points toward. He does not limit this to the sacraments in the narrowest sense, but applies to the various elements of the worship service. As signs, the rituals should be performed in such a way that they really act as signs. For example, it should be possible to perceive baptism as a bath, and the eucharist as a meal.[11] Lathrop believes the goal of designing an order of service is to integrate the various signs and symbols in such a way so they point to the fullness of the Christian message. The signs are not used appropriately if their meaning is not disclosed.[12] Therefore, an important criterion for evaluating a given worship service is whether or not it has profound

11. Lathrop, *Holy Things*, 164–74.
12. Ibid., 170.

symbolic meaning: "Liturgical criticism asks whether the assembly is symbolically strong."[13]

The primary symbol is not the various rituals within the service, but the very fact that the church comes together for worship:

> The local church-assembly is itself, as gathering, the primary symbol. By its participation, by its communal mode of song and prayer around Scripture reading, meal keeping, and bathing, it is being transformed into a primary witness to the identity of God and the identity of the world before God.[14]

Lathrop sees the congregation gathered for worship as symbol, sign, or witness—a reality that primarily points beyond itself. The rituals of the service are brought in from other contexts, albeit transformed (*broken*), and given a new meaning through their *juxtaposition* with other signs.

For example, this is reflected by Lathrop's understanding of the worship as a fellowship. On the one hand, he sees it as necessary for new Christians to be part of smaller groups where they can learn the faith. On the other hand, these groups have to be brought into the larger fellowship of the worship service. Lathrop describes this as less intimate and more symbolic: "But the groups must be turned toward the liturgical assembly, toward the larger, less intimate, more symbol-making gathering."[15]

In chapter 5 I have argued that the church's task is not only to symbolize or point to the fullness of communion between God and humanity and one another as realized in the kingdom of God, but also to *anticipate* this fellowship by being in fellowship with one another. The church as a fellowship is not only a *symbol* of fellowship, but a sign that partakes in, and thereby anticipates, the fellowship it points to.[16] In my opinion, Lathrop places too little emphasis upon the anticipatory character of the sign. It is not sufficient for worship to symbolize fellowship without also *being* a fellowship. Only by being a fellowship, worship symbolizes the fellowship of the kingdom. The church at worship *is* a fellowship from which other aspects of the church's character of fellowship flows from the source of fellowship as it unfolds during worship.

---

13. Ibid., 162.
14. *Holy People*, 49. Cf. p. 21.
15. *Holy Things*, 122–23.
16. See chapter 2.

Worship: As Gathered in the Name of Jesus

A result of emphasizing worship as fellowship means those taking part in worship are not primarily be understood as individuals who are engaging in their own personal devotions. Even if we participate in worship as individuals and having individual interpretations to what is actually going on in the service, worship is nevertheless still something we do *together*. Not only do we do "something" together, but we do the things Christians have always done when they have come together in the name of Jesus: reading and preaching the Word, praying together, celebrating the meal instituted by Jesus, and initiate new members to the fellowship through baptism. These actions are not merely symbols of something beyond (invisible or future), but are actions constitutive of the Christian fellowship in the now. To be a Christian fellowship is to do these things together.

Given that we do things *together* means we cannot understand those who go to the service as being an audience at a show or concert, etc. Firstly, this is to assume there is a dichotomy between those who *perform* and those who watch and listen. Although this tendency is not unusual, it is deeply problematical in terms of what worship should be. Secondly, it reduces the relationship between the participants to a minimum. The interaction between the audience at a show or concert is usually very minimal and confined to a sharing of certain common rules of conduct on that premise. In the service participants do not relate only to those on the stage, but to each other as worshippers, even if different people of course may have different functions and tasks in the service.

The church service also differs from a performance because it is not only a fellowship during the service, but it presupposes the existence of a fellowship prior to the coming together for worship as well as the continuing existence of this fellowship after the service. This does not mean that the worship service is primarily a meeting place for old friends. It is important not to confuse intimacy with fellowship.[17] The fellowship of the service should be open enough to welcome the guest and stranger into its midst. At the same time, the gathering for worship presupposes the existence of a fellowship that gathers, and continues to exist after the service is ended. These two forms of the fellowship constitute each other:

---

17. In addition to Gordon Lathrop (see above), we also find a similar critique made by Patrick Keifert in *Welcoming the Stranger*. Keifert believes the intimacy ideal is problematical because the church service is a public and open event. This topic is explored in chapter 5.

the fellowship of the service needs the fellowship that is already there before the gathering. At the same time the fellowship that follows after the service is there only because the fellowship has been assembled for worship: it is through worship that the church becomes a fellowship in Christ, is maintained, and equipped to carry out its mission in the world.

The uniqueness of the Christian worship service is it not only points beyond itself into the future towards a different reality, but it is also in an incomplete manner, a sign and anticipation of what it signifies. Not only does it anticipate fellowship between God and humans, but it *is* also an encounter with God. It is not only a sign of fellowship, but *is* Christian fellowship. At the same time, it is *also* a sign that anticipates the consummation of God's kingdom. Part of the uniqueness of the church service is it simultaneously a sign, as well as an anticipation of the kingdom. While it is clear that the *relationship* between these aspects can be understood and emphasized differently. How we regard the relationship between the church service as a *realization* of something, and worship as a *sign* and *symbol* of something, is an important variable in understanding the relationship between the various Christian worship traditions.

Symbolic elements are not stressed so much in the more *low church* traditions. What is of more importance is the direct experience, be that of salvation, of God or Christian fellowship. This is especially true in Pentecostal and Charismatic circles where the immediate experience of the Spirit's presence is paramount. In more *high church* traditions the use of sign and symbol play a far greater role, both in terms of rituals and objects. The symbolic often gives emphasis to the invisible dimensions of Christian fellowship and points beyond the present experience to the future or transcendent.

Taken to their extreme, both high and low church traditions can lead us astray. An understanding of worship as a place where everything is realized and all can be experienced immediately, is not consistent with the fact that God's kingdom is not yet fully realized. An understanding of worship as something that only points to the beyond to the transcendent and future does not tally with the message that the kingdom of God is at hand, and that Jesus actually has promised to be present when people gather in his name. There would be very few examples of traditions in which the church service is either understood as a complete expression of a realized eschatology, or as being purely symbolic. Most traditions, however, would hold both of these elements together with different degrees of emphasis: Jesus is made present in worship, and worship points beyond to a future realization.

This duality of present and future should influence how signs in worship are shaped and performed. It is important to remember that a sign is not just purely symbolic, but is participatory in that which it signifies. As the eucharist anticipates the feast in the kingdom of God, it is important that it is celebrated in such a way that communicants have the feeling that they are really participating in a banquet meal. It is true that this is a meal with stylized and symbolic movements, but it still remains a meal of eating and drinking together. In many cases, the celebration of the eucharist has been reduced to a religious ritual that has very little resemblance of a meal. With baptism too, there can be so little use of water that the resemblance of washing can become very remote.[18]

To acknowledge the use of signs in worship means we must consciously be aware of elements that might inadvertently act as signs that *contradict* the Christian message. By our actions, we can effectively undermine the words spoken. For example, this can happen if a service endorses the discrimination or exclusion of a particular group of people. A worship service in which, e.g., people of color are not given access, acts as a sign against the teaching of the gospel that is the very basis of Christian worship. In a similar way this is true if the church service endorses a differentiated treatment of those present, e.g. on the basis of social position. In the Letter of James such a distinction between the rich and the poor is regarded as a form of unacceptable behavior:

> For if a person with gold rings and in fine clothes comes into your assembly, and if a poor person in dirty clothes also comes in, and if you take notice of the one wearing the fine clothes and say, "Have a seat here, please," while to the one who is poor you say, "Stand there," or, "Sit at my feet," have you not made distinctions among yourselves, and become judges with evil thoughts? . . . But if you show partiality, you commit sin and are convicted by the law as transgressors. (Jas 2:2–4, 9)

A worship service that should be a sign of the reality of God's kingdom can be a sign of the quite the reverse—a sign of the sin and injustice that

---

18. For Gordon Lathrop an important issue is that signs truly represent "wholeness and integrity." See for example Lathrop, *Holy Things*, 164–74.

still reigns in the world. The gospel is therefore a constant point of reference by which the church and its worship must be judged.[19]

WHAT SHOULD AND SHOULD NOT BE INCLUDED IN THE WORSHIP SERVICE

By suggesting the possibility of turning worship into a sign that might be in contrast to the gospel we have implicitly raised the issue of what *cannot* be included in Christian worship. A good place to start to answer this issue is to see the service as being gathered *in Jesus' name*. If the service takes place in a *different* name other than the name of Jesus, it is obviously something other than Christian worship. This can occur if the prayers and worship are addressed to someone other than God in Christ, or if the message preached is something other than the Christian gospel. Furthermore, in a Christian worship service, Christian prayer should not be combined with non-Christian forms of prayers or the Christian gospel with other conflicting messages. Such a contradictory message need not necessarily be an alternative *religious* message, but can also be a secular-based alternative to the Christian faith.[20] This is not to say everything that does not have an explicit reference to the gospel should be excluded from worship. On the contrary, the service is a place where everything that is part of the human experience can be included, so long as it serves the purpose of the service, i.e., to gather people in the name of Jesus.

To say that human experience can be included in the service includes those areas of human life perceived as difficult. This applies to all human suffering, pain, and desire, even when this takes the form of an experience of abandonment and doubt of God. The Psalms of the Old Testament show us that complaining to (and even accuse) God is part of the experience of a believer's relationship to God. The fact that life's problems do belong in the worship service, witnesses that *sinful people* have their place there—the Christian church is always a fellowship of sinners. Moreover, this fellowship is a community of sinners who also *confess* their sins, ask

---

19. In 1 Corinthians 11 Paul criticizes the church in Corinth for making a similar distinction in connection to the church's celebration of the eucharist—were some remained hungry while others are satiated. It is probable that Paul is making reference to this issue when he says: "Whoever, therefore, eats the bread or drinks the cup of the Lord in an unworthy manner will be answerable for the body and blood of the Lord" (v. 27).

20. This does not exclude the possibility of praying and sharing with people of other faiths. What I am referring to here is specifically within the context of Christian worship.

for forgiveness, and seek to turn away from evil, and do good. The service cannot be a place where people simply maintain or trivialize sin.

What unites people in worship is the belief in the one God who has revealed himself through Jesus Christ. In many other questions Christians may be divided e.g., political beliefs. Although political and social engagement is a natural consequence of Christian faith, Christians may support different political strategies and parties. Worship, on the other hand, should not be the place for the promotion of political ideologies or programs. Having said that, preaching can and should highlight the fact that the Christian message has political and social overtones and can comment on current or controversial topics.

Related to the question of what can be included in Christian worship, is the question of what *has to* be included in the service for it to be a gathering in the name of Jesus. The most obvious answer to this question is worship needs to include the means of grace in which Jesus is present by the Word and the sacraments. To clarify, it is important to make two modifications to this statement. Firstly, I will make a comment about the relation between the Word and the sacraments. On the one hand, I believe it would be inappropriate to make the sacraments a necessity for every worship service. On the other hand, the *Word* is a necessary component for every service. The way the Word is used may take different forms (readings, sermon, and so on), but it is not possible to talk of a Christian worship without the name of Jesus being mentioned. This does not mean that the eucharist (and for that matter baptism) does not naturally belong in the church's worship, although there may be differing opinions about their frequency. Even in churches where the eucharist is celebrated often, there is still room for church services where the Word alone can represent the presence of Jesus.

Secondly, the presence of Jesus cannot be separated from the people gathered. If there is not a congregation present there is no worship. It is not enough if people are only physically present. To be Christian worship, there need to be people who come together to actively seek God in Jesus' name. This means that *prayer* is an essential part of Christian worship. Prayer is essential, not primarily as individual prayer, but a shared activity where people pray together and shape the service as an act of common prayer. To illustrate, we can give the example of the difference between a church service and a church concert: the gospel may be clearly expressed by what is sung in a church concert (e.g., in a cantata by Bach).

The concert might even become an opportunity for individual devotion, but remains outside of the domain of common prayer and worship. When a cantata is performed as part of a service, however, it may become part of the worship of the church.[21]

Such an understanding of the basic elements of a church service can be summed up by Luther, who says in the church "nothing else may ever happen in it except that our dear Lord himself may speak to us through his holy Word and we respond to him through prayer and praise."[22]

Christian worship must be basically understood as an expression of God's encounter with people, while also being people's encounter with God. In worship both God and people are interacting, even if theologically speaking God's interaction is always understood as the basis. The duality of divine and human interaction in worship has often been interpreted by the distinction between the sacramental and the sacrificial dimensions of worship. While the sacramental dimension is God giving us his gifts, the sacrificial dimension is what we bring God in prayer, praise, and confession. Such a distinction is not to imply that it is possible to differentiate so easily between these two aspects of the church service. Although some parts of the service are easier to differentiate than others, both the sacramental and the sacrificial are present in all parts of the service. For example, the eucharist is God's gift and is also an offering of people's prayer and worship. Prayer means humans turning to God and is based upon what God has done for us and in us (cf. Rom 8:26).[23]

VARIOUS ELEMENTS OF THE WORSHIP SERVICE

In the previous paragraph I have asked: what are the *necessary* components of a church service, the absolute minimum that needs to be there in order to be Christian worship. In a similar vein, we also need to consider the *breadth* and *depth* of a worship service and how the various possible elements of a worship service are related to the fundamental character of worship as *gathering in the name of Jesus*. Without wanting to infer that this is an exhaustive list, in the following points I will now examine the

---

21. Many of the great works of sacred music were originally written to be part of the church service. To play these arrangements outside of the worship context is to change their purpose and original intent of meaning.

22. "Sermon at the Dedication of the Castle Church in Torgau" (1544), *Luther's Works*, vol. 51, 333 (WA 49:588).

23. Brunner, "Zur Lehre vom Gottesdienst," 192.

Worship: As Gathered in the Name of Jesus

possible breadth of elements in Christian worship. I will also show how these various elements can be related to the constituting role of worship in the life of the church.[24] None of these elements can stand *alone*. It is only when you put all the different elements together that we can truly have a church service. Although the order of service can be followed in very different ways, there appears to be some common patterns. Lathrop uses the term *ordo* to denote the meaningful pattern in the liturgy.[25]

Scripture Reading

An important element of Christian worship service is the reading of passages from the Bible. The reading of the Bible connects those gathered for worship to the story of Jesus' life, death, and resurrection. The four Gospels have a unique position as they most directly convey this story. Passages from other writings found in the New Testament also belong to the dissemination and understanding of this story. They create a bond to the original disciples that Jesus gave his promise to that he would be present when they gathered in his name. Passages from the Old Testament were read in the first Christian church services (1 Tim 4:13) and have their place in worship as they give a testimony of God's interaction with the people of Israel. Although the biblical texts were written by human authors, they are for those gathered understood as the word of God. By the Spirit, Jesus is made present through the words of the Bible.

Preaching

The message of the gospel is not only conveyed through the reading of biblical passages, but also through the preached exposition of the message. Preaching in a worship service may take many different forms, and even though preaching clearly has things in common with other forms of public speaking, it remains unique in the setting of a church service. In a service, the sermon has its centre in the biblical message of Jesus. Preaching applies the message of the biblical writings to a specific situ-

---

24. For a further discussion about the different elements of a church service see, for example Brunner, "Zur Lehre vom Gottesdienst" and the liturgical handbooks of Schmidt-Lauber et. al., *Handbuch der Liturgik,* and Bieritz, *Liturgik.*

25. "Meaning occurs through structure, by one thing set next to another. The scheduling of the *ordo,* the setting of one liturgical thing next to another in the shape of the liturgy, evokes and replicates the deep structure of biblical language, the use of the old to say the new by means of juxtaposition." Lathrop, *Holy Things,* 33.

ation and context. Those who preach, are not to do this for their own benefit, but are to preach a message on behalf of God to the assembled congregation. Preaching should not only apply to the individual, but to the congregation as a fellowship. The goal is not to make Christian preaching *original*, but to preach the same gospel which has been taught since the time of the apostles. Equally true, the gospel should be interpreted in new ways for different circumstances for those present. In this way preaching connects the Jesus of history to his second coming. It is a making present of Jesus in the now for all those gathered.

Other Spoken Words

Alongside Scripture reading and preaching, a church service may also have a number of different forms of speech. These can be pre-formulated in the shape of liturgy, or can be more improvised. A service may allow for different opportunities to respond to what has been preached, for example, through testimonies from church members. Clearly there is an overlap between the giving of testimonies and preaching. Spontaneous forms of speech that are charismatically inspired messages are described in the New Testament as "prophecy" (1 Cor 12:10, 14:1–25). The New Testament also assumes that speaking in tongues and the interpretation of tongues is a type of inspired utterance in Christian worship, although Paul does warn against excessive usage of this speech in services (1 Cor 14). Today these charismatic utterances are again more common in the worship influenced by the Pentecostal and Charismatic movements.

A particular form of speech are different forms of *performative words*. These words not only communicate a certain meaning, but are intended to call upon the presence and promises of God, his forgiveness and blessing. Examples include: the greeting at the beginning of a service, absolution after confession, the greeting of peace before the eucharist, and the blessing at the conclusion of the service. These performative words are usually given by the worship leader, but they may also be given by the congregation e.g. by wishing each other the peace before receiving the eucharist.

A special feature in many worship traditions is *antiphonal reading* (or singing), either between groups in the church or by the worship leader and congregation. Antiphonal reading expresses the unity of the fellowship in worship as there is no division between audience and performer.

Worship: As Gathered in the Name of Jesus

A particular form of interactive spoken word (refrain) is when the congregation responds to what is being taught or preached, for example, with a loud "Amen." In more informal worship forms the congregation may respond with spontaneous shouts and applause.

Another feature of many orders of services is creedal confession such as the Nicene or Apostles' Creed. This enables the congregation to speak out their common belief about God the Father and his deeds through the Son and in the Spirit.

Most services are likely to contain more prosaic forms of speech, for example, information and announcements about various aspects of church business. In the deepest theological sense, this part of the service shows the connection between worship and church life outside the service. When announcements are made about the forthcoming service this links the one service to the next in a continuous chain.

Prayers

Although the whole of the service really is to be understood as a prayer, it will also contain elements more explicitly set aside as prayer, where the church consciously turns to God. The prayers may be devised in advance, or they can be more improvised and spontaneous during parts of the service. They can be read by one person and followed by the congregation, or the congregation might say them together. The service might also include moments of silence, where each individual has the space to silently lift up their own prayers to God.

There are normally various types of prayers and petitions in the service. One form of prayer is the essential prayer of invocation of the presence of God. For example, a prayer in its Aramaic form that is preserved from the early church, is "Maranatha!" ("Our Lord come!" 1 Cor 16:22). This expression can be seen as both a plea for the presence of Jesus in the here and now, and a plea for his second coming to happen soon. This plea shows how the service brings these two forms of Jesus' presence together. Another form of prayer is that of supplication for the Lord to show his mercy as typical expressed in the cry "Kyrie eleision" ("Lord, have mercy," see e.g., Matt 17:15).

An indispensable form of prayer is that of *praise*. This is when the congregation glorifies God for who he is and what he has done. There are *prayers of lament* that cry out and complain before God for not intervening in the suffering of the individual and peoples. The service also has *penitentiary prayers* where the congregation confess their sins and seek absolution.

At the heart of the service are the prayers of *intercession*. This is when the congregation pleads on behalf of the world and the church in prayer to God. In many orders of worship a shorter or longer section is reserved for such intercessory prayers. These prayers may take the form of more general concerns and be linked to current affairs, for example, prayers of healing from illness. Intercessions can also correspond to prayers of thanksgiving for answers prayer.

Many Christian traditions practice *ministry prayer* as a part of the service. This is when individuals are prayed for, often with in conjunction with the laying on of hands. In the Pentecostal and Charismatic traditions this is particularly common where there is the expectation of immediate divine intervention, for example, to heal. This prayer may include the entire congregation, or it may be led by various ministry teams during the service with an invitation to come forward for ministry prayer.

In large sections of the Christian tradition, the Old Testament Psalms have played a central role in the church's life of prayer. The Psalms may be used as a text for common prayer, or are applied as a source of inspiration for personal devotions.

Singing

Singing is really nothing more than a particular form of what I have discussed in the previous two points. However, singing is such an important and notable element in almost all forms of Christian worship that it should be mentioned separately. Congregational singing creates a unique form of collective participation in prayer, praise and confession. Singing can also take the form of antiphony between groups in the church, for example, between the choir and the rest of the congregation, or between the church service leader/choir master and the congregation.[26]

---

26. In many churches singing is accompanied by instrumental music, for example, the organ. When used appropriately, a musical instrument is an important accompaniment for singing in the church. However, the musical instrumental should not be so dominant that the fellowship element of church singing is overshadowed. The potential benefits of singing unaccompanied can be shown by the worship life of such churches where, out of principle, they have renounced instrumental music in worship, which has in return helped develop a special form of congregational singing (e.g., the American denomination Churches of Christ).

Worship: As Gathered in the Name of Jesus

Silence

A common element in many orders of services is silence. The time allowed for silence, be it seconds or minutes gives people space for private prayer and reflection. Silence can remind people that the service is not just about being with other people, but about being with God. Silence may provide an opportunity to call to mind the presence of God. There is a biblical precedent that God is not only present in words and actions, but also in silence (1 Kgs 19:12–13; Isa 30:15). However, the use of silence should not be evoked in such a way in the service as to move from collective worship to individual devotion.

Signs and Symbols

The most profound rituals and signs of the service are found in baptism and the eucharist. This is evidenced by the fact that the sacraments not only point toward another reality, but those who receive the sacraments become a part of this reality. Through the use of water in baptism we are incorporated into fellowship with the crucified and risen Christ. In the eucharist, the bread and wine become Christ made present in body and blood. The baptismal and eucharistic sacraments are not silent rituals and signs, but are celebrated with word and prayer. Through the combination of words, prayers, and rituals the sacraments signify and make present the triune God in a profound way.[27]

The worship service can also have a variety of other signs and symbols that do not have the same sacramental characteristics of baptism and the eucharist. What these signs and symbols have in common is they support and reiterate what else happens in the service. As a rule they are much more than illustrations, but integrated elements in the service. Together with what is said in word and prayer they lift the congregation together in their worship of God.

Many of the signs and symbols in the service are performed by using only the body. When the congregation stands together, this expresses that they are standing in the presence of God. When kneeling, they are bowing before God. When folding hands together, they are focusing in on prayer. With lifted hands, they are praising God in worship or reaching out to God in need. When signing with the cross, they are marking themselves and others with the cross of their Lord. When giving a handshake or hug,

---

27. See chapter 2 concerning baptism and the eucharist.

they are expressing the fellowship of the believers. When performing the laying on hands, they are evoking the Spirit in a special way for the blessing of a ministry. In some traditions the provocation or ecstasy of the congregation is seen as being an expression of the presence of the Spirit.[28]

Other signs may require the use of one or more material elements. This is true of water for foot washing, incense to accompany worship, and bells for the call to prayer. In the Orthodox tradition, icons play a central role as a medium of worship and devotion. In some traditions the use of holy water serves a reminder of baptism.

The use of clothing and textiles are also signs used in the worship service. A white baptismal dress is a sign of what happens in baptism, and a stole around the neck indicates that you have been given a specific ministry in the church. At the same time, these signs are potentially problematic in they run the risk of dividing the church into two: those *officiate* (clergy) and those who *participate* (laity).

Some objects have a purely practical function, but through time they have taken on the character of a sign. For example, this is true of lectionaries, hymnals and liturgical books, chalice and paten, baptismal font and jug. The fact that such objects have both a practical and a symbolic function is obviously something that has to be taken into account when designing them. This is a particular challenge in the face of the trivialization that often characterizes with the use of new practical aids such as the printed order of service or video projector.

Sacrifice

An understanding of the worship service as sacrificial offering is one of the most disputed debates in the history of theology (primarily in regards to the eucharist). What is agreed, however, is the Christian church does not offer a sacrifice in the same manner as the Old Testament temple worship. Rather, it is based upon Jesus' one sacrifice that occurred once and for all (Heb 7:27, 9:12, 10:10). The debate about the Roman Catholic doctrine of the mass as a sacrifice is indication of the differing views about how the sacrifice of Jesus is made present in the eucharist. The reformers criticized this understanding of the eucharist as it seemed to imply a repeated offer-

---

28. For example, moving and crying aloud in the Laestadian tradition in northern Scandinavia (Finnish: *liikutukset*) cf. Gjessing, "Laestadianism," 193; and the kind of shaking and falling in the Spirit of the so-called "Toronto Blessing" of the 1990s, cf. Poloma, *Main Street Mystics*.

ing of Christ's sacrifice.[29] What remains uncontroversial, however, is to see worship as a sacrifice of praise where the church presents itself as an offering of thanks to God.[30] The eucharist and the other parts of the service can be interpreted in these terms, even if in some parts of the service the sacrificial element is more concretely expressed. This occurs when the bread and wine—produce from the earth and refined by people—is lifted up for use in the eucharistic meal and when money or other goods are collected for various projects in or outside of the church. This last type of offering expresses, in a unique way that the church does not worship only for its own sake, but for the sake of the world. Offerings of money and goods thus become both a sign and a concrete expression of what it signifies.

Music and Art

Besides being a vehicle for words through singing, music also has its own special place in the church service. Even though acoustic music is devoid of words and prayers, it can create an atmosphere that complements and highlights words and prayers. The same applies to other art forms like painting, architecture, textiles, and dance. The textual and spoken can be viewed as a form of art, for example, hymns, texts, and liturgy. These should all work towards the highest possible standard, literary and artistically speaking. The sermon may be seen at its peak, as a form of literary art, even if it is not the only yardstick by which it should be measured. The church house too, with its architecture and decor can speak of an art that bears witness to God's beauty and presence.[31]

---

29. A result of the various ecumenical conversations between Roman Catholics and Protestants has shown that the seemingly polarized positions are not as insurmountable as originally believed. Harding Meyer argues that despite these different theological positions, it is still possible to come to a basic theological consensus about the doctrine of the eucharistic, including the meaning of the eucharistic sacrifice. Meyer, "Der sich abzeichnende evangelisch/katholische Konsens."

30. As Melanchthon explains in Apology to the Augsburg Confession (Apol. art. XXIV, para. 16–65), what is required is a fundamental distinction between the two types of offerings. Kolb and Wengert, *Book of Concord*, 260–69. Melanchthon distinguishes between "the atoning sacrifice, that is, a work of satisfaction for guilt and punishment" and the sacrifice of praise "rendered by those who have already been reconciled as a way for us to give thanks or express gratitude" (para. 19).

31. Brunner, "Zur Lehre vom Gottesdienst," 313–32.

The fact that art has its place in the worship service is not only for practical reasons, but is grounded upon theological reasons as well. We are exhorted to bring our best in worship, as reflected in the New Jerusalem: "People will bring into it the glory and the honor of the nations" (Rev 21:26). Through its multiplicity and richness of interpretation, art has the distinctive ability to convey the understanding of worship as sign. What is required of art within a worship setting is what it represents must be consistent with the message that is being communicated and witnessed.

THE TIME, PLACE AND FORM OF THE WORSHIP SERVICE

In order to worship it is necessary to gather at a certain time and at a certain place. In principle it can be at any time or place, even if not all times and places are equally convenient. When worship is celebrated regularly, it usually has a certain pattern in both terms of time and place. Some churches hold their services in premises which are also used for other purposes, which was the pattern in the early church. When a church building or another venue is designed primarily for the worship service, this allows for the possibility to design it in a particular way relevant for the service, e.g. including a pulpit and a communion table. When it comes to decorating the room this varies greatly between Christian traditions. While some traditions would want to keep the church building as simple as possible in order not to draw attention away from the message, other traditions will use images and other forms of art to highlight the different aspects of what the service signifies. The design of the church building involves fixtures and equipment as well as the architectural layout inside and out.

In the same way as elements of the church service can be signs that contradict the gospel, so the design of the place of worship can create difficulties too. For example, the interior can create divisions between different groups in the congregation, whether this is the clergy who are separated from the laity, or by reinforcing societal divisions by reserving special pews for the rich.

The regularity of the worship service also leads to the establishment of fixed worship times. Early in the history of the church *Sunday* was reserved as the day in the week that corresponded with the day of the week when the Lord Jesus rose from the grave.[32] Many Christian traditions fol-

---

32. This is already documented as early as the year 150 by Justin Martyr's First Apology. *First and Second Apologies*, chapter 67, p. 71.

Worship: As Gathered in the Name of Jesus

low a pattern where worship services vary according to their place within the liturgical year.

Over time, as often happens, places and times where church services are celebrated can take on the character as holy places or holy days. In the New Testament, however, holiness is related to the holy God and those who share in God's holiness.[33] Thus, the church service becomes a place of sanctification where people meet the holy God and share in his holiness. As a place for such an occasion the space for worship deserves respect. For example, it should not be used for anything that contradicts true worship. This does not mean that place of worship has any inherent sanctity devoid of the *communion of saints* as gathered.

The same can be said of Sunday as a *holy day*. Sunday does not have any special holiness other than it is a day set apart for church worship. This idea is encapsulated by the classical view of Luther's explanation of what it means to hallow the day of rest as found in the Little Catechism: "We are to fear and love God, so that we do not despise preaching or God's Word, but instead keep that Word holy and gladly hear and learn it."[34]

We find differences in the actual format of the worship service. This applies to what aspects are emphasized and how they are formatted. The reasons for the differences are partly due to the various theological and ecclesial traditions. It is also due to governing context in which worship takes place and the people assembled. This vast variation should not be seen as a problem, but more as a richness and resource. This does not mean that everything is just as good: traditions and specific church services should be assessed critically. To do this, it is necessary to consider the theological basis for worship, the context in which it takes place, and the people who attend the church service. It is a confirmation, enrichment and a challenge to being aware of the fact that other Christians also gather for worship in different ways, in the name of Jesus.

Although a worship service can be shaped in many different ways, it is clear that the actual service must be ordered with a specific and set pattern in mind. Notwithstanding the variations and occasional exceptions, a church service should contain the minimum of coherence and continuity. Too overly restrictive and spontaneous forms of worship can inhibit worship that is truly alive.

33. See chapter 2 for a description of the church as holy.
34. Kolb and Wengert, *Book of Concord*, 352.

The worship service has always included elements and patterns that exist (or have existed) in other contexts. In particular, some aspects have been adopted from the public sphere: public buildings, theaters, lecture halls/classrooms, concert halls, etc. Therefore, it is not uncommon that there is a correlation between the development of the idiom of church service and developments found in contemporary society. For example, it is usual for the sermon to be influenced by the general ideals of public speech, even if it preserves its own genre-related bias. Likewise, it is only natural for church music to be influenced by the styles found in contemporary music.

To be influenced by and adopting contemporary forms of expression, is not only a cultural necessity, but is theological necessary. This can be seen from a theology of creation perspective: the church is part of the created world and carries the world with it in its encounter with God in worship. This can also be seen from the idea of church as being sent into the world. To use the forms that are completely foreign to the culture would shut the church off from the world, rather than making itself available to the world.[35]

The fact that the church by its worship uses forms that are also found in other places, does not mean what happens in the church service is the same as in other contexts where these similar forms are used. Although the service might have some elements in common with the concert or lecture, this does not mean it *is* a concert or a lecture. When using forms found in other contexts these must be done with an awareness that they are lifted up unto *another* plane. A worship service is not a religious form of a theatrical play, concert, or lecture, but a very special kind of event. The church may well make use of the theater, concert, or lecture influences in their activities and programs, but these measures never *replace* the worship service. This also applies to the teaching aspect of a church's life. For example, it is a questionable practice when children are taken out of worship and offered in its place something that normally happens in a school.[36]

---

35. See chapter 4 for a discussion about the relationship between the church and the world.

36. The majority of *Sunday schools* include elements of worship (e.g., song, prayer, and preaching) that would make it natural to interpret them as a worship service for children. If this is so, then the term *school* creates a difficulty, because what is happening here is something more than that of a school setting. In other words, the term school is to misrepresent what is actually happening, namely worship.

Even if worship shares various elements with other spheres, they are shaped in a certain way by being part of the service. A sermon has much in common with other forms of public speaking, but is also something unique and has on its own form. Likewise, church music will have much in common with other forms of music, but it is still shaped by the fact that it is used in a worship service. The challenge lies in trying to distinguish between what *has to be* different, and what has *become* different in virtue of a particular church tradition. The *otherness* of a worship service must not be over-emphasized in such a way that legitimizes a separation from the culture at large. One should be particularly wary of archaic forms which live on by virtue of their own value without having any contemporary relevance to justify it. We should also be sensitive to certain cultural forms (e.g., forms of music) that appear to be more religious than other forms. Even if some forms have a long tradition in the church, this does not give them a monopoly at the exclusion of other forms of expression that are for example more common in the contemporary culture.

THE WORSHIP SERVICE AS A RITUAL

A characteristic of the church service is that it *repeated* again and again. This creates a pattern and regularity in the service, even if the details and forms might vary from time to time. This means that the service can be understood as a *ritual*. As a ritual this means the church service can be scrutinized by using general theories of ritual. Research about rituals has become a rapidly growing interdisciplinary field of research which has contributed to an increased understanding of church worship.[37] Although worship from a theological perspective is unique compared to other human rituals, it is nonetheless a human phenomenon with clear similarities with other rituals.

When we speak of worship as ritual, this includes not only the more formal and liturgical order of services, but also more informal worship forms which often have the same ordering and contain largely the same elements over and over again.[38] This illustrates how, amongst other things,

---

37. See for example, Heimbrock, *Gottesdienst*, who interprets Christian worship through theoretical perspectives using religious studies, social anthropology, sociology of religion, psychology of religion and pedagogy. A more practical theological perspective of ritual theory can be seen in, for example, Modéus, *Mänsklig gudstjänst*. Albrecht, *Rites in the Spirit,* gives a theory of ritual approach to Pentecostal and Charismatic worship.

38. The shape of ritual is different in cultures than emphasize the oral tradition over

ritual primary takes place, not within books or fixed forms, but within the lives of those who partake in the service. The *rubric book* is nothing other than a tool for the ritual. To perform a ritual, by its virtue of being a ritual, is not to preclude spontaneity, improvisation and variation.

To make a corrective to a one-sided cognitive approach to worship, we can apply a ritual theoretical perspective. Such a cognitive approach is particularly widespread within the Protestant tradition, where learning and cognitive understanding has often been the central focus of worship. To understand the church service as a ritual includes far more than just the cognitive, however. Among other aspects, worship as a ritual:

- Has a special ability to create structure and meaning. As transcending the framework of everyday life and gives meaning and structure to everyday life.
- Creates and maintains fellowship between those participating.
- Symbolizes what cannot be fully expressed through words. The ritual carries the sign character of the worship.
- Incorporates not only humanity's intellectual faculties, but also the body.
- Creates a space where people are opened up to have religious *experiences*.[39]

Ritual theory not only helps us to understand what happens in a church service, but it also might make contribution to how the service could be shaped. Not least, it could provide a corrective to the idea that the church service that is not fully comprehendible has no value. This is not to say that cognitive is of no value in the church service. For a ritual to be part of worship means it is interpreted and conveyed in light of a Christian understanding of God and his work in Jesus Christ. This does not prevent the ritual from being *open* for individual interpretation, as not everything is overtly defined. At the same time, there is good reason to caution

---

the written tradition. For example, Pentecostal and Charismatic worship embodies an oral worship culture, where the ritual is internalized in the worshippers rather than codified in written text. Cartledge, *Encountering the Spirit*, 60–61.

39. Heimbrock, *Gottesdienst*, 8 (our translation): "In my opinion, it seems to be meaningful to ask how worship as a ritual, not only provides a space for learning, but also has a certain anthropological, inner psychological and interactive role to play, where people can relate inner experiences and collective interpretive patterns to understand these experiences in relation to each other."

against a *ritualism* which makes the implementation of the ritual an end in itself devoid of understanding and participation. This overemphasis was one of the issues confronted by the reformers who believed that worship should be in the vernacular and not in Latin.

THE WORSHIP SERVICE AS A PLACE TO EXPERIENCE GOD

It is worth making some remarks about the church service as a place of religious *experience*. This is an issue not only of interest in ritual theory, but is in the highest degree, a theological issue. The claim that Jesus is present when people gather in his name (Matt 18:20) raises the question of whether divine presence can be *experienced*, and if so how? These questions are addressed in very different ways according to different theologians and Christian traditions.[40]

Within Pentecostal and Charismatic Christianity there is often an understanding that the experience of God's presence is a relatively direct experience of the Spirit's work, both within the individual and as a manifested presence in the worship service. The extended time of singing during worship is designed to make worshippers receptive to the experience of God's presence.[41] The value of this view is it takes seriously the experience of the presence of God as something concrete. Its difficulty lies in "the collapse of worship into immanentism" as James H. S. Steven has observed in his analysis of Charismatic worship.[42] Namely, it confuses personal feeling and ambiance with the presence of God.

At the other end of the scale, we find the approach that emphasizes the *sacramental* character of God's presence. This stresses the objective dimension of God's presence through visible means. Thus, we are relieved from the striving for subjective spiritual experiences, and can have peace of mind in something outside of oneself.[43] The danger of such an accentuation of the objective may be that it binds God's presence so closely to

---

40. Matthias Zeindler gives an extensive overview in his book on the experience of God in the church. Zeindler argues that the local congregation and its social interaction is the primary place to experience the triune God. Zeindler, *Gotteserfahrung*.

41. Albrecht, *Rites in the Spirit*, 237–51. "At least in part, the apparent goal of the worship service is to allow the worshipers to have a heightened sense of the presence of the divine" (ibid., 239).

42. Steven, *Worship in the Spirit*, 194.

43. An example of this view can be found in Ola Tjørhom's "materialist spirituality." Tjørhom, *Embodied Faith*.

the physical reality of the sacraments that the opportunity of experiencing of God becomes problematical—where we are not to experience, but are simply called to *believe* in God's presence (in the Word and the sacraments). This too is a type of immantentism, as the experience of one's own faith is the closest we can come to experiencing God. However, this is not a necessary consequence of a sacramentally oriented spirituality: in many cases the practice of a sacramental understanding of God's presence is combined with a more mystical understanding of God experience as mediated through prayer and contemplation.[44]

THE WORSHIP SERVICE OF THE REAL CHURCH

The understanding of the worship service should be, above all, anchored ecclesiologically: we cannot understand worship correctly unless it is founded upon a comprehensive understanding of the identity and mission of the church. At the same time the worship service plays a central role in this understanding: to be a Christian church is to gather in Jesus' name. The church service is not just one of many activities of the church's life. It does not represent just one sector or area of activity, but is itself the unifying point in the life of the church. The church service is the church in its compacted form.

An ecclesiological basis for understanding the church service is not just a general principle, but is to say that the worship service should be rooted in the actual church as it exists in a certain time and space. It is not a congregation in a general sense that comes together to worship, but the actual and real church. This means that the daily life of the congregation and its members should be understood in light of the Word, and brought to worship and lifted up in prayer to God. The church service will be characterized, not only by timeless theological truths, but by specific people that make up the congregation, and by a specific context to which they are a part of.

A critical issue is to consider whether the church service gives room to and expresses what it means to be a Christian church in each specific place. There is, for example, something wrong if diaconal ministry is something that takes place in all other contexts, but does not have its roots in the church's worship service. There is something amiss when children and young adults do not have their place in the church service.

---

44. Cunningham and Egan, *Christian Spirituality*, 123–42.

Worship: As Gathered in the Name of Jesus

There is something amiss if the church service is a place where only a few are active, while most retreat into being passive spectators. Finally, there is something amiss if the church service is only an internal affair for a particular group, which is not open to the outside world.

This is partly a question of whether the actual members of the congregation are allowed to express their faith and concerns, or whether it is monopolized by certain groups in the church. However, there is also the issue about the various aspects of the church's identity and calling is expressed in worship. In the church service the church remembers its calling and its destiny. The church should also recognize that it is not fully what it is destined to be, but it exists in the tension between the old and new, in an *already and not yet* state. To see the church service as a means to glorify or justify itself, is obviously a contradiction in terms to what the church service should actually be about. Instead, each worship service should have elements of self-examination and confession. The church service should not only reflect the actual church, but should confront the church by God's calling and God's grace.

The acting subject of the worship service is, theologically speaking, the church as a fellowship. However, in order for the fellowship to worship, some form of leadership is required. This leadership is more than a role as moderator or chairman, but is about leading the congregation in their prayers, adoration and worship, preaching and celebrating the eucharist. This task has often been assigned to a particular person who is called and ordained.[45] This means that the basic function of Christian leadership is to execute the central aspects of the church's worship. This is shown, for example, by exhortation to the church leader Timothy: "Give attention to the public reading of scripture, to exhorting, to teaching" (1 Tim 4:13).

To lead the church in worship does not mean the congregation is passive under the leadership of the pastor or the priest. In the New Testament we get a glimpse of the first Christian worship service that is clearly a place where everyone contributes in their own way. For example, concerning what happened when the church in Corinth came together, Paul writes: "When you come together, each one has a hymn, a lesson, a revelation, a tongue, or an interpretation. Let all things be done for building up" (1 Cor 14:26). This is not only an example from the early church,

---

45. See the discussion in chapter 6.

but also corresponds to a basic understanding of those who worship at the church service as being those who come together in Jesus' name. Worship that reduces the congregation to that of spectators is deeply problematical. It is also important to point out that participation and involvement can take many forms. For example, to listen attentively to the sermon, praying along with the prayers and singing along to the hymns are all outlets of active participation.

The Christian fellowship lives in the constant alternating motion of assembling and sending. Whatever happens in the church service should not remain there, but is sent out into the world. Therefore, the natural conclusion of a worship service is that of *sending*: from coming together in the name of Jesus to the sending out in Jesus' name in everyday life. Faith and the presence of God are not left in the church building, but carried out into the world. In its most profound way, it is God who sends us out. During the church service the church is being prepared to be sent out by God and to do God's mission. A church in mission is also a worshipping church. The church worshipping is also a church being sent out in mission.

9

The Universal Church as the Fellowship of Local Churches

A*n understanding of the* church as a fellowship of people who gather in the name of Jesus, means the local congregation is the basic form of the church. The congregation is the place for the presence of the risen Christ and the anticipation of the kingdom of God. This is to say each congregation is truly and fully church. This does not mean that denominations or broader ecumenical fellowship of churches do not have any theological significance. The fellowship of the church is not only a fellowship within a certain congregation; it is also the fellowship between congregations.

In fact, each congregation is not the only place where the risen Jesus is present, or the only place that anticipates the eschatological fellowship. The presence of Jesus, through the Spirit, is not restricted to any one place. He is present *everywhere* and *at all times* whenever people gather in his name. The church is not just local, it is also *universal*.

THE UNIVERSAL CHURCH

The idea of the church's universality is readily interpreted by some as denoting the church's invisibility. While the local congregation is a comparatively specific entity, the universal church is far more complex to recognize. The difficulty of grasping the universal church in its totality does not mean it is invisible. The fact that something is impossible to fully comprehend or delineate, does not mean that it is not tangible or possible to experience. Understood as the sum of all the various congregations gathered in Jesus' name, the universal church is concrete reality, even though no one except God will ever have full overview of this reality.

The universal church is no less visible than any other universal variables such as "humanity." As the sum of all human beings and human societies, humanity is a concrete and empirical reality, even though no one could ever have a complete overview of what this term really refers to.

The idea of the universal church is not only an idea about universality in space (in the whole world), but it also concerns time, i.e. it includes Christian churches of the past and potentially of the future too. Christians that gather in the name of Jesus *in the now,* also belong to the same universal church of the *past,* and to those who will gather in the *future* until the final consummation. Therefore, the universal church is an entity that remains open to historical investigation.

The understanding of the universal church as a fellowship of congregations does not mean that the universal church is nothing more than the sum of its parts (in the sense of a pure multiplication of all local churches). A theological understanding of the church also includes the notion of the *unity* of the church. This notion of unity is immediately contradicted by the reality that the church is characterized by splits and divisions. It is therefore important to emphasize that the church's unity is rooted Christologically and eschatologically. The church is one because it is the same Christ who is right in the middle of every fellowship gathered in his name, even if these communities do not fully acknowledge one another. Each congregation in their own location anticipate and share the same eschatological fellowship between God and humanity in the kingdom.

The fact that unity is Christologically and eschatologically rooted is not to say that it only belongs to the future, or is just a form of pure, idealistic unity. The church's unity should be understood as analogous to the church's holiness.[1] It is something the church fully partakes of by its relationship to Jesus and the forthcoming kingdom of God. At the same time the church is called to realize this holiness in here and now: The church is holy, and is therefore called to be holy; the church is one, and is therefore called to realize oneness.

Church unity and catholicity are integrally connected.[2] As there is only one church, the church cannot be limited to a particular place or a particular time. The one church is the church that has been in the world since the time of Jesus and continues to gather in Jesus' name at different

---

1. For a presentation concerning the holiness of the church see chapter 2.
2. For a description of the church as catholic see chapter 4.

The Universal Church as the Fellowship of Local Churches

places and at different times. On the one hand, unity and catholicity are attributes of the universal church. On the other hand, unity and catholicity are attributes of the local congregation. As the place where Jesus Christ is present and where the eschatological communion between God and humanity is anticipated, the local congregation manifests the one, catholic church.

However, this understanding of the local church as being a manifestation of the one, catholic church is threatened if this church does not also recognize other churches as being manifestations of the same reality—and allowing this recognition to have practical outcomes. Just as an individual is not called to be a Christian alone, so this is true of churches who meet in Jesus' name—they are not called to be a church alone, but churches together as part of the church universal. To be part of the one, catholic church is thus to live in community with other churches that are part of the same universal church. The universal church is more than the *sum* of the churches in different places and different times—it also is *the relationship and fellowship* between these churches. As the church is a pilgrim church in this world moving towards its eschatological destiny, to a greater or lesser degree, this community will always be an imperfect community—often characterized by disunity.

Miroslav Volf points out that an eschatological definition of the church's catholicity makes it possible to bring together the church's unity with the unity of humanity, and the whole of creation within the final consummation. In the words of Volf: "The catholicity of the entire people of God is the ecclesial dimension of the eschatological fullness of salvation for the entirety of created reality."[3]

When the church is said to be catholic in the here and now, it is in anticipation of this being fulfilled. As anticipation, the catholicity of the church is imperfect and incomplete because there is a difference between eschatological and historical ecclesiology.[4] Volf stresses that catholicity is not something that just applies to the universal church, but also applies to the local congregation. Catholicity is given in the local congregation as anticipation of the consummated fellowship of the kingdom. At the same time, catholicity is expressed in relationship to other churches: "One

---

3. Volf, *After Our Likeness*, 267.
4. Ibid., 267–68.

mark of the catholicity of the local church involves its *relations to other churches*."[5]

In the New Testament, the idea of the universal church is not given a lot of prominence. When the Bible speaks of *church* (*ekklesia*), this is principally with reference to the local churches in different parts of the Roman Empire. Church unity is chiefly that of unity and cohesion within the local congregation (Rom 12:16, 15:5; 1 Cor 1:10; 2 Cor 13:11; Phil 2:2, 4:2). Some passages do seem to use the term in a more general sense, for example, when Paul talks about having persecuted "the church of God" (1 Cor 15:9; Gal. 1:13; cf. Phil 3:6). The idea of the same church existing in different places is portrayed by Paul when he greets the local congregation in Corinth: "To the church of God that is in Corinth, to those who are sanctified in Christ Jesus, called to be saints, together with all those who in every place call on the name of our Lord Jesus Christ, both their Lord and ours" (1 Cor 1:2).[6]

The understanding of different churches as being part of one, universal church is also shown by the way Paul maintains communication between churches. This was true of the particular churches Paul had founded, but clearly he also presupposes fellowship between these churches and the churches that he had not founded, such as in Jerusalem and Rome. For example, the relationship between these churches is illustrated by the gift that Paul gathered for the church in Jerusalem (Acts 24:17; Rom 15: 25–28; 1 Cor 16:1; 2 Cor 8–9; Gal 2:10). Paul also shows how the local congregation is part of a common Christian tradition, for example when he writes in 1 Corinthians 7:17: "This is my rule in all the churches" (cf. 1 Cor 4:17). Paul's own ministry, and not least by his own letter writing, appears to have had a unifying function between the churches—a function that his letters continue to have well after his death. For Paul, the communion between the churches was something concrete and real. This was not some sort of abstract notion of a universal church, rather it is a concrete fellowship between the churches. The universal church is nothing less than those "who are sanctified in Christ Jesus, called to be saints, together with all those who in every place call on the name of our Lord Jesus Christ, both their Lord and ours" (1 Cor 1:2).

---

5. Ibid., 274.

6. See Hvalvik, "All Those Who in Every Place," and "The Churches of the Saints." The following paragraph is also attributed to Hvalvik.

The Universal Church as the Fellowship of Local Churches

The idea of the different churches being part of a larger community is also reflected in the post-Apostolic writings from the end of the first century and beginning of the second century. In one of the early Christian writings, the Martyrdom of Polycarp, one local congregation greets other churches in the following way: "The Church (*ekklesia*) of God which sojourns in Smyrna, to the Church of God which sojourns in Philomelium, and to all the sojournings of the Holy Catholic Church in every place. 'Mercy, peace and love' of God the Father, and our Lord Jesus Christ be multiplied."[7]

At the beginning of the second century we can already see how *bishops* were given a decisive role for maintaining the unity of the church (with a focus being primarily the unity within each congregation). By the beginning of the third century, Cyprian saw the bishop as having a more clearly defined role in protecting the unity of the universal church, i.e. the unity between the local churches. When bishops recognize one another and are in fellowship with each other, this unifies the church as a communion.[8]

CHURCH SPLITS AND MOVES TOWARDS UNITY

From the very early beginnings of the history of the church, there was both unity and division. Ecumenical councils helped to clarify the basis for continued unity, but these councils also led to splits between those who did and did not agree with the councils' decisions. In the early church the issue of Christology and the doctrine of God were serious divisive controversies. As a result of differences within Western and Eastern church traditions, including disagreements over the role of the bishop of Rome (the pope) in the universal church, the unity of fellowship eventually broke down during the eleventh century between the Roman Catholic Church in the West and the Orthodox churches of the East ("the Great Schism" 1054). In the sixteenth century the Reformation led to a major split in the Western church. This in turn, led to the formation of a number of new churches. Most notably in Protestantism, these splits have continued to occur resulting in vast variety of different denominations. In the present context, what distinguishes these different denominations from each other can vary immensely (teaching, tradition, practice, ordained

---

7. *Apostolic Fathers*, vol. II, 312.
8. Bakke, "Episcopal Ministry."

ministry, culture, language, etc.). There is also a variance to what degree these denominations choose to recognize and cooperate with each other.

Church history has not only been marked by splits, but also by the various attempts to create unity. During the twentieth century, for example, there was the emergence of a comprehensive ecumenical movement. This movement has continued to grow in influence and has led to ecumenical organizations and collaborative efforts with several participating denominations, the largest being the World Council of Churches (WCC, founded 1948).[9] Churches have also drawn closer to each other through bi-lateral conversations about doctrine. In many instances, such conversations have led to the withdrawal of previously held condemnations. In some cases, conversations have led to closer fellowship and even mergers between churches.[10] For example, the Church of Norway has gained a closer relationship with other Lutheran churches through the Lutheran World Federation, has established communion with the Methodist Church, with Reformed churches (through the Leuenberg Concord), and with some Anglican churches (via the Porvoo Agreement).

It is not difficult to see how historical and social processes have contributed to shaping the modern ecumenical movement. For example, we can see how globalization has led groups into closer ties with each other, which previously had been relatively separated from each other. We can see that churches have come together as a result of secularization and a weakened position in many societies.[11] The basis of this rapprochement has been a shared understanding of important theological and ecclesiological themes. A fundamental conviction being that unity belongs to the identity of the church, and that unity that cannot be realized by one church alone, but only through churches together. Another important aspect that has come as a result of rapprochement is that church unity is necessary, not only for the sake of the church, but also for the sake of the church's witness in the world. According to John 17:21, Christian unity is the starting point for the world to believe that God sent Jesus.

---

9. For an overview of the ecumenical movement see FitzGerald, *Ecumenical Movement*.

10. Tjørhom, *Kirkens enhet*, 26–51.

11. In 1967 Peter Berger pointed out that sociological factors undergirded the modern ecumenical movement and rapprochement led to churches became more and more like each other, for example, through the development of central bureaucratic structures. *Sacred Canopy*, 141–45.

The Universal Church as the Fellowship of Local Churches

How we perceive the goal of the ecumenical work lingers as an unresolved question in the ecumenical movement, i.e., how we think the unity we seek should be shaped. Is it sufficient that we simply recognize each other as Christian brothers and sisters, or must there be greater recognition that will lead to a full-organizational integration? Is the goal of unity to merge all Christian denominations into one large church, or are we content with more modest goals?

What remains important to elucidate is church unity is not the same as uniformity. On the contrary, the diversity of Christian traditions is a blessing and expresses the varsity of the gifts of the Spirit. At the same time, not all forms of diversity are consistent with the unity of the church. To recognize any kind of ecclesial pluralism and simply accept the status quo is a contradiction to the call to realize the unity of the church.[12]

How the goal of the efforts for unity might be conceived can be summed up by the renowned General Assembly of the WCC declaration made at New Delhi, 1961:

> We believe that the unity which is both God's will and his gift to his Church is being made visible as all in each place who are baptized into Jesus Christ and confess him as Lord and Saviour are brought by the Holy Spirit into one fully committed fellowship, holding the one apostolic faith, preaching the one Gospel, breaking the one bread, joining in common prayer, and having a corporate life reaching out in witness and service to all and who at the same time are united with the whole Christian fellowship in all places and all ages in such wise that ministry and members are accepted by all, and that all can act and speak together as occasion requires for the tasks to which God calls his people.[13]

This declaration stresses that unity is something visible, but does not focus on the organizational. Instead, it stresses the importance of a "fully committed fellowship" in common witness, worship and service.

Since this declaration was made there have been various proposed models to try and work with the correlation between unity and diversity.[14] The model "unity in reconciled diversity" seeks to give room to a certain degree of ecumenical diversity, while also wanting to see a reconciling

---

12. Tjørhom, *Kirkens enhet*, 52–73.
13. *New Delhi Speaks*, 55.
14. For an overview of different ecumenical models see Meyer, *That All May Be One*.

process between the churches at an institutional and structural level.[15] In the context of doctrinal differences the use of the concept "differentiated consensus" confirms what is essentially agreed while acknowledging the remaining disagreements, it makes a distinction between what is church dividing and what is not.[16] Such a model was used in the *Joint Declaration on the Doctrine of Justification* between the Roman Catholic Church and the Lutheran World Federation.

UNITY BETWEEN LOCAL CHURCHES

The efforts of the ecumenical movement are mainly related to the relationship between various denominations and confessional traditions. However, this issue is only one aspect of the wider question of unity between local churches within the framework of the universal church. This requires us to consider how the unity between congregations and local churches within the same denomination is to be theologically interpreted. Is this just a practical matter, or does it have a deeper theological meaning? In light of this, how should we understand the ecclesiological status of denominations and regional churches?

Indeed, within some denominations the relationship between local churches is a matter of great theological significance. Not least, this is true of the Roman Catholic Church and the Orthodox churches, where the unity of local churches via bishops is essential to ecclesial identity. In Protestant traditions, due to the emphasis placed upon the local congregation as the primary form of church, theological reflection concerning the connection between congregations within the denomination or the confessional tradition is usually not fully developed. A reason for simply taking these connections for granted is the fact that existing ecclesial structures are often the result of historical and political processes that are dominated by interests other than just theological ones. For example, this is true of many former and existing state churches.

The lack of such theological reflection is often manifested in a denomination's inability to deal with internal conflicts and controversies. While developing an ecumenical mindset towards other churches, the same ecumenical principles are not necessarily applied within internal

---

15. Tjørhom, *Kirkens enhet*, 62–64; Meyer, *Versöhnte Verschiedenheit*, vol. I, 101–19.

16. Tjørhom, *Visible Church*, 85; Rusch, *Ecumenical Reception*, 118–30; Wagner, *Einheit*.

The Universal Church as the Fellowship of Local Churches

affairs. Lack of theological reflection in this area is often supported by theologically understanding the church as either the local congregation or the universal church, while all levels between the local and the universal is viewed as just a matter of practical concern. Such a viewpoint does not take into account that the local church belongs to, and relates to, the universal church in and by its relation to other local churches. The universal church is manifest by its fellowship between local churches. The fellowship of local congregations within a certain denomination is one form of such fellowship, and is in no way theologically indifferent.

How churches relate to one another concerns the *local church's catholicity*, to paraphrase Miroslav Volf. A church that isolates itself from other churches denies its catholicity. How churches actually relate to each other and the way different Christian traditions understand these relationships will vary. In the Congregationalist tradition, to which Volf belongs, this tradition has largely accentuated individual church autonomy. As Volf points out, even within this tradition, one is obliged to have an *openness* of relationship to other churches:

> The minimal requirement for catholicity with regard to relations between churches is the *openness* of each church to all other churches. A church that closes itself off from other churches of God past or present, or a church that has no desire to turn to these churches in some fashion, is denying its own catholicity. A church cannot reflect the eschatological catholicity of the entire people of God and at the same time isolate itself from other churches.[17]

Such "openness" is the *bare essential* of what it means for a congregation to communicate its catholicity. A church that *only* shows openness, but will not commit to binding agreements demonstrates its catholicity in very incomplete manner: "Openness to other churches should lead to a free networking with those churches, and as the image of the net also suggests, these mutual relations should be expressed in corresponding ecclesial institutions."[18]

It is obviously unrealistic to expect every local congregation to have the same binding commitments to *all* other churches. In their own way, the fact that there are committed relationships between *some* churches is an expression of the church's catholicity. A denomination manifests

---

17. Volf, *After Our Likeness*, 275.
18. Ibid.

and promotes the church's catholicity by being a fellowship of churches. This is based upon the condition that the denomination does not become a *closed* community which precludes fellowship with other churches and denominations. Fellowship between the churches within the same denomination and traditions and the continuing ecumenical openness should supplement and enrich each other.

No denomination or confessional tradition can, at this point in history, claim to represent the universal catholic church in its *entirety*. Some traditions have made such claims to be the only true church. These claims have been an important part of the history of church splits and divisions, but in most cases today such positions have either been abandoned or greatly modified.

TYPES OF UNITY

When it comes to fellowship within a denomination or confessional tradition, and in the context of inter-denominational fellowship, there are two rather different forms of fellowship between churches. Theologically speaking, we should still look for the same basic elements in these two forms of fellowship where they can mutually illuminate each other: In ecumenical contexts where fellowship often operates very informally it is advantageous to raise the levels of mutual commitment. Within the denomination where fellowship is often understood in predominantly legal and organizational terms it is necessary to remember unity in faith and ministry as the source for church unity.

Based upon key ecumenical documents, Ola Tjørhom suggests there are five aspects for ecclesial fellowship. These five aspects must all be present before we can truly speak of church unity:[19]

1. Unity in faith and confession
2. Unity in sacramental life
3. Unity in offices and ministry
4. Unity in mission
5. A mutually committed life—with love as the bond of unity

---

19. Tjørhom, *Kirkens enhet*, 74–99.

The Universal Church as the Fellowship of Local Churches

Each of these aspects can be applied within denominations and confessional traditions, as well as within the ecumenical community at large. Each of these aspects will usually be only partially fulfilled. In comparison to the wider ecumenical community, these aspects will usually (but not always) be more fulfilled within a denomination. There will always be some denominations that will have a greater degree of unity with some churches compared to others. Or, to be more precise, some are further away from unity in their mutual relationship than others. Even though the degree of unity among Christian groups and churches will vary, we cannot be contempt with the lack of unity that exists. At the same time, it is required to distinguish between what is necessary to achieve true unity, and where we may differ without jeopardizing unity. A feature that further complicates the issue is when Christian traditions have different views about what creates and what breaks down unity. What is a critical precondition for one tradition may be viewed as insignificant for another tradition.

When it comes to "unity in faith and confession" (1), we can see that Christian churches share a normative source, namely the Bible. Returning to the church's shared source has proved to be a necessary prerequisite in ecumenical methodology.[20] Acknowledging the formal normativeness of Scripture is not sufficient however. Most churches will have some notion of a center within the Bible, and in order to achieve true unity it will be necessary to agree upon what this center may be. In the Lutheran tradition, this center has been identified as the *gospel* (as supported by a Pauline perspective, for example in Romans 1:16 and Galatians 1:6–9). According to the Augsburg Confession art. VII "it is enough for the true unity of the church to agree concerning the teaching of the gospel and the administration of the sacraments," while on the other hand "it is not necessary that human traditions, rites, or ceremonies instituted by human beings be alike everywhere."[21] Other traditions do not operate with the same sharp distinction between the "gospel" and "human traditions," even if they share the conviction that some issues are more important than other, and that it is easier to tolerate differences in some questions than in others. For example, in more recent Roman Catholic theology,

---

20. For an example of this line of thought, see *Joint Declaration on the Doctrine of Justification*.

21. Kolb and Wengert, *Book of Concord*, 43.

the idea of a "hierarchy of truths" has emerged giving different weights of emphasis and importance between doctrinal truths.[22]

At various times throughout the history of the church there have been attempts to summarize the main content of belief through various confessional documents. These documents have, in part, been a means to protect church unity, but they have also served as a tool for demarcation. The most unifying document of this type as still today recognized by most Christian groups is undoubtedly the Nicene Creed of the fourth century. Other confessional documents like those from the Reformation period serve, to a greater extent, to maintain unity within a specific tradition and as a means to highlight the differences between traditions. Terms such as *confession* and *confessional* (from Latin *confessio*) signifies on the one hand, the divisions between churches: their confessions of faith being *diverse*. On the other hand, different confessions and confessional traditions can also be seen as various attempts to express the content of the *same* Christian faith.[23] Problems arise when this results in a form of *confessionalism* that makes a tradition the only expression of the truth.

Unity of doctrine and confession is not only obtained when Christians seek a closer fellowship with each other. In certain cases, unity has to be protected by refusing collaboration and fellowship. Doctrines that claim to be Christian, but in reality deny the central content of Christian belief in God and salvation is to remove the very foundation for fellowship. In such cases we are no longer just talking about theological disagreement, but about outright heresy. This may apply to certain groups that by their deviant doctrines have placed themselves outside Christian fellowship.[24] It can also apply to certain individuals and groups that have removed themselves from the fellowship of doctrine and confession of a particular church or denomination

In the history of the church, we can see how unity and disunity have become polarized as absolute categories, allowing no room for compromise. Without complete doctrinal agreement, this would often lead to

---

22. *Teachings of the Second Vatican Council.* Decree on Ecumenism par. 11, p. 195; Tjørhom, *Kirkens enhet*, 65.

23. For example, the Augsburg Confession does not suggest the founding of a new church, but rather outlines that the evangelicals were in line with the church's doctrine and tradition.

24. This applies to, for example, non-Trinitarian churches like the Church of Jesus Christ of Latter-Day Saints and Jehovah's Witnesses.

mutual condemnation and excommunication. A similar pattern can also be seen in ecclesial debates today, when the question of whether disagreement about certain controversial issues destroys communion within the church. With this in mind, I believe it is necessary to have a more nuanced view about church unity and disunity. There may be a unity of certain fundamental beliefs, while being divided about other issues that do not have the same status. This is not to disvalue the less important issues, which can also be serious obstacles to fellowship and collaboration—even within each denomination.

In the case of "unity in sacramental life and celebration" (2), this concerns how congregations and churches acknowledge each other's sacraments and worship. Fundamentally, this is to recognize each other's *baptism* i.e., it is not necessary to be baptized again when moving from one denomination to another. In the Western church, the rejection of re-baptizing (even if this was performed by a heretic) has been the prevailing view since the third century.[25] The practice of Baptist and Pentecostal churches to re-baptize people who are baptized as babies continues to be a serious obstacle to Christian unity.

A more overt form of ecclesial fellowship is when we pray and worship together. The ultimate expression of Christian fellowship is when we acknowledge the validity of each other's eucharist, preside over the eucharist together, or share in each other's eucharistic celebration. Such a move remains a controversial issue in ecumenical circles. While Protestants often hold onto the claim that we can partake in each other's eucharist without having achieved unity at all points, the Roman Catholic Church understands eucharistic fellowship as the *goal* of ecumenism, rather than a signpost along the way.[26]

The question of "unity in office and ministry" (3) is interpreted differently according to different ecclesial traditions. This becomes an important issue for church unity for churches that perceive certain offices as being constitutive in the life of the church. This applies particularly to the Roman Catholic Church, Orthodox churches and the churches of the

---

25. Schlink, *Doctrine of Baptism*, 206–10.

26. While acknowledging the central role of the bishops, the Second Vatican Council Decree on Ecumenism does allow Roman Catholics to pray with other Christians in an ecumenical context: "Such prayers in common . . . are a genuine expression of the ties which still bind Catholics to their separated brethren." *Teachings of the Second Vatican Council*, Decree on Ecumenism, para. 8, pp. 192–93.

Anglican Communion. Most notably, this has been related to the ministry of the bishop and its place within a threefold pattern of ministry.[27] For churches that subscribe to the historic episcopal succession as being essential to the church's apostolicity, this can be perceived as a "deficiency" in other churches and a hindrance to unity until this is resolved.[28] For other churches it is difficult to accept that a particular pattern of ordained ministry should be a prerequisite for church unity, or that the church's apostolicity depends upon the historical episcopal succession. One possible way to accommodate these different traditions can be found in the Porvoo Agreement between Anglican and Lutheran churches. Here it is recognized that the churches without the historical succession may have preserved their apostolicity while maintaining that succession is still a valuable *sign* of apostolicity and therefore to be welcomed.[29]

Despite ecumenical developments concerning the ordained ministry, the idea of a common understanding and practice across different traditions seem to be quite illusive. It is a great paradox that a ministry that is presented as a sign of unity in many cases becomes an obstacle to greater Christian unity. An alternative approach could be to see variety in ministerial patterns as reflecting the diversity of the Spirit's gifts (see chapter 7) and to consider how these different ministerial patterns could enrich and complement each other.

The question of "unity in mission" (4) indicates how the unity of the church is not only to serve its own interest, but is of crucial importance for carrying out the mission God has given to the church. A divided church will also be divided in its testimony and ministry to the world. In addition, many tasks are so vast that they cannot be completed by local congregations and individual churches alone. What is required is collaborative ministry where churches work together in mission. A good example of this, within the ecumenical movement, is the *Life and Work* branch. This was established to facilitate practical cooperation between churches as undergirded by a *love your neighbor* ecumenism.[30]

---

27. This is also stated the last section of the Lima document *Baptism, Eucharist and Ministry*. Cf. the discussion above in chapter 7.

28. *Teachings of the Second Vatican Council*, Decree on Ecumenism, para. 22, pp. 181–83.

29. *Together in Mission and Ministry*, para. 46-54, cf. Tjørhom, *Kirken—troens mor*, 93-94.

30. FitzGerald, *Ecumenical Movement*, 87–92; Tjørhom, *Kirken—troens mor*, 96.

The Universal Church as the Fellowship of Local Churches

The last point Tjørhom suggests is, "a mutually committed life—with love as the bond of unity" (5). As love is the real bond of unity, all relationships and structures are but mere empty shells without love. This applies to both the internal life within a particular church or denomination and within the ecumenical community. Tjørhom captures this insight as follows:

> When all is said and done, it is love that is the basis and overflowing quality that overrides all the other criteria for unity. Love is the foundation of our unity of ministry and the driving force in our longing for unity. Without love, our ecumenical commitment will not only be empty, it will be as dead as faith is without works.[31]

The church as a fellowship of love is applicable, not only to the local congregation, but between churches as well. Without love "which binds everything together in perfect harmony" (Col 3:14) there can be no real ecclesial unity, even if all the other factors are in place.

MUTUAL ACCOUNTABILITY

A fellowship between churches and denominations requires not only mutual recognition, but also assumes that there is a willingness to make a *commitment* to each other. Such a commitment implies a willingness to be accountable to each other. Everything a church or denomination does is of concern for the other. In the ecumenical circles the concept of *mutual accountability* has been promoted as signifying a shared and committed relationship to one another. Even if such a commitment should also affect organizational structures, it is primarily understood as a basic *attitude* between the churches in the way they relate to each other with reciprocal openness and commitment—with a willingness to both accept and give criticism. The basis for this commitment to each other is based upon the apostolic foundation as contained in the Scripture. First and foremost, it is upon this premise that churches can test their commitment to each other and fulfill their shared mission.[32]

---

31. Tjørhom, *Kirken—troens mor*, 99 (our translation).

32. In his PhD thesis Olav Fykse Tveit investigates "mutual accountability" as a basic ecumenical attitude. Tveit summarizes this as follows: "Mutual accountability as ecumenical attitude is a combination of reliability, faithfulness, trustfulness, solidarity, openness, and ability to give and take constructive critique." Tveit, *Mutual Accountability*, 310.

In principle, this mutual accountability is nothing more than the same reciprocal commitment that occurs within denominations and confessional traditions. They are local churches in alliance with each other as bound by confession and organizational fellowship.[33] It varies greatly how such communities are structured and function, and in some cases this is a relatively loose network of churches, and in other cases tightly, regulated organizations. Those with the loosest connections are churches that belong to the *Congregationalist* tradition. Although this does not preclude some collaborative organization, Congregational churches generally emphasize individual church autonomy.

The churches in the *episcopal* tradition are tied to the diocese under the supervision and leadership of the bishop. The various bishops and dioceses remain in fellowship with each another, normally under the leadership of specially commissioned bishops, such as archbishops, patriarchs, or as is the case in the Roman Catholic Church, the Pope.

A *synodical* tradition binds churches together through collective bodies such as councils and meetings (synods). Local churches send their own representatives to these councils and synods. Even if synodical bodies are dominated by pastors and other ordained ministers, governance is still based upon a representative system with democratic elements. The synodical tradition is predominant in Reformed and Presbyterian churches.

Many churches combine different elements from these models. Some churches that traditionally have had an episcopal church structure have also adopted a synodical system, like the Church of England and the folk churches of Norway, Sweden and Finland.

Within different denominational structures we often find a large proportion of authority given to regional and central bodies, including in matters relating to the local congregation. In many cases, the distribution of authority between local and central bodies of the church is the result of specific historical circumstances, rather than from theological reasons. However, the delegating of authority can also be based upon a denomination's ecclesiological character as committed fellowship. In such cases, the mutual commitment to fellowship between local churches includes transferring authority to denominational bodies and agencies. Such an

---

33. Tveit makes a similar point: "The applicability of mutual accountability as ecclesiological premise could be extended far beyond that [sc. inter-church relations], because any fellowship—in or between churches—requires qualities of relation." Ibid., 311.

The Universal Church as the Fellowship of Local Churches

ecclesiological interpretation of denominational authority helps to *qualify* and *limit* the central authority of the churches. Firstly, it is important that authority is not so extensive that it does not provide sufficient space for each congregation to shape their own inner life. Secondly, it is important that denominational bodies and agencies do not act as some form of detached and independent ecclesial government, but are true to their mandate to represent the churches by which they are elected.

Bodies and agencies at a regional and central level should keep in mind that they are really at the service of the churches and the fellowship of churches. The idea of a national church as the primary unit and the various congregations are representatives or branches is highly problematical. Such bodies and agencies have no independent ecclesiological validation other than being at the service of the churches, enable the fellowship between the churches, and solve the tasks that local churches cannot solve on their own.

We can also understand ecumenical organizations and communities as being representative of the above. Although they seldom have the committed character of denominations, this does not mean they are to be understood as mere interest groups with no ecclesiological status. These bodies, both through their existence and through their activities, can encapsulate the fellowship of the church's unity and catholicity between churches and denominations. This idea is reflected in the increasing use of the term *community of churches* to denote certain ecumenical organizations, while the understanding of this community is shaped by insights from *communio*-ecclesiology.[34] An example of this can be found in the Lutheran World Federation, which in 1990 changed its constitution from understanding itself as "a free association of Lutheran churches" to "a communion of churches which confess the triune God, agree in the proclamation of the Word of God and are united in pulpit and altar fellowship."[35]

The fellowship between congregations and churches as characterized by a mutual commitment, is also expressed in the concept of *oversight* (Greek: *episkopé* and its derivatives such as *episkopos,* bishop).[36] In

---

34. Cf. the discussion of koinonia/communio ecclesiology in chapter 5.

35. Mortensen, *From Federation to Communion,* 216–46; Nordstokke, "Ecclesiological Self-Understanding of the Lutheran World Federation."

36. It is important to distinguish between pastoral oversight exercised within each community (as in Acts 20:28 and 1 Pet 5:1–4), and oversight as exercised in the com-

churches that have episcopacy, oversight is exercised through the bishop's ministry. Oversight can also be understood as a more general function and can be exercised by someone other than the bishop. Oversight may for example, be attributed to synods, or to people who do not have the title or have been ordained as a bishop. A more general understanding of the concept is expressed in the Lima document, which claims that a supervisory ministry "in some form" is necessary in order to safeguard the church's unity.[37] We can also find a similar definition in the Faith and Order document: *The Nature and Mission of the Church*. This document states that oversight first served to keep the various local churches together as one fellowship during the time of the early church: "The purpose was to hold the local congregations in communion, to safeguard and to hand on apostolic truth, to give mutual support and to lead in witnessing to the Gospel. All these functions are summed up in the term episkopé."[38] The document also points out that this oversight may be exercised in different ways, both through synods and by individuals (bishops). No matter what form the oversight takes, it is crucial that it includes a personal dimension (someone has made it their personal responsibility), a collegial dimension (as exercised in fellowship of shared responsibility), and has a communal dimension (that oversight is rooted in the fellowship of all the baptized).[39]

CHURCH ORGANIZATIONS AS MINISTERING ON BEHALF OF THE CHURCHES

Elements that bind the relationship between churches and denominations are not simply structures for oversight and governance. In churches and in the ecumenical community, there are also a number of institutions and organizations that support and assist local churches, or minister on behalf of the churches. These are not only the denominations' own organizational bodies, but include a number of independent organizations and institutions that are either owned by churches or denominations, or are self-governed.

---

munion of churches. For example, in the New Testament Paul's ministry to the churches is seen as an outworking of the latter.

37. *Baptism, Eucharist and Ministry*, Ministry, para. 23, p. 25.

38. *Nature and Mission of the Church*, para. 91, p. 24.

39. Ibid., para. 94-98, pp. 25-26. In the Porvoo Agreement *episkopé*/oversight is primarily directed toward the episcopal office, but is also used as a more general term.

The Universal Church as the Fellowship of Local Churches

If we take Norway as an example, ever since the establishment of the Norwegian Bible Society in 1816 and the Norwegian Missionary Society in 1842, there has been a long tradition of Christian voluntary organizations. There has been a growth in such organizations and institutions ever since, especially those involved in mission and diaconal ministry. These organizations contribute partly to the work of the local church, partly to solving tasks that are of such a nature that cannot be fulfilled by a single congregation, for example, foreign missions, the establishment of hospitals and other diaconal institutions, and building schools (theological and general education). While some organizations and institutions define themselves as part of a particular denomination, others have a more ecumenical character, i.e. they minister on behalf different denominations, for example, Norwegian Church Aid.

While in some contexts such organizations and institutions are more formally independent from official church structures, in other contexts there may be a move towards more formal ties. Instead of being independent missionary societies, in many cases such missionary work is led by a department within the denomination's own headquarters.[40] This development has been supported by theological arguments, for example, the missiologist Olav G. Myklebust who argues that because mission is a central part of the church's assignment it should be taken care of by the church itself and not by an independent society.[41] A similar line of argument could be raised for the diaconal ministry as well. The difficulty with this position proposed by Myklebust is that it identifies the church with central ecclesial bodies and denominational headquarters. However, if we are to take seriously the local congregation as the primary unit of church, such a conclusion is not so obvious. Both denominational agencies and independent organizations may be of service to churches and fulfill tasks on behalf of the churches. For both of these types of organizations there is a risk they can forget their original reason for their existence and start treating local churches as being either their customers or branches. The formal connection to congregations will usually be closer if these organizations are integrated within the denomination's organization. At the same time, a more independent position could lead to a greater creativity and diversity in fulfilling the task at hand, and it could also make it easier

---

40. For example, in the Church of Sweden missionary work is integrated in the department for International Affairs.

41. Myklebust, *Misjonskunnskap*, 101–11.

to minister on behalf of the wider ecumenical community of churches. In my opinion, there is no clear-cut answer to how these tasks should be organized. What is important is that these organizations and institutions are perceived and act as bodies operating on behalf of the churches and the fellowship of churches.

The missiologist Ralph D. Winter distinguishes between two different types of church structures which he believes are of equal ecclesiological importance. He proposes that two basic kinds of structures are found throughout church history, one which he calls *modality* and other *sodality*. The modality structure is the permanent church structure as primarily being related to the local congregation. This structure represents the backbone and stability of a church's life. The sodality structure on the other hand, is mobile and flexible, and is suitable focusing upon specific needs. To support his argument, Winter gives historical examples, for example he mentions the monastic movement, various revival and renewal movements, and various missionary organizations. Winter believes we need both structures in the church for the church to carry out its mission. It is important that the structures recognize and are in concord with each other. At the same time, he warns against integrating the two structures too tightly that can, for example, lead to the attenuation of the priority of mission.[42]

Winter's distinction between the two structures undoubtedly points out some important aspects of how the church functions. One is left wondering, however, if such distinctions are too simplistic. In many cases, the movements Winter describes as expressions of *sodality* often have traits of the local congregation as well, for example they have their own worship services. This applies to monastic communities as well as to other types of movements. The problem with Winter's model is that the dynamic and outward looking focus is removed from the understanding of the local church and left to the sodality structure. Neither the local congregation nor denominational structures can be so rigid that they neglect to take into account the call to renewal and mission. Although the church in many cases needs the help from outside agencies to fulfill certain tasks, it is important that these tasks are understood as belonging to the church even if they are aided by the help of external organizations. The ecclesial identity of such mission organizations and diaconal organizations is,

---

42. Winter, "Two Structures of God's Redemptive Mission." Cf. Eriksen, *A Twofold Structural Model.*

CHURCH AND SMALL GROUPS

As a fellowship gathered in Jesus' name, the local congregation is the basic ecclesial unit. At the same time, the local church cannot stand alone as the church, but is established through its openness to, and communion with, other churches. Even with such an understanding, the question of the basic ecclesial unit is still not fully clarified. In fact, in many cases it is not easy to distinguish between a congregation and a fellowship of congregations. For example, this applies when a local congregation has a number of different worship services. Some churches, for example, may use different buildings or have different times for their services and often these services will have different groups of people attending. Is this then, one congregation with different services, or is it different congregations with one, shared organizational structure?

It is not always clear what we mean by a worshipping community, for example, are youth worship services in reality a youth congregation? When we gather in Jesus' name in a Bible group is this a congregation? What actually is the relationship between the *small group* and the fellowship of the church as a whole?

In the New Testament, the *house church* was the basic unit of the Christian gathering. In the lack of other places to worship, Christians met in the homes of church members, preferably those with larger premises. In several places in Paul's letters he writes of gathering "in the house of" someone in the congregation (Rom 16:5; 1 Cor 16:19; Col 4:15; Phlm 2).[43] In the Acts of the Apostles we read that the home continued to be the meeting place for the church (Acts 2:46, 8:3). There are indications that these house churches were part of a larger community in the same city. According to Acts 2:46, Christians met in homes as well as in the temple. In 1 Corinthians 14:23 we see the "whole church" (*ekklesia hole*) coming together (see also Rom 16:23; 1 Cor 11:20–22, 14:35). However, we are still left with the issue of what exactly is the local congregation, is it the house church itself, or the community of house churches? The situation was not necessarily the same for all places—what was appropriate in

---

43. The same Greek phrase *kat oikon ekklesia* is used in all the references cited.

Corinth was not necessarily appropriate for other cities. New Testament scholars generally have differing opinions about the matter.[44]

Various denominations have also interpreted the question of the church's basic unit differently. In Roman Catholic and Anglican traditions the *diocese* is understood as the basic unit of the local church. In contrast, Lutherans perceive the local worshipping congregation as the basic unit, with the diocese acting as the regional church unit.[45] However, this does not exclude the possibility of smaller units within the congregation. Reading Luther, the closest we can get to the house church of the New Testament is his emphasis upon the *family* as an important place for Christian education and nurture. Within Methodism so-called *classes* were types of small fellowships within the framework of the local church. With the Pietist revival movement we see small fellowships contained within the framework of the congregation (*ecclesiola in ecclesia*). In general, this movement did not regard these fellowships as new churches, but saw these as contributing to the renewal of the existing church.[46] For example, in the Church of Norway, under the auspices of Christian voluntary-run organizations the tradition of fellowships has continued right up until the present time. While some of these groups clearly can be seen as subgroups of the local congregation, others have become more like independent fellowships. In recent years, several of these fellowships have increasingly begun to see themselves as churches. As part of this self-identity as a church, these fellowships have, for example, started to administer the sacraments.[47]

In recent years we have seen the launch of *cell churches* as an ideal way to organize the church. The idea behind this concept is that all church members are to be part of a small group (*cell*), while still belonging to the church fellowship as a whole. The small group setting creates space for a more personal and closely-knit community. Advocates of cell church believe this structure based upon small groups, enables a more mission focus as cell groups can be more suited to engage in outreach.[48] A more

---

44. Sandnes, *New Family*, 96–97.

45. This difference of emphasis is reflected in North American Lutheran-Catholic dialogue document, Gros and Lee, *Church as Koinonia of Salvation*, 21–26.

46. Vigilius, *Kirke i kirken*.

47. Concerning this issue see Hegstad, *Kirke i forandring*, 92–101.

48. Potter, *Challenge of Cell Church*; Booker and Ireland, *Evangelism*, 141–57. The possibility to be part of a small group is a good thing, but it becomes in my opinion

The Universal Church as the Fellowship of Local Churches

radical version of the cell principle asserts that these small groups (or "house churches") *are* the church, and that the coming together of various cell groups is a meeting point for several churches.[49]

If we ask the question of whether or not a group consisting of a few individuals is large enough to be understood as a church, the answer is undoubtedly yes. When Jesus said he will be present when "two or three are gathered" in his name (Matt 18:20), a small group obviously falls within this category. However, when the members of a group are also part of a larger worship community, the group should not be regarded as a congregation, but *part of a congregation*. When several groups meet regularly for a joint worship service, this larger assembly is to be understood as church in its more comprehensive sense. This larger assembly should also be the primary venue for the administration of the sacraments. Furthermore, this larger assembly has a defined pastoral leadership, which is not usually the case at the group level.

When reflecting upon the question on what constitutes a congregation as distinct from groups, it is important to emphasize the gathering *in the name of Jesus* as constituting the church. Even if a congregation consists of several smaller groups, it still remains that the coming together for common worship makes this body a church. This is somewhat different in a context where there is no regular common worship. Fellowship with God and each other as gathered around the word and sacraments cannot be replaced by organizational and administrative structures. Theologically speaking, different worshipping assemblies that even meet under the same roof, but have no joint service together may rather be understood as several congregations worshipping side by side one another.

Traditional definitions of the term church are also being challenged by Christian fellowships that have the character of more free-flowing networks than specific groups. In his book *Liquid church* Pete Ward argues that Christian fellowship may take the form of changing networks and relations, rather than traditional ecclesial structures. A "liquid" church has no institutional form and does not require a weekly congregational

---

problematic if we *have* to be part of a small group to be part of the church. To do this is to not take into account that the personal and spiritual fellowship that small groups provide can also be found in other settings such as in marriage and the family. It should also be noted that the use of metaphor *cell* incorrectly gives the impression this organizational model is more *organic* than other organizational models.

49. Simson, *Houses That Change the World*.

meeting, but may consist of informal networks of communication. In his view, such developments should be encouraged in order for the church to find its place in an ever-changing culture.

There is, and probably should not be, any easy answer to the question of the basic unit of the church, and in how we are to distinguish between a church in the full sense of the word between groups within the church and other forms of fellowships and networks. In many cases the interplay between small groups, congregations, networks, and fellowship of churches all tend to merge into each other without clear demarcations of where one ends and another begins. Ultimately, this is not a question that *requires* a precise answer, because no congregation is ever the church alone but is always in fellowship with other churches. The church is *both* the local worshipping congregation *and* the fellowship of congregations. To be in fellowship means to be open to one another and be in relationship to one another. When circumstances allow, this is also to come together as a church in common worship and communion. This can happen both within denominations and within the ecumenical community at large. While such a fellowship of local churches can only be partial and incomplete and imperfection suitably describes the church's unity, it also anticipates a fellowship where the difference between the local congregation and universal church will one day be abolished in the eschatological fellowship of God's kingdom where "God may be all in all" (1 Cor 15:28).

10

Epilogue: Building Up the Real Church

What do we mean when we say we believe in the church? In this book I have argued that the church we confess is not another church *beyond* or *above* the church as we experience it. The church is a visible fellowship of people coming together in Jesus' name. This is the real church. To believe in the church means to believe Jesus' promise that when two or three are gathered in his name, there will he be in the midst of them (Matt 18:20). To believe in the church is to believe that the church is a sign and foretaste of the fellowship between people and God of the coming kingdom. Such a perspective implies that the church is both characterized by the presence of Jesus and by its eschatological destiny. As an anticipation of the kingdom to come, the church is still a part of this world and is marked by sin, unbelief, and division.

This duality of the church's existence means that the church is a pilgrim church. It is sent to the world with a mission to witness to the kingdom of God by word and deed. A church faithful to its calling will be a church in mission. The church is not here just for itself, but for the sake of the world. At the same time the church is of crucial importance for the realization of this mission, both as a sign of and an instrument for the kingdom of God. The fellowship gathered in Jesus' name is the very place where people can meet the risen Christ. A church that is faithful to its calling must be conscious of how it appears as a Christian community, both as a local congregation and as a fellowship of churches. For example, we are compelled to ask, how the fellowship of Word and sacrament can be an open community where even the stranger is welcomed.

The Real Church

The New Testament does not understand the church as something static and given once and for all. In many New Testament references, and especially Pauline corpus, the church is to be "built up" (Greek: *oikodome*).[1] This "building up" means the church is to move beyond its own fellowship and reach out to others. At the same time, it means building up the inner spiritual maturity and growth of those who belong to the Christian fellowship. When God gives gifts to the church, they are "to equip the saints for the work of ministry, for building up the body of Christ, until all of us come to the unity of faith and of the knowledge of the Son of God, to maturity, to the measure of the full stature of Christ" (Eph 4:12–13).

The real subject of this process is God himself. He is the one who gathers the church, builds it up and sends it out. This is not to exclude human cooperation, but presupposes it because God works in and through human deeds. As Paul puts it: "I planted, Apollos watered, but God gave the growth" (1 Cor 3:6).

For ecclesiology this means the task is not completed with theological interpretations of the church's reality. As I have pointed out in chapter 1, systematic theology is only one of several movements of a coherent theological process which, according to Don Browning points towards a strategic practical theology. For ecclesiology, this means dogmatic ecclesiology is to contribute to a practical ecclesiology, one that is worked out in the life and development of the congregation. One can therefore argue that *church development* is fundamentally a practical theological theme. A possible definition of church development could be as follows: An intentional effort to make the church better equipped to be what it is called to be, and do what it is called to do.[2]

Academic research on church development could certainly draw upon methods and angles from other academic disciplines such as organizational or educational development. However, work of development in the church has to take into account the peculiar character of the church, sociologically and theologically. On the one hand, church development should take into account the specific characteristics of the church as a social reality in the given context. On the other hand, church development should also be based on a theological understanding of the church: while

---

1. See 1 Cor 14:5, 12, 26; 2 Cor 12:19; Eph 4:12–16, 29.

2. A proposal for church development as a necessary task for practical theology is given in Birkedal et al., *Menighetsutvikling i folkekirken*.

it is a human community, it is also a result of God's presence and God's call. Whereas the task of dogmatic ecclesiology is to interpret theologically belief about the church, practical ecclesiology is concerned how this belief is to be lived out in practice—so that the church is "building itself up in love" (Eph 4:16).

The fact that the actual and present church is the real church means this is the *only* church. Whatever God does not achieve in and through this church, is not to be realized in an invisible and hidden church. If the church's call to unity, holiness, and catholicity is to be fulfilled, it is to be fulfilled in this church. If the calling of God upon the church is to be realized, it must be completed by this church. What makes this possible is the reality that the church is not left by itself. God acts in the world through imperfect people, for wherever two or three are gathered in his name, the resurrected Jesus Christ is there among them.

Bibliography

Aagaard, Anna Marie. *Identifikation af kirken*. Fredriksberg: Forlaget ANIS, 1991.
Aasgaard, Reidar. *"My Beloved Brothers and Sisters!": Christian Siblingship in Paul*. London: T. & T. Clark, 2004.
Albrecht, Daniel E. *Rites in the Spirit: A Ritual Approach to Pentecostal/Charismatic Spirituality*. Sheffield: Sheffield Academic, 1999.
Althaus, Paul. *Die letzten Dinge: Lehrbuch der Eschatologie*. 8. ed. Gütersloh: Mohn, 1961.
———. *The Theology of Martin Luther*. Philadelphia: Fortress, 1966.
The Apostolic Fathers. Vol. II. The Loeb Classical Library. Cambridge, MA: Harvard University Press, 1976.
Askeland, Harald. "Hva betyr det om kirken forstås som organisasjon?" In *Ledelse i kirken*, edited by Marit Halvorsen Hougsnæs, Frank Grimstad and Harald Askeland, 23–42. Oslo: Kirkens Arbeidsgiverorganisasjon, 2003.
———. *Ledere og lederroller: Om ledelse og lederroller i den lokale kirke*. KIFO Rapport 7. Trondheim: Tapir, 1998.
Augustin, Aurelius. *Concerning the City of God against the Pagans*. Translated by Henry Bettenson. London: Penguin, 1984.
Austad, Torleiv. "Kirche." In *Theologie der lutherischen Bekenntnisschriften*, edited by Horst Georg Pöhlmann, Torleiv Austad and Friedhelm Krüger, 169–85. Gütersloh: Chr. Kaiser/Gütersloher Verlagshaus, 1996.
Bakke, Odd Magne. "The Episcopal Ministry and the Unity of the Church from the Apostolic Fathers to Cyprian." In *The Formation of the Early Church*, edited by Jostein Ådna. Wissenschaftliche Untersuchungen Zum Neuen Testament, 379–408. Tübingen: Mohr Siebeck, 2005.
Banks, Robert J. *Paul's Idea of Community: The Early House Churches in Their Historical Setting*. Exeter: Paternoster, 1980.
Baptism, Eucharist and Ministry. Faith and Order Paper. Geneva: World Council of Churches, 1982.
Barth, Karl. *Church Dogmatics*. Authorised English Translation. Vol. I–IV, Edinburgh: T. & T. Clark, 1956–77.
Bassler, Jouette M. *Navigating Paul: An Introduction to Key Theological Concepts*. Louisville, KY: Westminster John Knox, 2007.
Bauman, Zygmunt. *Thinking Sociologically*. Oxford: Blackwell, 1990.
Berger, Peter L. *Invitation to Sociology: A Humanistic Perspective*. Harmondsworth: Penguin, 1966.
———. *A Rumour of Angels: Modern Society and the Rediscovery of the Supernatural*. London: Allen Lane, 1969.
———. *The Sacred Canopy: Elements of a Sociological Theory of Religion*. New York: Doubleday, 1967.

Bibliography

―――. "Sociology and Ecclesiology." In *The Place of Bonhoeffer*, edited by Martin E. Marty, 53–79. London: SCM, 1963.
Berger, Peter L., and Thomas Luckmann. *The Social Construction of Reality: A Treatise in the Sociology of Knowledge*. London: Penguin, 1971.
Best, Thomas F., and Günther Gassmann, eds. *On the Way to Fuller Koinonia: Official Report of the Fifth World Conference on Faith and Order*. Faith and Order Paper 166. Geneva: WCC Publications, 1994.
Best, Thomas F., and Wesley Granberg-Michaelson, eds. *Costly Unity: Presentations and Reports from the World Council of Churches' Consultation in Rønde, Denmark, February 1993*. Geneva: World Council of Churches, 1993.
Bevans, Stephen B. *Models of Contextual Theology*. Maryknoll, NY: Orbis, 2002.
Bevans, Stephen B., and Roger Schroeder. *Constants in Context: A Theology of Mission for Today*. Maryknoll, NY: Orbis, 2004.
Bhaskar, Roy. "Societies." In *Critical Realism. Essential Readings*, edited by Margaret S. Archer, 206–57. London: Routledge, 1998.
Bieritz, Karl-Heinrich. *Liturgik*. Berlin–New York: Walter de Gruyter, 2004.
Birkedal, Erling, Harald Hegstad, and Turid Skorpe Lannem, eds. *Menighetsutvikling i folkekirken: Erfaringer og muligheter*. Oslo: IKO-forlaget, 2012.
Bonhoeffer, Dietrich. *Sanctorum Communio: A Theological Study of the Sociology of the Church*. Dietrich Bonhoeffer Works. Vol. 1, Minneapolis: Fortress, 1998.
Booker, Mike, and Mark Ireland. *Evangelism—Which Way Now?: An Evaluation of Alpha, Emmaus, Cell Church and Other Contemporary Strategies for Evangelism*. 2nd ed. London: Church House Publishing, 2005.
Bosch, David J. *Transforming Mission: Paradigm Shifts in Theology of Mission*. Maryknoll, NY: Orbis, 1991.
―――. *Witness to the World: The Christian Mission in Theological Perspective*. London: Marshall, Morgan & Scott, 1980.
Bradshaw, Paul F. "The Effects of the Coming of Christendom on Early Christian Worship." In *The Origins of Christendom in the West*, edited by Alan Kreider, 269–86. Edinburgh: T. & T. Clark, 2001.
Browning, Don S. *A Fundamental Practical Theology: Descriptive and Strategic Proposals*. Minneapolis: Fortress, 1991.
Brunner, Emil. *The Misunderstanding of the Church*. London: Lutterworth Press, 1952.
Brunner, Peter. "Zur Lehre vom Gottesdienst der im Namen Jesu versammelten Gemeinde." In *Leiturgia: Handbuch des evangelischen Gottesdienstes*, vol. 1, edited by Karl Ferdinand Müller and Walter Blankenburg, 83–361. Kassel: Johannes Stauda-Verlag, 1954.
Cartledge, Mark J. *Encountering the Spirit: The Charismatic Tradition*. Maryknoll, NY: Orbis, 2007.
The Church for Others, and the Church for the World: A Quest for Structures for Missionary Congregations. Final Report of the Western European Working Group and North American Working Group of the Department on Studies in Evangelism. Geneva: World Council of Churches, 1967.
Collins, Raymond F. *The Many Faces of the Church: A Study in New Testament Ecclesiology*. Companions to the New Testament. New York: Crossroad, 2004.
Communio/Koinonia: A New Testament-Early Christian Concept and Its Contemporary Appropriation and Significance. Strasbourg: Institute for Ecumenical Research, 1990.

Bibliography

Cullmann, Oscar. *Christ and Time: The Primitive Christian Conception of Time and History*. London: SCM, 1962.
———. *Salvation in History*. London: SCM, 1967.
Cunningham, Lawrence S., and Keith J. Egan. *Christian Spirituality: Themes from the Tradition*. New York: Paulist, 1996.
Dahl, Nils Alstrup. *Das Volk Gottes: Eine Untersuchung zum Kirchenbewusstsein des Urchristentums*. Oslo: Dybwad, 1941.
Davie, Grace. *Religion in Modern Europe: A Memory Mutates*. Oxford: Oxford University Press, 2000.
Den norske Kirkes identitet og oppdrag: Uttalelse fra Kirkemøtet 2004. Oslo: Kirkerådet, 2004.
Die Bekenntnisschriften der evangelisch-lutherischen Kirche. 11. ed. Göttingen: Vandenhoeck & Ruprecht, 1976.
Doyle, Dennis M. *Communion Ecclesiology: Vision and Versions*. New York: Maryknoll, 2000.
Dulles, Avery. *The Catholicity of the Church*. Oxford: Oxford University Press, 1987.
———. *Models of the Church*. Exp. ed. New York: Doubleday, 1987.
Eastwood, Cyril. *The Priesthood of All Believers: An Examination of the Doctrine from the Reformation to the Present Day*. Eugene, OR: Wipf & Stock, 2009.
Elert, Werner. *Abendmahl und Kirchengemeinschaft in der alten Kirche hauptsächlich des Ostens*. Berlin: Lutherisches Verlagshaus, 1954.
Eriksen, Bent Reidar. *A Twofold Structural Model for Renewal and Mission with Special Reference to the Church of Norway*. Pasadena, CA: Fuller Theological Seminary, 1983.
Eriksson, Anne-Louise, Göran Gunner, and Niclas Blåder, eds. *Exploring a Heritage: Evangelical Lutheran Churches in the North*. Church of Sweden Research Series, vol. 5. Eugene, OR: Pickwick, 2012.
Etzioni, Amitai. *Modern Organizations*. Englewood Cliffs, NJ: Prentice-Hall, 1964.
Fagerberg, Holsten. *Bekenntnis, Kirche und Amt in der deutschen konfessionellen Theologie des 19. Jahrhunderts*. Uppsala Universitets Årsskrift 1952:9. Uppsala: A.-B. Lundequistska bokhandeln, 1952.
FitzGerald, Thomas E. *The Ecumenical Movement: An Introductory History*. Contributions to the Study of Religion, No. 72. Westport, CT: Praeger, 2004.
Frisby, David, and Derek Sayer. *Society*. Chichester/London and New York: Ellis Horwood/Tavistock, 1986.
Frostin, Per. *Luther's Two Kingdoms Doctrin: A Critical Study*. Studia Theologica Lundensia. Lund: Lund University Press, 1994.
Furseth, Inger, and Pål Repstad. *An Introduction to the Sociology of Religion: Classical and Contemporary Perspectives*. Aldershot, Hants: Ashgate, 2006.
Giddens, Anthony. *Sociology*. 2. ed. Cambridge: Polity, 1993.
Gill, Robin. *The Social Context of Theology: A Methodological Enquiry*. London and Oxford: Mowbrays, 1975.
Gjessing, Gutorm. "Laestadianism: A Revivalistic Saamish (Lapp)—Finnish Movement for National Liberation." *Ultimate Reality and Meaning* 2, no. 3 (1979) 188–204.
Green, Clifford J. *Bonhoeffer: A Theology of Sociality*. Grand Rapids, Mi: Eerdmans, 1999.
Gros, Jeffrey, and Randall R. Lee, eds. *The Church as Koinonia of Salvation: Its Structures and Ministries. Agreed Statement of the Tenth Round of the U.S. Lutheran-Roman Catholic Dialogue with Background Papers*, Lutherans and Catholics in Dialogue; 10. Washington, D.C.: United States Conference of Catholic Bishops, 2005.

Bibliography

Gudstjenestebok for Den norske kirke. Vol. 1-2. Oslo: Verbum, 1992.

Gullaksen, Per-Otto. *Stat og kirke i Norge: Kirkerett mellom teologi og politikk.* Oslo: Verbum, 2000.

Haag, Herbert. *Upstairs, Downstairs: Did Jesus Want a Two-Class Church?* New York: Crossroad, 1998.

Haight, Roger. *Christian Community in History.* Vol. 1-3. New York: Continuum, 2004-8.

Hauerwas, Stanley, and William H. Willimon. *Resident Aliens: Life in the Christian Colony. A Provocative Christian Assessment of Culture and Ministry for People Who Know That Something Is Wrong.* Nashville: Abingdon, 1989.

Healy, Nicholas M. *Church, World, and the Christian Life: Practical-Prophetic Ecclesiology.* Cambridge Studies in Christian Doctrine. Cambridge: Cambridge University Press, 2000.

———. "The Logic of Karl Barth's Ecclesiology: Analysis, Assessment and Proposed Modifications." *Modern Theology* 10, no. 3 (1994) 253-70.

———. "Some Observations on Ecclesiological Method." *Toronto Journal of Theology* 12, no. 1 (1996) 47-63.

Hegstad, Harald. "Én kropp—mange lemmer: Skisse til tjenesteteologi for Den norske kirke." *Halvårsskrift for praktisk teologi* 26, no. 2 (2009) 29-38.

———. *Folkekirke og trosfellesskap: Et kirkesosiologisk og ekklesiologisk grunnproblem belyst gjennom en undersøkelse av tre norske lokalmenigheter.* KIFO Perspektiv 1. Trondheim: Tapir, 1996.

———. *Kirke i forandring: Fellesskap, tilhørighet og mangfold i Den norske kirke.* Oslo: Luther, 1999.

———. "A Minority within the Majority: On the Relation between the Church as Folk Church and as a Community of Believers." *Studia Theologica* 53 (1999) 119-31.

Heimbrock, Hans-Günter. *Gottesdienst: Spielraum des Lebens. Sozial- und kulturwissenschaftliche Analysen zum Ritual in praktisch-theologischem Interesse.* Theologie & Empirie 15, Kampen-Weinheim: Kok-Deutscher Studien Verlag, 1993.

Hesselgrave, David J., and Edward Rommen. *Contextualization: Meanings, Methods, and Models.* Leicester: Apollos, 1989.

Hiebert, Paul G. *Anthropological Reflections on Missiological Issues.* Grand Rapids: Baker, 1994.

———. "Sets and Structures: A Study of Church Patterns." In *New Horizons in World Mission*, edited by David J. Hesselgrave, 217-27. Grand Rapids: Baker, 1979.

Hjelm, Norman A., ed. *I Have Heard the Cry of My People: Proceedings [of] the Eighth Assembly [of the] Lutheran World Federation, Curitiba, Brazil. January 29—February 8, 1990.* Geneva: Lutheran World Federation, 1990.

Hofius, Otfried. "Gemeinschaft mit den Engeln im Gottesdienst der Kirche: Eine traditionsgeschichtliche Skizze." *Zeitschrift für Theologie und Kirche* 89 (1992) 172-96.

Holze, Heinrich, ed. *The Church as Communion: Lutheran Contributions to Ecclesiology.* LWF Documentation 42. Geneva: Lutheran World Federation, 1997.

Honecker, Martin. *Kirche als Gestalt und Ereignis: Die sichtbare Gestalt der Kirche als dogmatisches Problem.* München: Chr. Kaiser, 1963.

Hope, Ludvig. *Kyrkja og Guds folk.* Bjørgvin: Lunde, 1923.

Huber, Wolfgang. *Kirche.* Stuttgart-Berlin: Kreuz, 1979.

———. *Kirche und Öffentlichkeit.* Stuttgart: Ernst Klett, 1973.

Bibliography

Hvalvik, Reidar. "All Those Who in Every Place Call on the Name of Our Lord Jesus Christ: The Unity of the Pauline Churches." In *The Formation of the Early Church*, edited by Jostein Ådna. Wissenschaftliche Untersuchungen Zum Neuen Testament, 123-43. Tübingen: Mohr Siebeck, 2005.

———. "'The Churches of the Saints.': Paul's Concern for Unity in His References to the Christian Community." *Tidsskrift for teologi og kirke* 78, no. 3-4 (2007) 227-47.

Hütter, Reinhard. *Bound to Be Free: Evangelical Catholic Engagements in Ecclesiology, Ethics, and Ecumenism*. Grand Rapids: Eerdmans, 2004.

———. *Evangelische Ethik als kirchliches Zeugnis: Interpretationen zu Schlüsselfragen theologischer Ethik in der Gegenwart*. Evangelium und Ethik 1. Neukirchen-Vluyn: Neukirchener, 1993.

———. *Suffering Divine Things: Theology as Church Practice*. Grand Rapids: Eerdmans, 2000.

Høeg, Ida Marie, Ole Gunnar Winsnes, and Harald Hegstad. *Folkekirke 2000: En spørreundersøkelse blant medlemmer av Den norske kirke*. Oslo: Stiftelsen Kirkeforskning, 2000.

Håkansson, Bo. *Vardagens kyrka: Gustaf Wingrens kyrkosyn och folkkyrkans framtid*. Lund: Arcus, 2001.

Ivarsson, Henrik. *Kyrkan och diakonin*. Lund: Gleerups, 1959.

Johnson, Andy, and Kent E. Brower, eds. *Holiness and Ecclesiology in the New Testament*. Grand Rapids: Eerdmans, 2007.

Joint Declaration on the Doctrine of Justification. Grand Rapids: Eerdmans, 2000.

Justin Martyr. *The First and Second Apologies*. Ancient Christian Writers 56. New York: Paulist, 1997.

Jüngel, Eberhard. *God as the Mystery of the World: On the Foundation of the Theology of the Crucified One in the Dispute between Theism and Atheism*. Edinburgh: Clark, 1983.

Keifert, Patrick, ed. *Testing the Spirits: How Theology Informs the Study of Congregations*: Eerdmans, 2009.

Keifert, Patrick R. *Welcoming the Stranger: A Public Theology of Worship and Evangelism*. Minneapolis: Fortress, 1992.

Kinnamon, Michael, ed. *Signs of the Spirit: Official Report Seventh Assembly, Canberra, Australia, 7-20 February 1991*. Geneva: World Council of Churches, 1991.

Kolb, Robert, and Timothy J. Wengert. *The Book of Concord: The Confessions of the Evangelical Lutheran Church*. Minneapolis, Minn.: Fortress, 2000.

Kraft, Charles H. *Christianity in Culture: A Study in Dynamic Biblical Theologizing in Cross-Cultural Perspective*. Maryknoll, NY: Orbis, 1979.

Kvalbein, Hans. *Jesus: Hva ville han? Hvem var han? En innføring i de tre første evangelienes budskap*. Oslo: Luther, 2008.

———. "The Kingdom of God in the Ethics of Jesus." *Communio Viatorum* 40, no. 3 (1998) 197-227.

Kümmel, Werner Georg. *Promise and Fulfilment: The Eschatological Message of Jesus*. Studies in Biblical Theology. 2nd English ed. London: SCM, 1961.

Küng, Hans. *The Church*. London: Search, 1981.

Kärkkäinen, Veli-Matti. *An Introduction to Ecclesiology: Ecumenical, Historical & Global Perspectives*. Downers Grove, IL: InterVarsity, 2002.

Käsemann, Ernst. "The Canon of the New Testament and the Unity of the Church." In *Essays on New Testament Themes*, by Ernst Käsemann, 95-107. Philadelphia: Fortress, 1982.

Bibliography

Lappegard, Sevat. "Folkekyrkjeteologi." In *Folkekirken—Status og strategier*, edited by Bjørn Sandvik. Presteforeningens Studiebibliotek, 107-31. Oslo: Den norske kirkes presteforening, 1988.

Lathrop, Gordon W. *Holy People: A Liturgical Ecclesiology*. Minneapolis: Fortress, 1999.

———. *Holy Things: A Liturgical Theology*. Minneapolis: Fortress, 1993.

Lathrop, Gordon, and Timothy J. Wengert. *Christian Assembly: Marks of the Church in a Pluralistic Age*. Minneapolis: Fortress, 2004.

Lincoln, Andrew T. *Paradise Now and Not Yet: Studies in the Role of the Heavenly Dimension in Paul's Thought with Special Reference to His Eschatology*. Cambridge: Cambridge University Press, 1981.

Luther, Martin. *Luther's Works*. Vol. 1-55. Edited by Jaroslav Pelikan and Helmut T. Lehmann et al. Philadelphia: Fortress, 1958-1986.

Martin, David. *Reflections on Sociology and Theology*. Oxford: Clarendon, 1997.

Meyer, Harding. "Der sich abzeichnende evangelisch/katholische Konsens im theologischen Verständnis der Eucharistie und die Frage der Eucharistie-Gemeinschaft." *Zeitschrift für Theologie und Kirche* 127, no. 2-3 (2005) 165-82.

———. *That All May Be One: Perceptions and Models of Ecumenicity*. Grand Rapids, Mich: Eerdmans, 1999.

———. *Versöhnte Verschiedenheit: Aufsätze zur ökumenischen Theologie*. Vol. I-II. Frankfurt am Main: Lembeck, 1998.

Milbank, John. *Theology and Social Theory: Beyond Secular Reason*. Oxford: Blackwell, 1990.

Modéus, Martin. *Mänsklig gudstjänst: Om gudstjänsten som relation och rit*. Stockholm: Verbum, 2005.

Molland, Einar. "Das kirchliche Amt im Neuen Testament und in der alten Kirche." In *Opuscula Patristica*, by Einar Molland. Bibliotheca Theologica Norvegica 2, 207-29. Oslo: Universitetsforlaget, 1970.

Moltmann, Jürgen. *The Church in the Power of the Spirit: A Contribution to Messianic Ecclesiology*. New York: Harper & Row, 1977.

Morgan, Gareth. *Images of Organization*. Updated ed. Thousand Oaks, Calif.: Sage, 2006.

Morris, Danny E., and Charles M. Olsen. *Discerning God's Will Together: A Spiritual Practice for the Church*. Nashville, Tenn.: Upper Room Books, 1997.

Mortensen, Viggo, Prasanna Kumari, Norman A. Hjelm, and Jens Holger Schjørring. *From Federation to Communion: The History of the Lutheran World Federation*. Minneapolis: Fortress, 1997.

Muthiah, Robert A. *The Priesthood of All Believers in the Twenty-First Century: Living Faithfully as the Whole People of God in a Postmodern Context*. Eugene, OR: Pickwick, 2009.

Myklebust, Olav Guttorm. *Misjonskunnskap: En innføring*. Oslo: Gyldendal, 1976.

The Nature and Mission of the Church: A Stage on the Way to a Common Statement. Faith and Order Paper 198. Geneva: World Council of Churches, 2005.

Neebe, Gudrun. *Apostolische Kirche: Grundunterscheidungen an Luthers Kirchenbegriff unter besonderer Berücksichtigung seiner Lehre von den Notae Ecclesiae*. Theologische Bibliothek Töpelmann 82. Berlin: W. de Gruyter, 1997.

New Delhi Speaks: The Message of the Third Assembly New Delhi 18 November—5 December 1961 with the Reports of the Assembly's Sections on Christian Witness, Service and Unity and an Appeal to All Governments and Peoples. London: SCM Press, 1962.

Niebuhr, H. Richard. *Christ and Culture*. New York: Harper, 1951.

Bibliography

Nielsen, Helge Kjær. *Han elskede os først: Om den bibelske begrundelse for diakoni.* 2nd ed. Aarhus: Aarhus universitetsforlag, 2003.

———. *Heilung und Verkündigung: Das Verständnis der Heilung und ihres Verhältnisses zur Verkündigung bei Jesus und in der ältesten Kirche.* Acta Theologica Danica XXII. Leiden: E. J. Brill, 1987.

Nielsen, Kirsten Busch. *Kirken, fællesskabet og teologien: Dietrich Bonhoeffers ekklesiologi.* Økumeniske Studier 3. Frederiksberg: ANIS, 1989.

Niesel, Wilhelm. *The Theology of Calvin.* London: Lutterwort, 1956.

Nissen, Johannes. *New Testament and Mission: Historical and Hermeneutical Perspectives.* New York: P. Lang, 1999.

Nordstokke, Kjell. *Det dyrebare mennesket: Diakoniens grunnlag og praksis.* Oslo: Verbum, 2002.

———, ed. *Diakonia in Context: Transformation, Reconciliation, Empowerment. A LWF Contribution to the Understanding and Practice of Diakonia.* Geneva: The Lutheran World Federation, 2009.

———. "The Ecclesiological Self-Understanding of the Lutheran World Federation: From 'Free Association' to 'Communion of Churches.'" *The Ecumenical Review* 44, no. 4 (1992) 479–90.

Pannenberg, Wolfhart, ed. *Revelation as History.* New York: Macmillan, 1968.

———. *Systematic Theology.* Vol. I–III, Edinburgh: T. & T. Clark, 1991–98.

Percy, Martyn. *Clergy: The Origin of Species.* London: Continuum, 2006.

Pettersson, Per. "The Church of Sweden in a Service Theoretical Perspective." In *Religions and Social Transitions*, edited by Eila Helander. Publications of the Department of Practical Theology, 188–207. Helsinki: University of Helsinki, Department of Practical Theology, 1999.

———. *Kvalitet i livslånga tjänsterelationer: Svenska kyrkan ur tjänsteteoretisk och religionssociologisk perspektiv.* Stockholm: Verbum, 2000.

Poloma, Margaret M. *Main Street Mystics: The Toronto Blessing and Reviving Pentecostalism.* Walnut Creek, CA: AltaMira, 2003.

Potter, Phil. *The Challenge of Cell Church: Getting to Grips with Cell Church Values.* Oxford: Bible Reading Fellowship, 2001.

Prenter, Regin. *Creation and Redemption.* Philadelphia: Fortress, 1967.

———. *Kirkens lutherske bekendelse: En aktuel theologisk udlægning af Den augsburgske bekendelse 1530.* Fredericia: Lohses, 1978.

Rasmusson, Arne. *The Church as Polis: From Political Theology to Theological Politics as Exemplified by Jürgen Moltmann and Stanley Hauerwas.* Studia Theologica Lundensia 49. Lund: Lund University Press, 1994.

Repstad, Pål. "Between Idealism and Reductionism: Some Sociological Perspectives on Making Theology." In *Religion and Modernity: Modes of Co-Existence*, edited by Pål Repstad, 91–117. Oslo: Scandinavian University Press, 1996.

Reumann, John. "Koinonia in Scripture: Survey of Biblical Texts." In *On the Way to Fuller Koinonia: Official Report of the Fifth World Conference on Faith and Order*, edited by Thomas F. Best and Günther Gassmann. Faith and Order Paper 166, 37–69. Geneva: WCC Publications, 1994.

Reuter, Hans-Richard. "Kirchenbegriff—Theologisch." In *Das Recht der Kirche*, edited by Gerhard Rau, Hans-Richard Reuter and Klaus Schlaich, 23–75. Gütersloh: Gütersloh/Kaiser, 1997.

Bibliography

Rikhof, Herwi. *The Concept of Church: A Methodological Inquiry into the Use of Metaphors in Ecclesiology*. London: Sheed, 1981.

Roloff, Jürgen. *Die Kirche im Neuen Testament*. Grundrisse zum Neuen Testament 10. Göttingen: Vandenhoeck & Ruprecht, 1993.

Rusch, William G. *Ecumenical Reception: Its Challenge and Opportunity*. Grand Rapids: Eerdmans, 2007.

Sandnes, Karl Olav. "Ekklesia at Corinth: Between Private and Public." *Tidsskrift for teologi og kirke* 78, no. 3–4 (2007) 248–65.

———. *I tidens fylde: En innføring i Paulus' teologi*. Oslo: Luther, 1996.

———. *A New Family: Conversion and Ecclesiology in the Early Church with Cross-Cultural Comparisons*. Studien zur interkulturellen Geschichte des Christentums 91. Bern-Berlin-Frankfurt a.M.-New York-Paris-Wien: Peter Lang, 1994.

Sannes, Kjell Olav. "Leadership and Ministry: An Evangelical Lutheran View." In *Mission to the World: Communicating the Gospel in the 21st Century. Essays in Honour of Knud Jørgensen*, edited by Tormod Engelsviken, Ernst Harbakk, Rolv Olsen and Thor Strandenæs, 314–28. Oxford: Regnum, 2008.

Schillebeeckx, Edward. *The Church with a Human Face: A New and Expanded Theology of Ministry*. London: SCM, 1985.

Schlink, Edmund. *The Doctrine of Baptism*. Saint Louis: Concordia, 1972.

———. *Ökumenische Dogmatik: Grundzüge*. Göttingen: Vandenhoeck & Ruprecht, 1983.

Schmidt-Lauber, Hans-Christoph, Michael Meyer-Blanck, and Karl-Heinrich Bieritz, eds. *Handbuch der Liturgik: Liturgiwissenschaft in Theologie und Praxis der Kirche*. Göttingen: Vandenhoeck & Ruprecht, 2003.

Scott, W. Richard. *Institutions and Organizations*. 2nd ed. London: Sage, 2001.

———. *Organizations: Rational, Natural, and Open Systems*. 5th ed. Upper Saddle River, NJ: Prentice Hall, Pearson Education International, 2003.

Senn, Frank C. *Christian Liturgy: Catholic and Evangelical*. Minneapolis: Fortress, 1997.

———. *The People's Work: A Social History of the Liturgy*. Minneapolis: Fortress, 2006.

Simson, Wolfgang. *Houses That Change the World: The Return of the House Churches*. Milton Keynes: Authentic Media, 2004.

Skarsaune, Oskar. "The Constantinian Turn." *Tidsskrift for teologi og kirke* 78, no. 3–4 (2007) 298–312.

———. "Det kirkelige embete: Fra presbyter til prest og biskop: Noen bibelske og oldkirkelige momenter." *Tidsskrift for teologi og kirke* 71, no. 3 (2000) 215–32.

———. "Det tredelte embete og det éne: Tjenesteordningene og ordinasjon/vigsling i Den norske kirke teologihistorisk belyst." *Tidsskrift for teologi og kirke* 70, no. 1 (1999) 21–29.

———. *In the Shadow of the Temple: Jewish Influences on Early Christianity*. Downers Grove, IL: InterVarsity, 2002.

———. *Troens ord: De tre oldkirkelige bekjennelsene*. Oslo: Luther, 1997.

Skjevesland, Olav. "Jesu hebredelsesgjerninger og diakonien." In *Diakoni og kirke*, edited by Andreas Aarflot, 9–32. Oslo: Luther, 1976.

———. *Levende kirke: Om nådegaver, tjenester og menighetsbygging*. Oslo: Luther, 1984.

———. "Ordinasjonen i Det nye testamente." In *Reform og embete*, edited by Per Otto Gullaksen, Torleiv Austad, Even Fougner, and Oskar Skarsaune, 199–212. Oslo: Universitetsforlaget, 1993.

Steven, James H. S. *Worship in the Spirit: Charismatic Worship in the Church of England*. Milton Keynes: Paternoster, 2002.

Bibliography

Stringer, Martin D. *On the Perception of Worship: The Ethnography of Worship in Four Christian Congregations in Manchester*. Birmingham: The University of Birmingham Press, 1999.

———. *A Sociological History of Christian Worship*. Cambridge: Cambridge University Press, 2005.

Sundberg, Walter. "Ministry in Nineteenth-Century European Lutheranism." In *Called & Ordained: Lutheran Perspectives on the Office of the Ministry*, edited by Todd Nichol and Marc Kolden, 77–92. Minneapolis: Fortress, 1990.

Synnes, Martin. "Teosentrisk eller soteriologisk tolkning av he basileia tou theou." *Tidsskrift for teologi og kirke* 70, no. 1 (1999) 54–74.

The Teachings of the Second Vatican Council: Complete Texts of the Constitutions, Decrees, and Declarations. Westminster, MD: Newman, 1966.

Tjørhom, Ola, ed. *Apostolicity and Unity: Essays on the Porvoo Common Statement*. Grand Rapids: Eerdmans, 2002.

———. *Embodied Faith: Reflections on a Materialist Spirituality*. Grand Rapids: Eerdmans, 2009.

———. *Kirken—troens mor: Et økumenisk bidrag til en luthersk ekklesiologi*. Oslo: Verbum, 1999.

———. *Kirkens enhet—for at verden skal se og tro: En innføring i økumenisk tenkning*. Oslo: Verbum, 2005.

———. *Visible Church—Visible Unity: Ecumenical Ecclesiology and "The Great Tradition of the Church."* Collegeville, Minn.: Liturgical Press, 2004.

Together in Mission and Ministry: The Porvoo Common Statement with Essays on Church and Ministry in Northern Europe. London: Church House Publishing, 1993.

Tveit, Olav Fykse. *Mutual Accountability as Ecumenical Attitude: A Study in Ecumenical Ecclesiology Based on Faith and Order Texts 1948-1998*. Oslo: The Norwegian Lutheran School of Theology, 2001.

Van Gelder, Craig. *The Essence of the Church: A Community Created by the Spirit*. Grand Rapids: Baker, 2000.

Van Gelder, Craig, and Dwight J. Zscheile. *The Missional Church in Perspective: Mapping Trends and Shaping the Conversation*. Grand Rapids: Baker, 2011.

van der Ven, Johannes A. *Ecclesiology in Context*. Grand Rapids: Eerdmans, 1996.

———. *Practical Theology: An Empirical Approach*. Leuven: Peeters, 1998.

Vigilius, Mikkel. *Kirke i kirken: Luthersk vækkelseskristendom—fra kirkelig bevægelse over organisation til kirkeligt opbrud*. Hillerød: LogosMedia, 2005.

Volf, Miroslav. *After Our Likeness: The Church as the Image of the Trinity*. Grand Rapids: Eerdmans, 1998.

———. "Community Formation as an Image of the Triune God: A Congregational Model of Church Order and Life." In *Community Formation in the Early Church and in the Church Today*, edited by Richard N. Longenecker, 213–37. Peabody MA: Hendrickson, 2002.

Wagner, Harald, ed. *Einheit—aber wie?: Zur Tragfähigkeit der ökumenischen Formel vom "differenzierten Konsens,"* Quaestiones Disputatae 184. Freiburg: Herder, 2000.

Wannenwetsch, Bernd. *Political Worship: Ethics for Christian Citizens*. Oxford Studies in Theological Ethics. Oxford: Oxford University Press, 2004.

Ward, Pete. *Liquid Church*. Peabody, MA: Hendrickson, 2002.

Welker, Michael. *What Happens in Holy Communion?* Grand Rapids: Eerdmans, 2000.

Bibliography

Wengert, Timothy J. *Priesthood, Pastors, Bishops: Public Ministry for the Reformation and Today*. Minneapolis: Fortress, 2008.
Wingren, Gustaf. *Creation and Law*. London: Oliver and Boyd, 1961.
———. *Gospel and Church*. Edinburgh and London: Oliver and Boyd, 1964.
———. *Luther on Vocation*. Philadelphia: Muhlenberg, 1957.
———. *Man and the Incarnation: A Study in the Biblical Theology of Irenaeus*. Philadelphia: Muhlenberg, 1959.
Winter, Ralph D. "The Two Structures of God's Redemptive Mission." In *Crucial Dimensions in World Evangelization*, edited by Arthur F. Glasser, Paul G. Hiebert, C. Peter Wagner and Ralph D. Winter, 326–44. South Pasadena, CA: William Carey Library, 1976.
Zahrnt, Heinz. *The Question of God*. New York: Harcourt Brace Jovanovich, 1969.
Zeindler, Matthias. *Gotteserfahrung in der christlichen Gemeinde: Eine systematisch-theologische Untersuchung*. Stuttgart: Kohlhammer, 2001.
Zizioulas, John. *Being as Communion: Studies in Personhood and the Church*. Crestwood NY: St Vladimir's Seminary Press, 1985.
———. "The Church as Communion: A Presentation on the World Conference Theme." In *On the Way to Fuller Koinonia. Official Report of the Fifth World Conference on Faith and Order*, edited by Thomas F. Best and Günther Gassmann. Faith and Order Paper 166, 103–11. Geneva: WCC Publications, 1994.
Østnor, Lars. *Kirkens tjenester med særlig henblikk på diakontjenesten*. Oslo: Luther, 1978.

Index

Aagaard, Anna Marie 35
Aalen, Sverre, 30
Aasgaard, Reidar, 100
actualistic understanding of the church, 103
Albrecht, Daniel E., 178, 197, 199
already and not yet, 30–31, 34, 47, 201
Althaus, Paul, 42, 45
angels, 46–47
Anglican, 11, 153, 155, 160, 173, 208, 216, 224
anticipation, anticipated, 2, 14, 31–34, 44, 50, 53–54, 71, 79, 86, 88, 102, 106, 179, 182, 203, 205, 227
apostle, apostles, 19, 21, 29, 50–51, 89, 144, 146–47, 155–57, 162, 166, 170, 176, 188
Apostles' Creed, 1, 15, 95, 189
art, 19, 134, 193–94, 213
Askeland, Harald, 127–28
Augsburg Confession, 7, 14, 19, 35, 41–42, 48–49, 133–34, 149, 151–52, 155, 158, 163, 193, 213–14
Augustine, 40
Austad, Torleiv, 41

Bakke, Odd Magne 207
Banks, Robert J., 28, 147
baptism, baptized, 19, 23, 36–37, 51–52, 54, 72–74, 81, 83–85, 98, 106, 110, 112–14, 117, 144–45, 148–49, 153, 156, 158, 161–62, 165, 179, 181, 183, 185, 191–92, 209, 215–16, 220
Barth, Karl, 7, 26–27, 29, 62
Bassler, Jouette M., 28
Bauman, Zygmunt, 58, 64
Berger, Peter L., 58–63, 139, 208
Bevans, Stephen B., 77, 82–84
Bhaskar, Roy, 59
Bieritz, Karl-Heinrich 173, 187
bishop, bishops, 144, 150, 152–53, 155–56, 159, 161–62, 164, 166, 168, 207, 210, 215–16, 218–20
body of Christ, 24–29, 53–54, 98, 100, 105, 130, 146, 149, 228
Bonhoeffer, Dietrich, 26–27, 29, 38, 60, 102–4
Booker, Mike, 224
Bosch, David J., 83
Bourdieu, Pierre, 58
Bradshaw, Paul F., 175
Browning, Don S., 3, 228
Brunner, Emil, 135–36
Brunner, Peter, 174–75, 186–87, 193

Calvin, Jean, 155
canon law, 135, 139–40
Cartledge, Mark J., 198
catholic, catholicity, 1, 8, 34, 38, 95–96, 177, 204–6, 211–12, 219, 229
cell, cell church, 224–25
charism, charisma, 146–49, 161–62, 166

Index

Charismatic, Charismatic movement, 11, 151, 173, 178, 182, 188, 190, 197–99
charismatic, 147, 162, 188
Christology, Christological, 3, 10, 27, 118, 207
church law, 137, 139–41
Church of Norway, 110–11, 140, 151, 162, 167, 208, 224
Church of Sweden, 132, 221
church service, 54, 113–14, 171, 174, 176, 178, 181–83, 185–88, 190, 193–202
clergy, clerical, 23, 112, 120, 124–25, 131–34, 136, 142–45, 148, 154, 164–66, 175, 192, 194
Collins, Raymond F., 9
communio, 12, 15–16, 26, 36–38, 60, 97, 102–3, 111–12, 219
communion, 1, 10–11, 15, 19, 23, 36, 48, 52–53, 72, 97, 102–3, 105–6, 135–36, 148, 153, 158, 160, 180, 194–95, 205–8, 215–16, 219–220, 223, 226
community, 5, 13, 15–16, 26–28, 33, 35–37, 39, 43, 47, 52–54, 56, 61–62, 65–66, 77, 80–81, 86, 91, 94, 97–98, 102–10, 112–16, 118–23, 125–26, 129, 131–32, 135, 137, 140, 142, 147–49, 153, 161, 168, 175, 184, 205, 207, 212–13, 217, 219–20, 222–27, 229
concrete, concrete church, 3–6, 8, 14, 17, 26–29, 43, 45, 60–61, 103–4, 112–13, 141–42, 152, 193, 199, 203–4, 206
confessional, 7–8, 11, 153, 160, 177, 210, 212–14, 218
contextual, 77–78, 154, 159
creation and redemption, 67, 73, 85
creation, theology of creation, 31–32, 42–43, 50, 53, 67–68, 70–75, 79–80, 85, 89–90, 93, 108, 196, 205
Cullmann, Oscar, 31
culture, cultural, 8, 75–79, 85, 95–96, 107, 121, 128, 131, 168, 179, 196–98, 208, 226
Cunningham, Lawrence S., 200
Cyprian, 207

Dahl, Nils Alstrup, 21
Davie, Grace, 111
deacon, 152–53, 155–56
denomination, denominational, 8, 11–12, 95, 124, 149, 152, 190, 210–15, 217–19, 221–22
diakonia, 89–92, 118, 157
diocese, 218, 224
diversity, 66, 76, 79–80, 93, 96, 106, 109, 120, 145–46, 152, 154, 156, 159, 163, 172, 209, 216, 221
division, 64, 79–80, 87, 128, 151, 160, 163, 165, 188, 207, 227
Doyle, Dennis M., 97
Dulles, Avery, 5, 12, 25, 95, 132
Durkheim, Emile, 57–58

Eastwood, Cyril, 159
ecclesia militans, 47
ecclesia triumphans, 47
ecclesiola in ecclesia, 17, 224
ecumenical, 7–9, 11–12, 53, 84, 89, 97, 106, 147–48, 152–53, 156, 163, 193, 203, 207–10, 212–13, 215–17, 219–22, 226
ecumenism, 10, 147, 214–16
Egan, Keith J., 200
ekklesia, 16, 117, 119, 135–36, 206–7, 223
Elert, Werner, 15
empirical, empirical church, 1, 3–5, 7, 10, 14, 17, 26–30, 56, 59–63, 65–66, 101–3, 114,

Index

empirical, empirical church (*cont.*) 130, 132–33, 139, 152–54, 178, 204
Eriksen, Bent Reidar 222
eschatology, eschatological, 2–3, 5, 13, 24, 26, 30–32, 34, 36–39, 41, 44–45, 47–48, 67, 73–74, 83, 87, 90, 95–96, 103–4, 115, 117, 182, 203–5, 211, 226–27
ethics, ethical, 13, 36, 60–61, 75, 78, 106–8, 117
Etzioni, Amitai, 130
eucharist, eucharistic, 15, 19, 36, 39, 52–55, 73–74, 85, 98, 102, 104–6, 113–14, 117, 148–49, 153, 156, 158, 160–62, 172, 174–76, 179, 183–86, 188, 191–93, 201, 215–16, 220
experience, 1–3, 14, 20–21, 34–35, 43, 45, 60–61, 64–65, 68, 101–4, 177, 182, 184, 199–200, 203, 227
experience of God, 104, 199

Fagerberg, Holsten, 133, 150, 167
family, 57, 71, 88, 100–1, 112, 116, 119–22, 224–25
fellowship, 1–2, 5, 10, 12–20, 22–31, 33–34, 37, 39–41, 43–44, 46, 51–52, 54–55, 65–66, 73–74, 81, 84–86, 91, 93–94, 96–109, 111–17, 119, 121–23, 125–26, 133–38, 142–49, 151, 153, 155, 157–59, 161, 163–65, 167–71, 176–77, 179–82, 184, 188, 190–92, 198, 201–9, 211–15, 217–28
FitzGerald, Thomas E., 208, 216
folk church, 8, 109–16, 118, 122, 129, 132, 165
Foucault, Michel, 58
free church, 113, 143
Frisby, David, 57
Frostin, Per, 94

Furseth, Inger, 58, 64–65, 110
Giddens, Anthony, 56, 58
Gill, Robin, 63
Gjessing, Gutorm, 192
gospel, 7, 9, 15, 19, 22, 24, 33, 42, 49–51, 64, 69, 72–74, 76–78, 80–82, 84–92, 95, 98–99, 106–8, 116, 124, 133, 144, 148–150, 152, 155, 163, 168, 176, 183–85, 187–88, 194, 209, 213, 220
governance, governing, 93, 133, 138, 166–67, 195, 218, 220
grace, 43, 63, 107, 144, 146, 167, 185, 201
Green, Clifford J., 26
Gullaksen, Per-Otto, 140

Haag, Herbert, 143
Haight, Roger, 5
Håkansson, Bo, 72
Hauerwas, Stanley M., 107–8
healing, healing ministry, 86–89, 146–48, 190
Healy, Nicholas M., 5–6, 12, 26, 29, 37, 40, 45, 64–65
heaven, heavenly, 18, 21, 39, 44–48, 96
Heimbrock, Hans-Günter, 197–98
heresy, 116, 214
Hesselgrave, David J., 77
hidden, hidden church, 1, 27, 39–40, 42–44, 106, 119, 229
Hiebert, Paul G., 115
high church, 72, 182
Hofius, 46–47
Holy Spirit, 20, 22–24, 30, 35–36, 42, 46, 49, 51, 54, 60, 81–82, 118, 137, 146, 148–49, 151, 156, 162, 170, 209
holy, holiness, 1–2, 15, 19–20, 22–24, 30, 33–38, 41–42, 46, 48–52, 54, 60, 74, 81–82, 96, 105, 115, 118, 134, 137,

243

holy, holiness (*cont.*)
143–44, 146, 148–49, 151, 156, 159, 162, 170, 173, 175, 179–80, 183, 186–87, 192, 195, 204, 207, 209, 229
Honecker, Martin, 103–4
Hope, Ludvig, 136
house church, 223–24
household, 39, 47, 71, 101, 116
Huber, Wolfgang, 114, 117, 124–25
Hütter, Reinhard, 108, 116–19
Hvalvik, Reidar, 206

Ignatius, 17
incarnation, incarnational, 29, 53, 63–64, 68
institution, institutionalization, 12, 15, 18, 40, 54, 65, 103, 126–127, 129–37, 139–41, 155, 157
invisible, invisible church, 1–3, 26–27, 29, 34, 38, 41–45, 57, 61, 102, 106, 112, 134, 181–82, 203, 229
Ireland, Mark, 224
Irenaeus, 68
Israel, 16, 21, 35, 49, 81, 117, 123, 174, 187
Ivarsson, Henrik, 89

judgment, judgment day, 32, 38–40, 44, 50, 69, 72, 88, 104, 123, 169
Jüngel, Eberhard, 64
justice, justification, 39, 48, 106, 117, 140
Justin Martyr, 113, 194

Kärkkäinen, Veli-Matti, 10
Käsemann, Ernst, 9
Keifert, Patrick R., 119–20, 169, 181
kingdom of God, 2, 13–14, 21, 23, 30–39, 44–45, 47–48, 50, 53–54, 71–72, 81, 83–90, 92–97, 101–2, 108, 138, 179–80, 182–83, 203–5, 226–27
koinonia, 12, 19, 23, 51, 53, 97–99, 104, 106, 219, 224
Kraft, Charles H., 76
Kümmel, Werner Georg, 31
Küng, Hans, 9–10, 16, 21–22, 32, 34–35, 37, 51–52, 95, 147–48
Kvalbein, Hans, 30–31

Lappegard, Sevat, 109
Lathrop, Gordon W., 66, 173, 179–81, 183, 187
lay, 100, 105, 124, 132, 136, 142–43, 145, 150–51, 164–65, 175
leader, leadership, 136, 146, 149–50, 155, 157–58, 162–63, 166–69, 188, 190, 201, 218, 225
Lima document, 19, 53, 148, 153, 156, 160, 216, 220
Lincoln, Andrew T., 46
liturgy, liturgical, 19, 33, 120, 162, 167–68, 171–73, 175–80, 187–88, 192–93, 195, 197
local church, 12–13, 16, 25, 95, 119, 155–56, 168, 180, 199, 203, 205–7, 210–11, 217–18, 221–24, 226–27
love, 17, 36, 69, 88, 91–92, 99–101, 105–6, 114, 135, 162, 195, 207, 212, 216–17, 229
low church, 75, 84, 171, 182
Luckmann, Thomas, 58–59
Luther, Martin, 15, 36, 38, 42, 74, 94, 105–6, 168, 186, 195, 224
Lutheran, 7–8, 11–12, 15, 41–42, 50, 66, 68, 75, 89, 94, 108–10, 133, 143–44, 149–52, 155, 160, 164, 173, 179, 208, 210, 213, 216, 219, 224

marks of the church, 66, 95
Martin, David, 63
Melanchthon, Philipp, 42–43, 193

metaphor, metaphorical, 27–28, 30, 130, 158, 225
methodological atheism, 62–63
Meyer, Harding, 193, 209–10
Milbank, John, 63–64
minister, 41, 143, 158, 160, 163, 166–67, 220–22
ministry, 11, 19, 43, 52–54, 83, 86–89, 91–93, 98, 133–34, 137, 142–68, 174, 190, 192, 200, 206–9, 212, 215–17, 220–21, 228
missio dei, 83–84
mission, 5, 11, 13, 80–87, 89–93, 96, 108, 112, 137–38, 141, 145, 150, 152, 154, 156–57, 162, 167, 182, 200, 202, 212, 216–17, 220–24, 227
missional, 13, 83–84, 124
Modéus, Martin, 172, 197
Molland, Einar, 160
Moltmann, Jürgen, 10, 13, 21, 96, 100
moral, morality, 13, 71, 75–76, 78, 106–8, 131
Morgan, Gareth, 130
Morris, Danny E., 169
Mortensen, Viggo, 219
music, 76, 186, 190, 193, 196–97
Muthiah, Robert A., 159
mutual accountability, 217–18
Myklebust, Olav G., 221

Neebe, Gudrun, 42
Neo-Lutheranism, 133, 144, 167
Nicene Creed, 1, 12, 21, 34, 95, 189, 214
Niebuhr, H. Richard, 79
Nielsen, Helge Kjær, 87, 89
Nielsen, Kirsten Busch, 26,
Niesel, Wilhelm, 155
Nissen, Johannes, 81
Nordstokke, Kjell, 89, 219

offering, 174, 186, 192–93
oikos, 116, 119
Olsen, Charles M., 169
ordained, ordained ministry, 43, 132–34, 144–45, 147, 149–51, 153–56, 160–64, 201, 207, 216, 218, 220
ordination, 161–63, 167–68
organization, 15, 18, 94, 112, 126–33, 135–39, 141, 218, 221
Orthodox, 10, 23, 155, 158, 164, 171, 173, 192, 207, 210, 215
oversight, 219–20

Pannenberg, Wolfhart, 10, 13, 31–33, 49, 51–52, 54, 93, 95
pastor, pastoral, 71, 132–33, 144–45, 149–52, 155, 158–61, 163, 167–68, 175, 201, 219, 225
Pelser, Gert, 28
pentecost, 17, 19, 24, 51, 117
Pentecostal, 172–73, 178, 182, 188, 190, 197–99, 215
Percy, Martin, 154
Pettersson, Per, 132
Pietism, Pietist, 122, 150–51, 224
pluralism, pluralistic, 76, 112, 209
polis, 13, 107–8, 116–17, 119
politics, political, 13, 16, 92–95, 107, 116–18, 175, 185, 210
Poloma, Margaret M., 192
Porvoo agreement, 11, 208, 216, 220
Potter, Phil., 224
pray, prayer, prayers, 19, 22, 24, 36, 38, 48, 75, 114, 122–23, 134, 161–64, 169, 173, 176, 180, 184–86, 189–93, 196, 200–2, 209, 215
preaching, 20, 30, 36, 43, 50–51, 78, 85–88, 90–91, 103–4, 133, 150, 155, 158, 168, 176, 181, 185, 187–88, 195–96, 201, 209
Prenter, Regin, 42–43

Index

presence of Jesus, 19–22, 24–25, 30–31, 33, 49, 54–55, 66, 185, 189, 203, 227
priest, priestly, 35, 70, 132, 152–53, 158–63, 174–75, 201
priesthood of all believers, 143, 150, 159–60, 166, 168
promise, 18–19, 21, 24, 30–31, 37, 68, 81, 103, 162, 187, 227
prophets, prophetic, 5, 21, 31, 50, 146–47, 157, 160
public, 75, 94, 116–121, 123, 129, 139, 147, 158, 162, 172, 181, 187, 196–97, 201

Rasmusson, Arne, 13, 107
Reformation, 40, 42, 139–40, 143, 157, 160, 166, 207, 214
Reformed, 155, 173, 208, 218
reification, reified, 59–60
Repstad, Pål, 58, 62, 64–65, 110
resurrection, 13, 20, 29–30, 45–48, 50–53, 72–73, 81, 85, 156, 187
Reumann, John, 98
Reuter, Hans-Richard, 140
revelation, 31, 45–47, 49–50, 65, 71–72, 176, 201
Rikhof, Herwi, 28
ritual, 120, 183, 197–99
Roloff, Jürgen, 9–10, 28
Roman Catholic, 5, 10–12, 25, 37, 40, 95, 131–33, 139–40, 143–44, 153, 158, 160–61, 164, 166, 172–73, 192, 207, 210, 213, 215, 218, 224
Rommen, Edward, 77
Rusch, William G., 210

sacrament, sacramental, 19, 41, 43, 49, 52, 55, 66, 73, 102, 104–5, 107, 129, 133–34, 136, 144, 150, 158, 163, 172, 179, 186, 191, 199–200, 212, 215, 227
sacrifice, 53, 69, 160, 174, 192–93

salvation, 24, 30–31, 33, 38, 40, 45–47, 49–51, 54, 69–70, 72–74, 80, 84–87, 90–91, 95, 108, 118, 123, 133–34, 145, 164, 172, 182, 205, 214, 224
Sandnes, Karl Olav, 28–29, 100–1, 117, 119, 147, 224
Sannes, Kjell Olav, 149–50
Sayer, Derek, 57
Schillebeeckx, Edward, 160
Schlink, Edmund, 51, 96, 147–48, 215
Schroeder, Roger, 82–84
Scott, W. Richard, 127–28, 131
Second Vatican Council, 10, 12, 132, 144, 155, 160, 166, 214–16
secular, secularization, 16, 35, 64, 71, 75–76, 82, 94–95, 118, 129, 157, 169, 208
Senn, Frank C., 173, 177
sermon, 108, 172, 185–87, 193, 196–97, 202
sign, 2, 14, 32–34, 43, 52–53, 55, 83, 85–88, 90, 95, 102, 105–6, 161, 179–80, 182–84, 192–94, 198, 216, 227
silence, 189, 191
Simson, Wolfgang, 225
sin, sinful, sinfulness, 5, 22, 26, 29, 31–33, 36–38, 40–41, 65, 68, 78–79, 85, 87, 90, 99, 115, 183–85, 227
singing, 188, 190, 193, 199, 202
Skarsaune, Oskar, 15, 143, 153, 160, 173
Skjevesland, Olav, 89, 146, 161
society, 6, 12–13, 56–61, 65, 71, 74–76, 78, 80, 92–95, 103, 107–10, 112, 118–19, 123, 131–32, 136, 138–39, 143, 157, 166, 196, 221
sociology, sociological, 12, 16, 26, 56–66, 79, 102, 110–11, 120, 126–28, 130, 132, 134, 136,

Index

sociology, sociological (*cont.*)
    139, 143, 164–65, 178, 197, 208
Sohm, Rudolph, 136, 140
spiritual, 12, 27, 45–46, 87, 94–95, 97, 99, 101–6, 123–24, 130, 136–37, 145–51, 157, 159, 161–67, 169–70, 199, 225, 228
Stahl, Friedrich Julius, 133–34
Steven, James H. S, 178, 199
Stringer, Martin D., 178
suffer, suffering, 53, 73, 75, 88, 92, 98, 100, 117, 184, 190
Sundberg, Walter, 133, 144, 150
symbol, 32–33, 173, 179–80, 182
Synnes, Martin, 30

Tertullian, 17
theology of ministry, 142, 145, 147, 151, 154, 159, 161
Tjørhom, Ola, 11, 70, 85, 94, 199, 208–210, 212, 214, 216–17
transcendence, transcendent, 45, 62–63, 182
Trinity, triune God, Trinitarian, 2, 14, 19, 22–23, 83, 97, 126, 191, 199, 214, 219
Troeltsch, Ernst, 65–66
Tveit, Olav Fykse, 217–18

unity, unity of the church, 9, 11, 23, 29, 48, 52, 95–96, 98, 106–7, 130, 145–46, 153–54, 156, 172, 188, 204–10, 212–17, 219–20, 226, 228–29
universal church, 25, 95, 177, 203–7, 209–11, 213, 215, 217, 219, 221, 223, 225–26

van der Ven, Johannes A., 4, 6, 12, 64–65
Van Gelder, Craig, 13, 83, 137–38
Vigilius, Mikkel, 224

visible, visible church, 2–3, 6, 14, 26–27, 29, 34, 38–44, 70, 85, 101–2, 104, 106, 111–12, 117, 134, 199, 204, 209–10, 227
Volf, Miroslav, 10, 17–18, 23, 28, 148, 164–66, 205, 211

Wagner, Harald, 210
Wannenwetsch, Bernd, 117
Ward, Pete, 225
Weber, Max, 57–58, 65–66
Welker, Michael, 52
Wengert, Timothy J., 66, 159
Wingren, Gustaf, 68, 72–76, 89–90, 109
Winter, Ralph D., 222
Word and sacrament, 41, 43, 49, 66, 73, 102, 104, 129, 133–34, 144, 150, 158, 163, 172, 227
Word, Word of God, 2, 19, 26–27, 41–43, 45, 49–50, 54–55, 66, 73, 102–4, 129, 133–34, 144, 150, 158, 163, 172, 181, 185–86, 195, 200, 219, 227
World Council of Churches, 12, 85, 106, 208
worship, worship service, 16–17, 26, 35, 46, 48, 54, 73–74, 81, 103–4, 109, 111, 113–14, 117, 119–23, 129, 156–58, 162, 164, 167, 171–202, 209, 215, 222–23, 225–26

Zahrnt, Heinz, 75
Zeindler, Mattias, 199
Zizioulas, John, 10, 23
Zscheile, Dwight J., 13, 83

Østnor, Lars, 89–90

www.ingramcontent.com/pod-product-compliance
Lightning Source LLC
Chambersburg PA
CBHW050850230426
43667CB00012B/2228